THE DIONNES

THE PIONEERS

THE DIONNES

ELLIE TESHER

Doubleday Canada

Canadian Cataloguing in Publication Data

Tesher, Ellie
      The Dionnes

Includes index.
ISBN 0-385-25843-7

1. Dionne quintuplets.   I. Title.

CT9998.D5T47 1999   920.0713   C99-931697-4

Front jacket photograph (top) by Peter Power/*Toronto Star*
Front jacket photograph (bottom) from the private collection of Cécile Dionne
Back jacket photograph from the private collection of Cécile Dionne
Jacket design by Gordon Robertson
Text and photo insert design by Heidy Lawrance Associates
Printed and bound in the USA

Published in Canada by
Doubleday Canada, a division of
Random House of Canada Limited
105 Bond Street
Toronto, Ontario
M5B 1Y3

BVG 10 9 8 7 6 5 4 3 2 1

To Merle and Philip,
who inspired my passion for justice.

CONTENTS

ACKNOWLEDGEMENTS

To my husband and friend, Vian Ewart, my heartfelt thanks for his unceasing enthusiasm for this book and his wise counsel, both personal and professional, during the course of my writing it. To my editor, Janice Weaver, my deep appreciation for her steadying confidence and her skilled, insightful direction, which were essential guides throughout the writing process.

This book was conceived with the enthusiasm of Gloria Goodman of Doubleday Canada, who first suggested it. It was nurtured at its earliest stages by encouragement from friends in publishing, Malcolm Lester and Barbara Coven, and other friends from the media and writing worlds, including Stevie Cameron, Marlene Hore, and Julie Rickerd. I was given great support by *Toronto Star* publisher John Honderich and my friends and colleagues at the *Star*. I was also given a generous vote of confidence by noted authors June Callwood and Pierre Berton, the latter having written a masterful history of the early Dionne era. The sage leadership of Doubleday editor-in-chief John Pearce and the proficient supervision of assistant editor Pamela Murray made them an excellent team, and I was fortunate to have them. I thank Peter Power of the *Star* for the powerful photo that helped connect me to the surviving Dionne quintuplets and their story, and that so appropriately graces the book's jacket.

I now believe there must be at least one major obstacle in every book's development. In my case, it was a severe back problem. I'm indebted to the amazing Anita Lorelli, the dedicated physiotherapist who took on both back and book as a joint challenge she was determined to see me through. The situation was eased by the diligent research of Susan Sutherland, along with the able computer assistance of Susan McGlashen and the systems wizardry of Kevin Omura. I thank Lisi Tesher for her multi-talented help at the computer at a time when it was most needed, and Stephen Tesher for his writer's sensitivity in providing morale boosts.

Thanks to Marlene Axler, Judd Feldman, Sandy Kivenko, and Stella Yeadon for their contributions to making the work easier.

Special thanks are owed to the remarkable Fay and Jimmy Rodolfos, who welcomed me into their home and their courageous lives. I also thank Rino Lolli for helping me with my transportation and for trying to improve my French, and Sister Claire Morin and the Congrégation des Petites Franciscaines de Marie in Baie-Saint-Paul, Quebec, for welcoming a stranger so graciously.

I wish to acknowledge the superb work of University of Toronto criminologist Mariana Valverde, whose academic papers on the unique political and cultural implications of the Dionne phenomenon served to inform and confirm my own perspective.

I'm very appreciative that Bertrand Dionne and Carlo Tarini, who are part of this story, shared unstintingly of their time and resources in the belief that the full account finally must be told.

Most of all, I wish to thank Cécile, Yvonne, and Annette Dionne for their sincere efforts to bring to light as much information as possible for this book. In so doing, they gave generously of their time and opened up their private adult lives to me with a trust and candour for which I'm deeply grateful. I also wish to thank the daughters of the late Marie Dionne for the important contribution they made by agreeing to the writing of this book.

The enduring significance of the Dionne quintuplets in the history of Canada can be told only as the story of five women whose lives were for ever altered by the bizarre circumstances that followed their unique birth. To finally put the pieces of this epic story together involved research, meetings, and interviews with far too many people for me to be able to mention them all. But I offer my appreciation to them, to the many *Star* readers who let me know they believed in the work, and to my friends, who never let my writer's world get too lonely.

Prologue: **THE FIGHT OF THEIR LIVES**

A GLITTERING CROWD of internationally famous personalities graced *Time* magazine's seventy-fifth anniversary gala on March 3, 1998. Assembled were the brightest lights in a galaxy of world leaders, scientists, intellectuals, film stars, sports legends, and business giants. They filled the landmark Radio City Music Hall at New York's Rockefeller Center with excitement merely by their presence.

They had gathered from all parts of the globe for a unique celebration honouring more than six hundred individuals who had been the newsmakers of the century. U.S. president Bill Clinton, former Soviet president Mikhail Gorbachev, computer titan Bill Gates, director Steven Spielberg, writer and Holocaust witness Elie Wiesel, and author Toni Morrison were there. So were baseball great Joe DiMaggio, broadcasters Walter Cronkite and Dan Rather, actor Lauren Bacall, and publisher John F. Kennedy, Jr. Special tributes honoured people who had died but remained woven into a twentieth-century tapestry of excellence, including civil rights leader Martin Luther King, inventors and aviation pioneers Orville and Wilbur Wright, filmmaker John Ford, comedian Lucille Ball, and former American president Franklin Delano Roosevelt.

But three newsmakers who had been known worldwide

since the 1930s—the surviving Dionne quintuplets—were missing. Annette, Yvonne, and Cécile Dionne had been included on the prestigious guest list, but they did not attend. The extraordinary circumstances of their lives had made them forgo a celebration of their own place in history.

The three pale, grey-haired women in worn winter coats drew no special notice on the early morning train ride from Montreal to Toronto that February day in 1998. They gazed out the window at bleak fields and, like travellers with no special mission, were resigned during the train's unexplained hour-long delay. Yet had the women boarded the train again the next morning, their remarkably similar faces would have been reflected in the front pages of all of Canada's major newspapers. Curious passengers would have read that those same patient women, Cécile, Annette, and Yvonne Dionne, were in the middle of the fight of their lives.

The surviving members of the once-famous Dionne quintuplets were headed into battle against a formidable force, the premier of Ontario and his Progressive Conservative government. The three shy and diminutive women were seeking a hefty cash settlement, along with a public inquiry into their past, from a single-minded political machine that had run roughshod over welfare mothers, civil servants, nurses, and labour unionists. The sisters had been stonewalled for years. The premier had even suggested once that they would die before a full study of their case could be done. The government had only recently come up with an offer—a pension of $2000 a month each and no inquiry—money that was to be put in the sisters' bank accounts whether they agreed to the deal or not.

Cécile, Annette, and Yvonne Dionne were about to stand up and tell Premier Mike Harris that his forced allowance wasn't good enough. They were going to reveal their incredible story to the world.

These women had travelled by train to Toronto once before. Then, they and their late sisters, Émilie and Marie, were celebrated five-year-old children who rode from the remote northern Ontario town of Callander with a fussing entourage in the Quintland Special, a private, specially painted red-and-gold train equipped with its own separate nursery. They were going to be presented to Britain's Royal Family, King George VI and Queen Elizabeth, an event that would inspire breathless page-one accounts in the newspapers of the day.

But in 1998, they made the trip to Canada's commercial and media centre to end a situation that was beyond the irony of comparisons to the past. Weary-looking from hard years and mounting ailments, these women would be photographed that day in plain sweat clothes and sweaters, holding a sign whose message was unimaginable for women who had brought a treasure trove in tourism dollars to the very province they now beseeched for help. Their sad faces became the very image of injustice.

To Mike Harris, Cécile, the sisters' spokesperson, presented a public-relations nightmare. Facing a phalanx of photographers and reporters with TV, video, and still cameras, klieg lights, and microphones, she described in a shaky voice what the frail sisters had endured in the previous fifty years: abuse, poverty, despair. This after a childhood of exploitation that started when they were wrenched away from their family in

3

the name of their own protection. Their sister Émilie had died at twenty, Marie at thirty-five. All five had suffered lasting negative effects from their bizarre childhood.

On March 6, 1998, within a week of the women's rare public appearance and the overwhelmingly sympathetic response of Ontarians, Harris, who had once callously told the women he was too busy to study their case and left it to his officials to reject their claim, performed a stunning reversal. The women would get a substantial settlement. They had won.

On Friday, February 27, 1998, I was in my Toronto home when I picked up the day's newspaper and was riveted by a photograph that conveyed pathos, suffering, and dignity at the same time. It was a news photo of Cécile, Annette, and Yvonne at their press conference, holding a sign that said, "Mr. Harris, We Want Justice, Not Charity."

As a news columnist for the *Toronto Star*, I am always looking for that special story that touches the public and captures its interest. Here was a truly Canadian story that spanned the decades, raised questions about governments past and present—and left everyone wondering how people whose lives seemed to promise a lifetime of prestige, glamour, and wealth could have fallen on such hard times. But how could I get inside the real story?

Through the office of Clayton Ruby, the women's lawyer, I was able to get a message to Carlo Tarini, the marketing whiz who was handling all of the sisters' press interviews. When Tarini called me the next morning, I launched into my most polished reporter's sales pitch to convince him to grant me access to the women. Tarini, however, was a master of media juggling and was being besieged by reporters from all over. He interrupted my pitch. "Look," he said, "I've got forty calls on my desk from people who want this story, the *New York Times*, Quebec reporters who've been working on it already—I owe something to them. Why should I give this interview to you?"

His cocksure manner triggered a response from me in kind. "I'm the one who'll get it on the front page of the *Toronto Star*, in the city where the premier lives, and that's the best route for the women to get their money."

It was brash but true, and it must have struck the right chord with Tarini. He gave me the nod for an in-depth interview. I flew to Montreal the same afternoon for what was to be the first reporter's look at the long, unknown years between the women's past fame and their present hardship.

As I walked into the suburban home where Annette Dionne once raised her children, and where the three surviving sisters then lived, I was struck by a sense that the life had gone out of the place. Poverty, illness, and depression, which had forced all three to move in together, hung in the air. The atmosphere was subdued, the lights dim, the interior drafty. The collected stuff of three women's lives littered tables and shelves, as if they no longer had the energy to clear it away. The wood floor was scratched bare, the faded and torn couch was near collapse. On the kitchen table were place-mats shredded almost beyond use, one covered with a palette of medications for the ailing sisters.

What I found most telling, however, was that Yvonne, Cécile, and Annette had not one visible keepsake of their celebrated former lives. Usually, people keep a special memento on the mantelpiece, on bookshelves, on a tabletop. Millions of photographs of the five famous sisters together as children and teens had made their way around the world; whole scrapbooks of Dionne quintuplet pictures still show up in people's attics and at garage sales. Yet, if the surviving sisters had held on to a favourite picture from that time, it was not to be seen. Nowhere was there a photo of the five girls together.

At sixty-three, Annette, Cécile, and Yvonne were nothing like the spunky seniors who grace contemporary retirement ads. Anyone could see they had endured difficult times. Pale and wan, they moved with the strain of pained hips and joints and sat somewhat hunched. Cécile walked slowly with a metal cane. Yvonne almost shuffled. Annette, trying hardest to be cheerful, was stooped. Their faces showed fatigue and anxiety. When they talked about the past, their mouths curved downward and their brows furrowed. They seemed almost apologetic about having to reveal unpleasant memories of losses and abuse. Never before had I come across people so wary but also so desperate to be heard. Yet somehow, the women still reserved a quiet dignity and polite manner.

A rapport was struck that Sunday between the three sisters and me. With my rudimentary high-school French and the sisters' relative though rusty familiarity with English, we entered into a unique conversation that deepened step by step. I leaned in closely, watching their eyes as they spoke. I repeated what they said in different ways, to test their meaning. These women were not naturally given to open expression of their feelings, with good reason: as youngsters, they were asked too many questions by the scientists who were probing them; as teens, they learned it was better to hide what they felt; as adults, they found few people they could trust. So it was no surprise that they spoke in a brief but direct manner, without embellishment or lengthy explanations. They told me of some of their mishaps and poor choices, and I shared some of mine, woman to woman.

Cécile, as spokesperson, was quicker to respond to my questions. But the two others had strong opinions when they spoke. Throughout that afternoon, the air was charged with the sisters' emerging emotions. They opened up wounds that had long been covered. Yvonne, usually the most reticent of the three, spoke plaintively of their separation from the rest of their family. Annette, with her arms folded tightly, told of the hurt of learning about what had happened to her trust-fund money only through archival documents. Cécile, twisting a piece of string from a frayed pillow, revealed the incredible sorrows of her adult life.

Towards the end of the interview, I asked about the *Time* magazine celebration. The women and Cécile's son Bertrand were to leave for New York two days later and stay overnight. Tarini said they were all set to go.

Cécile murmured low to me, "We're not going."

I asked aloud if their airfare had been paid, their hotel costs provided? Tarini said yes.

Cécile repeated an insistent but quiet "We're not going."

Once more Tarini spoke with assurance, this time smiling widely at Cécile as if to tell her that she needn't worry about anything.

Cécile looked at me imploringly.

Suddenly, I got it. "You don't have the right clothes? That's the problem?" I whispered.

She nodded several times, relieved that I had understood.

Of course it was the clothes. These were women who, as child stars, wore dresses and coats specially designed for them to meet royalty, to be photographed for worldwide publicity events, and to appear in Hollywood movies. But how could three impoverished and ailing women have come up with the money and effort required to find even simple dresses that would be elegant enough to take them to a ball with the likes of Sophia Loren, Barbara Walters, and Caroline Kennedy? They had already, long ago, lived their own version of the Cinderella story. They had learned painfully that there are no fairy godmothers.

Whatever instinct helped me catch on to why they wouldn't attend—whether it was compassion, intuition, a life-long career of reading people's feelings—it created a bond of trust between me and the sisters that ultimately led them to decide to talk openly to me about their little-known adult lives for this book. That incident also sparked my own desire to find out everything I could about what had happened to these world-renowned figures of Canadian history. Clearly, there was a vast period of the women's lives that had been kept hidden from the public. How had they come to be in a situation of total despair when they had once reaped a fortune for their government and themselves?

It was apparent to me then—and is far more so today—that a great injustice had been done to five innocent children and all their family members.

∽◦∾

The deal the sisters made with the Ontario government brought them and the late Marie's two daughters (Émilie had died unmarried) a total of $4 million, apologies from a chastened premier, and the surprise bonus of a judicial inquiry into what had happened to the money that had been set aside in a trust fund for the quintuplets' adult lives. A judge's investigation into the quintuplets' treatment while under government control would report back directly to the sisters and to the province's attorney-general.

In a global climate of economic restraint, in a politically conservative province, these timid women had roused the public and the press to outrage and forced politicians to rethink their strategy. A leader whose cutbacks to people on welfare, the homeless, and the health-care system had barely touched his ratings in the polls, had been pushed to change his style. The Dionne story, which had long since faded into the past, emerged again, an epic tale of lost glory that most people simply couldn't accept. It was time to bring history up to date.

1: LIVING WITH THE LEGEND

FOR JIMMY RODOLFOS, the teenage years in the blue-collar town of Woburn, Massachusetts, were sociable and energetic. Jimmy, the good-looking son of Tony the Greek barber, as his dad was called, was good at everything he did. His life in this quiet mix of farmland, tanneries, and basic shops tucked off the highway near Boston held promise as well as early success. His days were filled with school classes, student council, basketball, track, cross-country skiing in winter, and swimming every day at the local pond in summer.

He'd left his summer job as a short-order cook at 6 p.m. that steamy July 28, 1953. It was just ten days before his seventeenth birthday. Sweaty from his job and the muggy air, he hurried down to Horn Pond to cool off with a swim, just as he had done that same morning. He stripped again to his bathing suit and ran in as always with a shallow dive. But this time it wasn't shallow enough. His spinal cord took the hit. In a heartbeat, Jimmy Rodolfos was paralyzed from the shoulders down, a quadriplegic who had lost the use of his arms, legs, hands, and feet.

That same summer, pretty seventeen-year-old Fay White was suddenly struck with polio. She had been sleeping over at a girlfriend's house in Salem, Massachusetts, a town better known for its witch-hunts than for its working-class residents like Fay's divorced parents. There had been a weekend summer fair in the park near her friend's house, and Fay, intent on having fun, had put up with a headache all day. Unfortunately, the headache worsened, and soon she was sick to her stomach. Her legs started to feel the sensation of pins and needles, then weakened. The next day she slowly dragged herself to her father's nearby house, crawled up the steps, and asked for help to get home to her mother. The town doctor ordered an ambulance and diagnosed polio. Fay was paralyzed from the chest down, a paraplegic with no control of her legs or feet.

Jimmy and Fay met in the Massachusetts Hospital School for Crippled Children in Canton, Massachusetts. Despite its repellent name, the facility offered a pastoral campus, the friendship of dormitory life, and the only chance young people who couldn't walk or write on their own had to finish their high-school education and find a vocation. Jimmy had previously done some etching and pastel drawing, so he took easily to rehabilitation courses in mouth-painting, a skill that would later provide him with an income. Fay worked at the local YMCA as a secretary.

Although teachers and nursing staff tried to keep the sexes apart, and in particular tried to discourage Jimmy and Fay from thoughts of dating, the two fell in love. When Fay overheard talk of a doctor's report that Jimmy likely would not live beyond four or five years, she became determined that they would have together whatever time was possible. They were wed in Fay's church in October 1957—and were the only couple they knew of at that time with both partners in wheelchairs.

That was four decades ago, and for half of their long life together the Rodolfos have spent their days wrapped up in the very stuff of the Dionne legend—for legend is what the story has become, and nowhere is this more evident than in the Rodolfos' cluttered two-storey home, the centre of the Dionne Quint Collectors Club.

The myth of the enchanted Dionne childhood persists here despite the fact that time has changed everything else in Woburn. The town, now a high-tech industrial base, was made notorious in the 1980s as the site of a much-publicized court case, described in the book and film *A Civil Action*. Two major U.S. corporations were charged with contaminating local drinking wells; families lost eight children to leukemia. This landmark case ended with Beatrice Foods cleared of the charges in court, the families settling with chemical giant W.R. Grace, and Woburn no longer unknown.

Jimmy's grandfather's house, which was originally fashioned from a barn that had been pushed up and out to fit his eight children, had been torn apart again to accommodate Jimmy's and Fay's wheelchairs and give them a bedroom on the main floor. Now living on their own, Jimmy and Fay are both grey-haired and in their sixties.

Their house is like a time capsule full of Depression-era Dionne quintuplet memorabilia. Its rooms spill over with calendars, fans, plates, spoons—all promoting businesses or products with pictures of the five Dionne girls. There are personal items that once belonged to the sisters: jewellery, clothing, schoolbooks, early weight charts, gold lockets marked with each girl's name, two soft brown curls of baby-fine hair attached with a bobby pin. A Chicago reporter's notes, Papa Dionne's doodlings on a newspaper article, letters written by the doctor in charge of the quintuplets to an American medical specialist, original portraits and photos— all of it part of the voracious interest the media, the public, the doctors, and the quintuplets' own father had in the youngsters as public figures. Upstairs, in a spare room where some of the most valuable items are kept, five life-size quintuplet baby dolls stand in a crib that once was Émilie's. Covered with a plastic sheet to keep off dust, the dolls look like ghost babies watching over their belongings of old.

The Rodolfos are collectors at heart. Jimmy started by collecting pre-electricity-era irons, which he searched out at yard sales and flea markets. Back then, outings weren't easy; the couple had to depend on others to lift Jimmy in and out of the car and to push him in his wheelchair. Eventually, they bought a van with a hydraulic lift, and a motorized wheelchair for Jimmy.

While looking for irons at an antique show in January 1974, Jimmy had Fay's April birthday on his mind. With winter weather ahead, he realized he might not be able to get out again. He selected a few dolls and asked his wife to choose one for her gift. Fay picked a girl doll, a bald newborn. She cradled it in her arms, close to her chest. "Maybe there was a link to my not being able to have babies. I was drawn to it. We decided to collect dolls," Fay recalls.

The prized Dionne quintuplet dolls were a natural magnet. As with all collectors, the Rodolfos delighted in the hunt, seeking out dolls that were no longer made and increasingly hard to find. The most valued Dionne dolls were manufactured by the Madame Alexander Doll Company in New York, and had durable heads made of composition wood pulp and glue instead of fragile porcelain. When they were first created in the 1930s, one Dionne baby doll sold for $1.25. A set of all five snuggled in a wooden bed together cost $4.98. Today, collectors happily pay $1200 if they can find a set, and five life-sized baby dolls go for as much as $2500.

Two years after the quintuplets were born, a *Fortune* magazine article reported that the Dionne dolls had completely taken over Madame Alexander's business, bringing in the best sales in the company's history—$500,000 from the quintuplet dolls and their clothing in 1937 alone. Thanks to these tremendous profits, Madame Alexander and her husband, Philip Berhman, bought a French château-style house in Manhattan, the article goes on to say. Though they were barely toddlers, the girls were already making people rich.

The Rodolfos' first Dionne dolls were made by a different manufacturer; it cost them $225 for five babies in a basket. Soon, the couple were caught up in a single-minded pursuit. They sought out Dionne dolls only, and they read everything they could find about the sisters' miracle birth and the global fame that followed. In 1979, the Rodolfos created the Dionne Quint Collectors Club, which today—more than sixty years after the height of Dionnemania—still counts more than three hundred members from across the United States, Canada, and as far away as Holland.

So exuberant were the Rodolfos about their collection and club that they organized a Quintvention every five years. Members travelled to Woburn to see the Rodolfos' shrine-like home and to exchange Dionne collectibles. Whenever possible, the couple would feature special guests—Cécile's daughter, Elizabeth, was there in 1989, along with her cousin, a daughter of the late Marie. Several times, the Rodolfos invited the surviving quintuplets to attend; the women always sent back polite notes saying they couldn't make it.

Unknowingly, the couple had chosen to give their club the unit name that Annette, Yvonne, and Cécile Dionne least like: quint. It is a name that stamped the three women and their late sisters as a single entity with no individuality. As quints, they had no control; they were separated from the rest of their family for ever. "We were ashamed to be quints. I never thought we were miracle babies," Cécile says. Yvonne and Annette add, "We prefer the word 'sisters.'"

But neither the collectors nor people who had experienced the uplifting mania surrounding the babies in the otherwise dreary Depression years knew what being a quint meant in real life. How could they? All they saw was the image of care-free privilege that was fed by government-selected guardians to members of a hungry, and mostly uncritical, media. Jimmy Rodolfos, two years younger than the famed sisters, had in his youth read newspaper accounts and seen newsreels about the five little girls, and he believed they were living like fairy-tale princesses in Canada.

Of course, not all Dionne fans became official club members. Mabelle Tajan-Ponce, a Chilean woman, is one of the legion of people around the world who have always been intrigued by the quintuplets' story. People were drawn to them when they were just pathetic mites struggling for breath. They embraced them as they developed into lively, dimpled young-sters. And they remained fascinated with whatever glimpses they got of their grown-up lives.

In Chile, Tajan-Ponce grew up associating only a few items with Canada: the Royal Canadian Mounted Police, Eskimos, snow, and the Dionne quintuplets. When she was young, the local newspapers and magazines were full of stories about these amazing look-alike children. "It was a shock to see five of them at the same time. All the people spoke about that in Chile," Tajan-Ponce said. "For us, it was very sad to take chil-dren from parents. It was like a show, how they lived." She couldn't understand the difference between the Dionnes and a set of quintuplets who were born in Argentina to a wealthy textile manufacturer, Franco Diligenti, and his wife, in July 1943. The Diligentis were being brought up with their parents, and were photographed in magazines infrequently, while the Dionnes were raised in the public eye.

Today, Tajan-Ponce and her husband run a taxi company in Saint-Bruno, Quebec. They left Santiago in 1975 during the military regime of General Augusto Pinochet. One night, while driving home ten minutes before the state-imposed curfew, they were called to by military police, but the car windows were closed and music was playing on the radio. Their car was suddenly riddled with bullets. Tajan-Ponce and her husband were hit by fragments of bullets and pieces of glass from the shattered windows. Frightened for their lives and those of their three children, they knew it was time to get out. Eighteen months later, the family was in Quebec.

One day, Tajan-Ponce discovered not only that the Dionne sisters lived in the same town, but that two of them worked in the local library. "I thought, Can you imagine that they live here? I went downtown to try and see them. I went to the library, and there she [Annette] was and I watched her. Oh my God, it was so incredible."

From time to time, she caught sight of all three women in town. "They showed nothing about when they were famous. They are very humble, very quiet people. When I saw them on TV, I said to my children that twenty years ago I had heard about them. I remember a picture that showed at first they were very rich people with beautiful clothes."

Like countless others, Tajan-Ponce was a long-time Dionne follower who simply couldn't understand how the women's lives could have changed so dramatically.

As adults, the sisters have cooperated on two books that focus on the years when they were children and teens. In one, *We Were Five* by the American author James Brough, first written for *McCall's* magazine in 1963, the women revealed that they hadn't been as carefree and happy as people had believed them to be. But they so carefully skirted explicit details of pain and abuse that Annette now acknowledges that these can be found only "between the lines."

In *Family Secrets*, written by the French-Canadian author Jean-Yves Soucy and published in 1995, the three surviving quintuplets far more clearly described growing up in a troubled, abusive household. The book focuses on the years after their father won control of them from the government and they were moved, together with their family, into a massive home that was paid for from their trust fund.

Jimmy Rodolfos stopped reading that book after the first

three paragraphs. He disliked tarnish on his cherished shiny image of the quintuplets' fairy-tale past. He was disappointed, confused. "Why didn't they speak out sooner?" he asks, though he admits he missed the subtle hints in the earlier book. For her part, Fay says she understands that women might take years to gather the courage to speak out about abuse. But for both Rodolfos, immersed as they've been in the charmed aura of women they've never met, it's painful to accept. For them, the enduring fascination is with "those adorable babies and their miracle birth."

Says Fay, "Even knowing what happened, I still feel the same way about the Dionne phenomenon. I was told Jimmy wouldn't live long. We got married because they told us he didn't have much time. I identify with the quints that they survived; it was a miracle. They made people feel good, looking at healthy, happy babies. They were an inspiration."

Jimmy, too, speaks of inspiration. He went through a six-month period after his tragic accident when he raged aloud and wrestled with that eternal question: Why me? But he soon regained his determination not to let circumstances get the better of him. He found success as an artist, and was the first American to be invited to join the International Association of Mouth and Foot-Painting Artists. The arrangement allows for sales of his work through direct mail and has provided the couple with financial independence. But a bout of pneumonia in 1995 landed him in the hospital. Everything went wrong, and doctors said that three times he was near death. Jimmy was sure his days were numbered. He thought about applying to the Make a Wish Foundation, an organization usually associated with children suffering a fatal illness, to ask them to grant his special final request: a visit from Annette, Yvonne, and Cécile Dionne. Momentarily embarrassed by the memory, he adds a typical Rodolfos joke: "I think I'd jump out of my wheelchair."

The Rodolfos' devotion eventually led them to one of the rarest of quintuplet collectibles. A chance conversation in an American Midwest restaurant between a waitress and a member of the collectors' club revealed the existence of an original oil painting of Cécile. The portrait was the work of the noted artist and illustrator Willy Pogany, a native of Hungary who became successful in the U.S. He had been commissioned by the Karo syrup makers to paint a series of portraits of the quintuplets for the company's ads. Pogany had painted the girls from life, not a photograph, and he was one of only a few select artists permitted to spend hours each day at the Dionne nursery.

The waitress who owned the painting did not want to part with it at first. She had been married to the son of the president of Karo's New York ad agency. All five portraits had hung on his father's office walls. But days after the man died, four of the works were stolen. As if the thief hadn't enough time to get them all, Cécile's picture had been left behind. The other four portraits have never resurfaced.

The man's family took the remaining quintuplet portrait home; his widow later gave it to her son and his new wife. The couple ultimately divorced, and the waitress kept Cécile's portrait, carrying it with her through several moves. The Rodolfos negotiated with her for almost six years before she agreed to sell it. Fay drove herself and Jimmy in the van from Massachusetts to Florida to complete the deal. At last they looked upon the one-of-a-kind treasure—a beautiful rendition of Cécile at five, wearing an azure-blue dress, a bonnet, white gloves and holding a purse. Her face is tilted slightly, her eyes look upward with a tender, winsome smile. The portrait hangs in the Rodolfos' upstairs room. Coincidentally, just a few years later Cécile was given a copy of that same portrait, painted by a friend from a photograph of the original. It is the only likeness of herself that she keeps on view.

The quintuplets are shadowed by a popular image that survives through collectibles and dolls. As real-life individuals, they remain unknown. Just a few years ago, when Cécile lay in pain in a hospital with a blood clot in her lung and other complications following hip-replacement surgery, a nurse recognized that Madame Langlois, as she was listed, was a Dionne, one of the famous five sisters. The nurse, also a doll collector, enthused to her patient at some length about her "beautiful dolls" and how much she loved them, repeating the phrase of admiration and ownership several times: "My beautiful dolls. My beautiful dolls."

"Put your dolls away in the closet," a distressed Cécile told her firmly. "They are a thing of the past."

2: THE POLITICS OF A MIRACLE

IT TAKES MORE THAN an hour of driving on today's super-highways to get past the sprawl of Canada's largest city, Toronto, to the start of what is known as cottage country. Another hour north and the sleepy towns, fertile farm fields, and wooded bogs give way to a pleasureland of lakes and rivers where city folk can spend their weekends and be back in their offices on Monday. But that is not Ontario's true north. One must drive at least one more hour, past Huntsville—in summer, a bustling tourist town with cappuccino shops—for nature's dominance to become apparent. The craggy rocks of the Canadian Shield, which were blasted apart to form the highway, graduate to more rounded shapes moulded only by the force of the most recent ice age. The lowland woods are dense with white spruce and balsam fir, and thick sugar maples crowd the rolling hills. On a summer's night, a fortunate traveller may see the northern lights flashing riotous streaks of white and colour across the sky.

Just where the road passes an isolated truck stop and appears headed for endless wilderness, there's a sign showing an old wooden farmhouse and indicating that the Dionne Quint Museum is sixty kilometres away in North Bay, the small city that calls itself "the Gateway to the Far North." A city of some fifty-five thousand, North Bay has managed to survive through more bust than boom, picking itself up like a punch-drunk fighter with quirky defiance. An aerospace industry is growing there, and so is the population of retired folk. An adult-entertainment parlour does brisk business next to a Bible store. This is a place with north country attitude— "far enough away from Toronto," as locals like to say. Outdoorsy vacationers have always been drawn to the rugged countryside, its two bordering lakes, inexpensive tourist cabins, and superb fishing in bountiful Lake Nipissing.

But North Bay is far more famous for its past glory. In the 1930s, it was known to the far reaches of the globe as the home of the Dionne quintuplets, who were born in a nearby farming village to a family that already had five children. The extraordinary story of their birth and its sensational aftermath is documented in the museum that is the original Dionne homestead. Moved into the city in the 1980s, the historic farmhouse still attracts twelve thousand visitors in the months between May and October.

North Bay proudly boasts about its most-celebrated former locals, yet there is some ambivalence about the Dionnes' past among those who remember their early years. Anyone with an entrepreneurial spark suddenly made money on the quintuplets in those Depression days, when half a million people in the province were living on government relief. Even youngsters—the original squeegee kids—earned pennies by wiping the dirt off windows of cars that had snaked through dusty back roads to see the fantastic five children. Local businesses went from flat to frenzied. Today, old-timers revel in stories of the golden days of free-wheeling Dionnemania, when people with big cars and fur coats swarmed the region. But the story-tellers become uncomfortable when they're reminded of the effects on the little girls at the centre of the big show.

Verna Yarlasky, at eighty-one, was dismayed to hear that the surviving quintuplets had known poverty in their adult lives. The widely acclaimed "miracle birth" had catapulted Yarlasky's parents, like so many others, into sudden prosperity. The tourist camp they'd bought just two months before sat at the edge of Callander, a deflated former lumber-mill town that was three kilometres from the quintuplets' birthplace in the village of Corbeil. The Yarlaskys had accidently struck the mother lode. Suddenly townsfolk and outsiders alike were scrambling to put up motels, cabins, shacks—anything that would house the advancing armies of curiosity-seekers who were pumping cash into Callander and its surroundings.

Today, the Sunbeam Bungalows—a collection of modest efficiency cabins tucked in among the scented pines across from Callander Bay beach—still operate as a quiet fishing resort. But Yarlasky recalls the camp's heyday. "When the quintuplets were born, people slept all over the ground. It was amazing; everybody started to come up here." Her parents also owned the Callander Hotel, "the only eating place in town." Yarlasky remembers helping her sister, who was a hair-dresser, when she was asked to do the quintuplets' hair. "I still think of them as celebrities," she says with reverence even after six decades have passed. "It made me unhappy to learn they were unhappy."

Marguerite Audy's feelings are more complex, owing to her closer involvement with the Dionne story. She is the daughter of Donalda Alexandre Legros, the quintuplets' aunt

25

and one of two midwives who delivered the first three babies. At eighty-five, twice-widowed and practically bedridden in a North Bay nursing home, the thin, wiry woman has a feisty spirit and a sharp memory for the past, which she loves to recount. "I was twenty-one when they were born. In those days life was different. We were neighbours in a farming area. We didn't go out as much as today but visited one another's houses. After the quints were born the Dionnes' life changed. We all changed completely, too."

Audy's family left the farm and started a business in Callander, which they kept going for forty years. "It was a gift shop and a restaurant. The government expropriated our farm for a small amount of money to build the quints' playground. We didn't fight the government. We bought property in town and enjoyed the town. It happened at a poor time in the country, the Depression time; nobody had any money."

As a French-Canadian farm girl, Audy had helped out with chores until she was old enough to move to North Bay to do domestic work. "That's all there was for girls," she recalls. But with the quintuplets' record-shattering birth, new doors opened. She went to work with her mother in the gift shop, selling quintuplet memorabilia, Indian moccasins, British woollens and china, and serving in the restaurant. "It was very exciting. They [celebrity-seekers] came from all over the world —China, Japan, England, Scotland, Paris, Germany, Russia. It was a far cry from being a farmer's daughter. They came just to meet the people involved in the quintuplets' story. My mother was one of them, famous overnight. I never got over it. I still get emotional when I talk about it. We all prospered; we became much richer than when we were on the farm."

She remains thrilled by the memory of the long-ago drama, and loyal to the quintuplets as they were then. But with the primness of a disapproving relative, Audy is critical of their family strife and its public airing. "The parents were never ordinary again. People always pointed their fingers and talked. When they gained custody of the girls, people would say it was not a good idea. There was too much difference between the two sides of the family. The girls grew up like little princesses with no mother or father around.

"I didn't like their books," she goes on to say, referring to *Family Secrets* and *We Were Five*. "I didn't think it was proper to criticize the family. Everybody has a family feud, but it's a secret. They were a split family that didn't work out. You can't lay blame. If the government wanted to help, they could have built a big home with hired help for the five babies, and they would have all grown up together. That's what the community thinks."

More than sixty years later, the Dionne story still evokes powerful feelings in people. The vast majority are sympathetic to the quintuplets and their family, but some local people who were there when it all happened argue the past with leftover bitterness and envy. There is a small-town defensiveness about what went wrong. Some insist that the five sisters were lucky to be raised like royalty; others say they must have spent their money unwisely. Long-time families don't like to see their old neighbours airing their dirty laundry, as if worried that it reflects badly on them.

The Dionne story began in the dark, pre-dawn hours of May 28, 1934, when a twenty-five-year-old, sweet-faced farm wife

27

hovered between life and death during a terrifying premature labour. One by one, five of the tiniest babies ever seen were born. The first one could be held in the palm of an adult hand; each of the next four was smaller than the last. Amazingly, they looked exactly alike, five girls born at seven months and together weighing a total of only 13.6 pounds (the smallest, Marie, weighed less than two pounds). Their appearance, with their finger-sized arms and insect-like legs, was grotesque, their bodies blue. Only their dark eyes and impossibly long lashes showed human appeal.

Born in a simple backwoods farmhouse in a northern French-Canadian community, the frail girls were the first quintuplets ever to survive for more than a few days. Genetic experts calculated that the chances of a woman bearing even non-identical quintuplets were fifty-four million to one; the odds of five identical babies coming from one egg were considered incalculable. These babies were unique.

The first report of their birth began with a phone call from Oliva Dionne's brother Léon, who ran a garage in Callander and had driven his truck to his brother's barnyard for a load of manure. He noticed that the doctor was at the farmhouse—an uncommon occurrence in an area where neighbourly midwives assisted in normal births—and soon learned the astonishing news that he'd become an uncle to five identical baby girls.

When he got back to town, he phoned the editor of the *North Bay Nugget* and asked if a birth notice announcing the arrival of five babies at one time would cost more than the notice of a single birth. City editor Eddie Bunyan was sure this was a joke. Once convinced, he told Léon that there would be no cost at all, then sat down at his typewriter and pounded out forty-four words for the Canadian Press office in Toronto:

> North Bay, May 28—Mrs. Oliva Dionne, residing within a few miles of Callander, nine miles south of here, gave birth to five girls today. All were healthy, said Dr. A. R. Dafoe, Callander attending physician. Mrs. Dionne is 24 [sic] and had previously given birth to six children.

The report was sent by teletype machine to Toronto and wired to the Associated Press in New York. From there, the story was transmitted to the ends of the world by means of the technology of the day, cables that had been dropped beneath the seas.

Canada's largest newspaper, the Toronto Daily Star, was uncommonly conservative on the day of the birth. Its telegraph editor, who handled all wire stories, asked the paper's North Bay correspondent, Art Hill, to dispatch two hundred words, including an interview with the father, to add to the CP account. The resulting story appeared on page nineteen, the front page of the Star's second section, and turned to page twenty-one. On the second day, the Star ran a longer story, but still on page nineteen. Veteran Star newsman Jocko Thomas, who was then a cub reporter on the night police beat, says that the newspaper, which usually was known for its aggressive, no-holds-barred coverage of sensational stories, soon caught up with a vengeance.

The Reverend R.E. Knowles was a defrocked Presbyterian minister who had befriended the newspaper's owner and publisher, Joseph E. Atkinson, and was hired to write profile interviews. He commuted by train from his home town of Galt, Ontario, west of the city, to work at his Toronto office, just a few doors down the hall from Atkinson's. On May 30, two days after the quintuplets' birth, Knowles' seatmate on the train was a young newsman from Chicago, Charles Blake, a hotshot reporter for the *Chicago American*. Blake said he was on his way to Toronto, and from there on to Callander, to write about the fascinating newborns. Knowles hadn't read the small story about the five babies, nor it appeared had Atkinson, whom he told about it.

In a flash, the publisher was on the phone to his son-in-law, Harry C. Hindmarsh, the paper's managing editor, who immediately dispatched ace reporter Gordon Sinclair and Fred Davis, a freelance photographer the paper regularly used in those tight days of minimal staff. The two men, along with a hired nurse, were driven to the little-known northern town in a special car the *Star* reserved for its crack reporting teams. Their driver was Queen's Park reporter Keith Munro, who would edit Sinclair's daily reports on the infants as they struggled to stay alive. The newspaper also sent along five complete layettes of babies' clothing and later dispatched incubators to North Bay (but only four, since Blake had brought one with him from Chicago).

All over the world, people were soon caught up in what was being touted as the latest wonder of the world. On June 24, 1934, the *New York Times* reported that there had been only thirty-two authentic instances of the birth of quintuplets; the first was in 1694 and the most recent was in 1923. The Dionnes already held the record for survival. Five seemingly healthy brothers had been born in Kentucky in 1896, but by the fourteenth day all had died. In 1866, in Lisbon, Portugal, one girl of a quintuplet set lived for fifty days, but after her no other quintuplet had lived longer than two weeks.

The odds against the Dionnes were even more fantastic. The original single egg that Elzire Dionne carried had split *in utero* and created twins, Yvonne and Annette; it split again to form Cécile and possibly another twin; and split a third time to create Émilie and Marie, described as the only "mirror twins" (Émilie was left-handed while all the others were right-handed, and Émilie and Marie had hair whorls that twirled in opposite directions). The possibility of a sixth embryo was suggested when Alan Roy Dafoe, the doctor who had seen Elzire because of severe swelling during her pregnancy, reported that she had had pains at the beginning of her third month and had passed an egg-sized object.

All five newborns fought a Sisyphean battle to hold on to life, labouring over every breath through their first shaky days and weeks in a crowded house with no electricity or indoor plumbing; beset by pesky flies; exposed to the germs of other children, curious neighbours, relatives, and invading strangers. Their epic struggle to survive inspired such soaring optimism that the fragile infants captured the world's imagination. And no wonder. Daily progress reports of a half-ounce gained or a fevered crisis passed were the happiest pieces of news available in a world weary from widespread unemployment and the looming threat of war. Long before fertility drugs made multiple births common enough to spark parental support groups, the birth of the Dionne quintuplets seemed a metaphor of hope for a pessimistic world.

This was the cruel era when the world had been plunged into economic stagnation. Five years had passed since the infamous New York stock-market crash set off a rash of suicides among people who had lost their fortunes. Nearly everyone else was still barely scraping by. In Canada alone, 1.5 million people were on welfare, and countless more lived from hand to mouth. Each day, the reports that these five scrawny infants were holding on against all odds were the most encouraging news around.

The media hoopla that followed the Dionne quintuplets' birth fed the public's appetite for happy news of the girls. Interest was fanned by news organizations bent more on competition than investigation, and by a newly elected Liberal government, under Premier Mitchell Hepburn, that swiftly recognized the babies' enormous political and economic value.

Their father, Oliva Dionne, was unprepared for the whirlwind of sudden challenges and decisions he faced. He and his wife, Elzire, had had no warning that their family would suddenly double in size, and that they would have five more children in need of food and costly care. Even more alarming to the couple, the newborns drew a barrage of reporters, hucksters, and bothersome crowds to their farmhouse door.

The first, swift challenge came from Dr. Dafoe, the Callander doctor who was called in to help deliver the quintuplets. He arrived after the village midwives, Marie Jeanne Lebel and Donalda Legros, had already delivered the first two infants and as a third was on the way. The doctor delivered the last two babies, then left to arrange for a nurse to watch over the sickly newborns whose mother was near death. He also needed to find a supply of milk, as Elzire had never been able to breast-feed.

Dr. Dafoe had come to Callander twenty-five years before, grateful to find a town where he could practise medicine far removed from professional competition in Toronto, and from the pressure of his ambitious mother and hard-driving physician father, who were pillars of their small-town community of Madoc, in eastern Ontario. An awkward-looking short man with an overly large head, Dafoe stammered in personal conversation and kept aloof from all but a few associates. He had married a public health nurse who died of a brain tumour when their only son, William, was seven. Devastated by his loss, Dafoe sent his son away to a boarding school and grew ever more reclusive. In all his years in the region, he had never learned the language of his many French-Canadian patients. When the historic Dionne birth shone an international spotlight on the obscure country doctor, Dafoe was fifty-one, had diabetes, and expected nothing else from life but to work and retreat to his favourite pastime, reading.

Dafoe's long-time strength as a physician in the northern wilds had been his respect for common-sense methods, clean water, and fresh air. With the premature quintuplets, his reviving remedy of two drops of rum in ten drops of water, along with a risky enema procedure, had helped keep them alive. But these awesomely tiny creatures were still faltering. Dafoe turned to his brother, a prominent Toronto obstetrician, for advice. Dr. William Dafoe in turn called on Canada's authoritarian pediatric expert, Dr. Alan Brown of Toronto's Hospital for Sick Children. With such weighty backup, Dafoe took aggressive charge of the quintuplets. He refused to let the parents even hold their babies, and demanded that the other children be sent away from the house in which he and two nurses now held sway. Whether caused by a clash of cultures between the anglophone physician and the francophone farmer or a personality conflict between two stubbornly independent men under extreme pressure, the rift between Oliva Dionne and Dr. Dafoe was immediate and lasting.

As far as Dafoe was concerned, the quintuplets' father was simply unable to comprehend the dire threat that infectious germs posed to the infants. The Dionnes' parental rights were dismissed, and Dafoe was quickly cast by the watchful press as the quintuplets' only hope for survival. None of the mostly English-speaking press pack who hung about for hours on the Dionnes' property in search of stories took into account that the couple had already raised five children in the same serviceable log farmhouse that the reporters were now describing as a shack. Oliva was portrayed as a simple-minded peasant unfit to raise the miracle children. Elzire was practically ignored.

Within days, a confused, distraught Oliva Dionne made a fateful mistake. He had been pressed by a couple of slick entrepreneurs from Chicago to allow the quintuplets to be exhibited at the Century of Progress Exposition at the Chicago World's Fair in exchange for a payment that would end his financial worries. The deal had been sweetened by a down payment of $100 ready cash—a sum equal to a month's wages hauling gravel for the government, when he could get the work. Unsure of what to do, Dionne turned for guidance to his parish priest, who encouraged him to go ahead. But in truth, Father Daniel Routhier had more than the babies' best interests at heart; he had his eye on a percentage of the money so he could build a new church. He told Dionne that the babies' birth was a miracle from the Creator, and that something—he and Dionne settled on seven percent—was owed in return.

Dionne also sought advice from the babies' physician, in this case respecting his professional knowledge. Dafoe is reported to have responded positively to his query about the offer, saying that the babies were unlikely to live long and that Dionne might as well make money while he could. Dionne insisted that the contract include a clause assuring that the babies would not be moved without their doctor's consent.

Elzire's role in the matter is more elusive. When Oliva approached her about the contract, she refused to sign, making the deal invalid. Why she refused will never be known. When she was asked, she told an American reporter that she was never shown the contract, and that Oliva had changed his mind within twenty-four hours of signing.

That didn't stop the press, of course, who were starved for fresh stories to appease their editors and frustrated by the Dionnes' refusal to talk to them. They sounded the alarm over the quintuplets being sold for exhibit in a circus-like sideshow, even as baby Marie was reportedly at death's door. The spectre of such display taking place in the United States, the smugly dominant country south of the border, made it even worse. That's all that was needed for the cocky new Ontario Liberal government of Mitchell "Just Call Me Mitch" Hepburn to barge into the situation and take control.

﹌☙﹍

Mitch Hepburn had inherited his grandfather's dairy farm in Elgin County, in southern Ontario, plus part of his sizeable estate of stocks, bonds, cash, and mortgages. As a novice federal Liberal candidate in 1926, Hepburn was propelled to victory by his whirlwind oratory and personal dynamism, and went to Ottawa as a back-bencher at age thirty. Eight years later, running as a provincial Liberal, he became, on June 19, 1934, the youngest premier in Ontario's history. Shortly after, he arbitrarily flexed his new political muscle against Oliva Dionne, a powerless, hard-scrabble farmer, with disastrous results for the Dionne family and for the five little girls the government was meant to protect.

Dionne and Hepburn had a few similarities, though these were largely obscured by their vast difference in social station. Both were stubborn, determined men born to farming. Hepburn was just seven years older than Dionne and had little more education, having completed only grade ten. In his election campaign he had wooed Franco-Ontarian voters, aware of their influence when they voted as a bloc. But as one man facing another, the two were of vastly different worlds. Unlike Dionne, Hepburn was a gentleman farmer who prospered on one of the largest farms in his township. While Dionne was a family man trying to eke out a living, Hepburn was a womanizer whose reckless drinking and affairs had to be covered up by his aides so as not to ruin his political career.

A volatile and erratic personality, Hepburn seized hold of Dionne's babies in an opportunistic move at a time when he and his wife, Eva, were childless. He showed no compassion in what he did to Dionne and his family. Nor did he see the stunning contradiction when he and Eva, encouraged by a government promotion that used the quintuplets' first birthday to introduce Adopt a Child Week, gave a home to an orphan boy, Peter. A year later, they adopted a daughter, Patricia; she was followed four years later by Helen.

It was the public's spontaneous reaction to the birth that impressed the wily and populist Hepburn, and he seized on the chance to play the role of the hero saving the struggling infants from certain death (which is what he claimed would be their fate if the Chicago showmen or other exploiters got their hands on the helpless girls). On July 26, 1934, the five sisters were removed, by a judicial order quietly arranged in surrogate court in the District of Nipissing, from their parents' authority. They were placed under the two-year guardianship of four provincial appointees. Their grandfather, Olivier Dionne, was the only guardian linked to the family. The others were Dr. Dafoe, his friend Ken Morrison, and William H. Alderson of the Ontario Red Cross, who had arranged for the shipments of mothers' milk to nurse the infants. This would turn out to be only the first of three guardianship acts that would control the girls until they were twenty-one.

The author and historian Pierre Berton, who wrote *The Dionne Years* in 1977, said that Oliva Dionne was reported to have been easily encouraged to sign the first guardianship agreement with the province because of the huge medical and nursing costs involved with keeping his daughters alive. The Red Cross initially was paying for all care, but there was no defined arrangement. Berton wrote that years later, a bitter and outspoken Dionne said he had signed under duress because Dafoe and Alderson threatened to cut off the shipments of mothers' milk.

Once the province had control of the girls, all the other power grabs and exploitations were possible. And they followed as surely as bees to honey. Just four days after the guardianship was announced, the next extraordinary plan was unveiled. For the first time ever, a special hospital would be built for the benefit of just five citizens. It would have the best medical equipment of the day, as well as all the modern conveniences, like electricity and indoor plumbing, which were absent in the rest of the area. Dr. Dafoe would run it, and nurses and other staff would live there along with the babies. But there would be no place for the family. The girls would be isolated from their parents and siblings even though the hospital was erected across the road from the Dionne's home.

And so it was that on a rainy September day in 1934, the still-delicate quintuplets, just three and a half months old, were moved to their new dwelling, the Dafoe Hospital and Nursery, which became their home for nine years.

Their parents suffered from the start. Bereft of their babies, stunned by the doctor's rigid control over their visits, swarmed by curious and often rude onlookers, and deeply wounded by being described in the press as dumb and uncaring people, Oliva and Elzire lost battle after battle to hold on to their role as parents of the quintuplets.

The couple came from sturdy Norman families who had farmed the stubborn, rock-strewn fields in northeastern Ontario for two generations and who were respected in their small, isolated community. Waves of French-Canadian settlers began arriving from Quebec in 1888, following the Canada Pacific Railway line as it opened up Ontario's forested northland. Olivier Dionne, the quintuplets' grandfather, had worked in New England cotton mills until he saved enough money to buy three hundred acres of Corbeil farmland and build a home in 1896. Oliva Dionne was born in that house, and would later purchase it from his father for his own family. Elzire Dionne's father, Moïse Legros, also from Quebec, had a farm a short distance away. Elzire was known among her neighbours as devoutly religious, a quality much admired in a French-Catholic community where the parish church and its priest dominated all aspects of life.

Like his father before him, Oliva Dionne lived off the barely fertile land by farming in the summer and trapping and hunting in the winter. He picked up cash by hauling gravel with his wagon and horses, renting out his hay bailer, and selling fox pelts in North Bay. Slim, with large dark eyes and unruly thick hair, he stood out from his neighbours for more practical reasons. At thirty-one, he was one of the few men around who had proudly refused to go on welfare, though the hard times had pushed him to take out a small mortgage on his farm. He owned one of only two vehicles in the area; had nine years of schooling, which was more than most; and spoke English better than many. His resourcefulness would later help him adapt to a far different role as a crusader fiercely determined to regain control of his famous daughters. But in the dizzying hours after their birth, he was simply a young man facing expenses and outside influences that were beyond his understanding.

For her part, Elzire Dionne had known dramatic change

by the age of seven, when her mother died. She was forced to leave school at eleven to look after her seven brothers. As a teenager with an angelically pretty face and a reserved manner, she caught the eye of the most eligible bachelor around. Marrying at sixteen made her a younger bride than was usual for Corbeil, but she was already used to home-making and doing her share of work in the fields. The notion of having a large family was second nature to her, so much so that as a girl she had collected more than ten dolls, eerily fore-shadowing the babies she would bear. By the time she gave birth to the quintuplets, the twenty-five-year-old already had five other children ranging in ages from eleven months to almost eight years. A sixth child, baby Léo, had died of pneumonia at one month.

The quiet and predictable lives of Oliva and Elzire Dionne were shattered by the sensationalized birth of the five baby girls, an event that suddenly exposed the humble farming family to the world's scrutiny. Elzire was reportedly embarrassed to have birthed such a brood, but she consoled herself through religion, convinced that what had happened was a divine event. Whatever had brought these children to them, the strong-willed couple was determined not to give them up passively.

The father's fight began with frustrated acts of defiance. In one instance, he crawled through a drainpipe to sneak into the nursery. In another publicized episode, reported by the *Mail and Empire* (which became the *Globe and Mail*), a flurry took place at the Dafoe Hospital and Nursery when Oliva and Elzire Dionne arrived for a visit with their five baby girls. The father was carrying a suitcase, a signal to reporters that the couple would attempt to move in. A uniformed guard convinced them to turn back rather than be arrested. In the article, Dr. Dafoe was quoted as saying that the parents had access to the hospital at all times. No members of the press checked to see if this was true in practice. It was not.

Pierre Berton, whose book focused on the Dionne quintuplets' unusual childhood experience and the era that spawned it, points out that there existed at that time in Ontario an underlying racism towards French Canadians, particularly rural farmers who persisted in having large families at a time of declining English population growth. This racist disdain—whipped up by fanatics into fears of being overrun by a minority—made the snatching away of these celebrated children acceptable to the English majority. The public was content with news reports that merely echoed official government pronouncements.

But Oliva soon picked up political smarts and got help from Franco-Ontarian lobby groups that were advancing French education rights, and he eventually hired lawyers to push what became an obsessive drive to regain control of his daughters. In the early days, the only newspaper that consistently took issue with the government's involvement was the French-language *Le Droit* of Ottawa, a paper read mostly by French Canadians, whose opinions on the matter were ignored for a long time. When other francophone newspapers later took up Dionne's fight and railed against the government for preventing the youngsters from rejoining their family, the issues stressed were more often political—language and education—rather than the personal loss to five children of an everyday family life.

Elzire remained largely behind the scenes. She understood English, which her husband often spoke, but would not speak it to strangers. As a result, she was even more silent with reporters than her husband was, and really opened up only to one sympathetic French-speaking American reporter, Lillian Barker, who talked her way into the farmhouse and Elzire's confidence a year after the birth. Writing in a gushing, "sob sister" manner, the flamboyant Barker penned several serialized articles and two later books based on the family's views, one of which was so inaccurate that it was ultimately removed from sale in Canada.

Elzire also found a sympathetic ear in Almanda Marchand, the founder and president of the Fédération des femmes canadienne-françaises (FFCF). After a visit to Corbeil in April 1935 and a meeting with her group's North Bay chapter, Marchand sent a report supporting the Dionnes' parental rights to Premier Hepburn through Paul Leduc, a French-Canadian Cabinet minister. Marchand reported that Elzire had said at the meeting that she was anxious that the quintuplets' board of guardians include her and two other women, both mothers, who could understand her longing to be with the babies as much as possible.

Marchand was a member of an élite and wealthy French family that lived in Ottawa, and she knew how to work the political system. She was also a Liberal whose voice got heard by those in power. In June 1936, she convinced Ontario's welfare minister, David Croll, that the nursery should be renamed the Dionne Nursery rather than the Dafoe Hospital and Nursery. David Welch, a professor of social work, wrote in a special 1994 Dionne edition of the *Journal of Canadian*

Studies, "It was typical of the women of the time and shows the important role of the mother," that the women's lobby groups were among the first to mobilize.

Though Elzire depended on her husband in outside matters, she was a strong presence in her own household and tried to assert herself in the quintuplets' lives in whatever ways she could find. Out of frustration, she sometimes didn't visit the girls for weeks at a time; yet she would raise a fuss about their nutrition or the way their hair was being styled. As part of her plan to win her children back, she offered to continue her own schooling and to learn English. She also made it clear that she wanted all her children to have educational advantages that were not available in the tiny rural village of Corbeil. Through the supportive voice of the French vice-president of the Ontario Liberal Women's Association, she is reported to have expressed concern that the quintuplets' so-called progressive education might make her other children feel inferior. And in a rare public statement, given to *Le Droit* one year after the girls' birth, she thundered: "I will no longer give birth to children for the government."

Her anger and resentment also naturally spilled out in confrontations with the babies' nurses, who were instructed to restrict her involvement. In one incident, Elzire took two visiting cousins over to see the quintuplets, who were asleep on the nursery's porch at the time. As the party approached, a nurse appeared, screamed, "Don't you come up these steps!" and slammed the door in Elzire's face. Accounts of other tumultuous scenes occurring in front of the children were recorded by some members of the staff, who rarely saw these eruptions from the mother's perspective. Nurse Yvonne

Leroux wrote in her diary, "There is a terrible undercurrent of everything hateful going on." On March 18, when the Dionnes threatened to move into the hospital, Leroux wrote, "He and She came over with trunks and walked in and sat down." In that instance, the provincial police were able to smooth over the dispute, and the Dionnes went home. "The trouble is all this emotional upset is a terrible strain on us and the babies sense it and become difficult to handle," wrote Leroux. Eventually, Elzire let greater periods of time elapse between visits—she did not come across the road for two months, for example, after her daughters turned two.

Meanwhile, Dr. Dafoe went from unknown rural physician to internationally acclaimed country doctor who had saved the lives of the miracle quintuplets. He was brought by a publicity-seeking drugstore chain, the Liggett Company, to New York and embraced by the world's most sophisticated press. He was taken to Washington to meet President Franklin Roosevelt. He was nominated, in 1934, for the Nobel Prize for Medicine (but lost to a trio of American physicians). His fame spread not only because of news reports, but also because of the many photographs and frequent newsreel films of the babies and their doctor that were allowed under contracts negotiated by the guardians. All monies received were to be paid into a trust fund for the quintuplets. Some fees, however, were paid directly to Dafoe for his part in promoting products or caring for the girls during the filming of movies and advertisements in which they appeared. Most notably, he received three annual cheques of $10,000 for his role as technical adviser to Twentieth Century Fox, which produced three feature films starring the girls. (The first of these, *The Country Doctor,* was a Hollywood version of Dafoe's life, and was the box office hit of 1936.) To be fair, some companies wouldn't sign deals that excluded the physician, whose image they considered to be an asset. When he died, Dafoe, who for years had treated patients who had no money to pay him, left an estate of $182,466, almost all in stocks and bonds—the equivalent in today's dollars of well over $1 million. Money was flowing everywhere, with huge amounts coming back out of the girls' fund to pay for running the hospital, staff salaries, and expenses.

In 1935, Oliva Dionne finally got a chance to make some money, too. He and Elzire were invited to tour Chicago, Detroit, and several other midwestern cities and to appear briefly on stage as the world's most famous parents. It would prove to be the second terrible mistake Oliva Dionne would make. The media continued to portray the couple as foolish country bumpkins. In fact, the ridicule was so intense that it embarrassed many Canadians and fanned the fire of opportunism in the calculating mind of Hepburn, who was still riding high as the saviour of Ontario's best-known natural resource.

Within weeks of the notorious Dionne tour, a second guardianship plan was quickly rammed through the legislature despite opposition dissent. On March 25, 1935, the quintuplets became "special wards of His Majesty the King" until they reached eighteen. The old guardians were paid off and a new set was appointed. Ontario's welfare minister, David Croll, was named "special guardian" and given unlimited control over the children, their estate, and the appointment and activities of the "active guardians." These were Dr. Dafoe and Judge Joseph A. Valin, a Franco-Ontarian and Liberal whom Pierre Berton described as "approaching senility" at the time he was appointed. Oliva Dionne was also included, as the "natural guardian." Since Dionne boycotted all meetings for the first three years, Dafoe was effectively in charge of all day-to-day decisions regarding the five girls and Croll was in control of their finances.

An editorial in the *Mail and Empire* said the aim of the guardianship act was "not to remove the children but to surround them with the care and opportunities in life they could not otherwise have." Days later, the *Star* quoted a United Press story that said the government's plan was to "build up the Dionne quintuplets' trust fund in a manner which will permit the financial care of Mr. and Mrs. Oliva Dionne and the five elder Dionne children, as well as the famous girls." The article added that "the government cannot withdraw money from the trust fund." Fine sentiments, but any journalist who had bothered to look could have found out easily how expenses approved by the government-appointed guardians had begun leaching the fund. Indeed, a claim by Croll that the government was administering the fund "without cost of any kind" was a blatant lie, yet no enterprising reporter looked to the court records of the periodic passing of accounts by a judge to check this assertion.

The creation of Quintland was the next step, and from a public-relations point of view it was a brilliant move. But its five child stars, who were put on display there, quickly realized that they were like caged animals in a zoo. "We were a freak show," Cécile says simply. That reality would become the sisters' everlasting shame.

3: DIONNEMANIA

QUINTLAND WAS Canada's first entertainment theme park, though it offered a glimpse of a human miracle instead of amusement-park rides. There was a carnival atmosphere, with hucksters and hype and give-aways of so-called fertility stones that were culled daily from a local quarry. One contemporary writer described the scene as "the greatest Midway attraction of all time."

Where could tourists find a more wholesome, feel-good escape than in a quaint area where some people spoke a different language, and where they were treated to the never-before-seen spectacle of five indistinguishable little girls prodded by nurses to dance, twirl, clap, and perform antics? What could give the viewers more satisfaction than knowing that the children's superior care and the public's free admission was the gift of a generous government that was also providing a secure future for its treasured little leading ladies? So effective was the government's propaganda campaign that there are people who still believe today, despite anything they read to the contrary, that the Dionne quintuplets were the luckiest children alive.

Of course, no one who visited Quintland liked to acknowledge that they had been to a freak show. And it was easy to be

47

deceived. Even before they had reached one year, the girls were baby-doll perfect: large, dark eyes with thick, curled lashes that swept their glowing cheeks; button noses; rosebud lips; and thick, reddish-brown hair that the nurses shaped into finger curls. Happy in each other's constant company and attended to for every physical need, the sisters beamed sunny personalities with giggles and smiles. People flocked to the far-flung hospital to see them from their earliest days, and the nurses obliged by bringing them to the porch outside, holding them aloft one at a time and calling their names. Sometimes, when one of the girls was ill, another would be brought out under two different names.

To accommodate the increasing numbers of visitors, a viewing gallery around the children's outdoor playground was opened on July 1, 1936. Curious onlookers crowded into the strange, darkened corridor of the horseshoe-shaped gallery, convinced that the children didn't know they were being watched because of the barrier of thickly meshed dark screens on the outside of the windows. The Toronto psychologist Dr. William E. Blatz, who helped design the structure, described it thus:

> The building, the first of its kind ever to be built, is a U-shaped structure consisting of a single passageway entered from the base of the U, through which the visitors walk to one of the two exits at the extremities…. The outer wall of this passageway is windowless, and the inner side affords a view of the enclosed space and is protected by glass and a fine-mesh wire screen.

As the passageway is relatively dark, the screen disperses the light coming in from without so that onlookers are invisible to anyone in the play-ground.

Years later, Annette revealed that it was not so. Émilie had blown the whistle on the deception as far back as age five. One day when the sisters were taken, on schedule, to the outdoor playground area that was enclosed on three sides by the observatory, Marie held up a toy monkey. Émilie told her, "Put that down, or people will think there are six of us."

But none of this seemed to matter to an exhilarated public that was invited, free of charge, to witness these sweet children at play for a half-hour, twice each day, throughout the summer months. Rain or shine. People took up the invitation in droves. Hundreds would line up four abreast at least an hour and a half before each showing of the quintuplets. In the viewing gallery, two hundred people at a time would move through the passageway in two diverging lines. A massive parking lot that could hold a thousand cars at a time was built, and a huge canvas screen was erected between the nursery and the playground so the crowds could see the girls only from the viewing gallery.

Quintland was a gold-mine that brought a rush of wild boom times to the North. During the eight years the viewing gallery was open, almost three million people went there to see the girls and spend money in the area. Whole convoys of Canadian soldiers moving through the province were diverted to Quintland to see the wondrous spectacle. The Hollywood movie star Bette Davis visited in the fall of 1939 and announced that she would never play in a movie with the girls because they would certainly steal the show.

A 1938 *Harper's* magazine article, which assessed only American tourist spending, estimated the youngsters' enormous worth to the province. "The value of the American tourist traffic to Ontario, even in a depression year, is said to be between $100,000,000 and $125,000,000. According to the conservative reckoning of the Dominion Government's Travel Bureau in Ottawa, the five little charmers near Callander are directly responsible for at least a fifth of the gate.... They are a twenty to twenty-five million dollar attraction and, as such, one of Canada's most important businesses." The writer, Merrill Denison, went on to explain, "Capitalized at four per cent [the going rate for the times], these Quint-inspired revenues make the Dionne girls a $500,000,000 asset to Ontario." Put simply, it would take a half-billion-dollar investment to generate as much money as the girls drew annually from U.S. tourists who travelled to see them.

The *Harper's* article was quoted forty years later by author Berton and the 1938 estimates have been used by journalists ever since. But translated into today's dollars, the figures for the girls' value to the province are even more staggering: the Dionne quintuplets brought in to Ontario the equivalent of $250 million a year, making them an asset that would be worth $5 billion today.

Thanks to these overnight celebrities, the rugged stretch of highway leading to Quintland was paved, tourist cabins sprang up like dandelions, and local people who'd been living from day to day made money in every way imaginable. People swarmed Callander, a town that would once have had difficulty accommodating seventy-five visitors. Those who were lucky enough to find a room could park themselves in a comfortable chair and watch the unending line of traffic crawling towards what one journalist called "the most spectacular, if most refined, sideshow on earth." From the crack of dawn to long after nightfall, cars bearing a wide assortment of U.S. state licence plates rolled though the village at the incomprehensible rate of one per minute. Wrote one observer: "Callander is now at the crossroads of America."

Anyone related to the Dionne story, from the midwives to relatives and eventually the girls' own father, went into business signing autographs, selling souvenirs, pumping gas. Denison described the Dionne effect as "rural rehabilitation.... The five girls, in their fifty-two months of existence, have helped save a sizeable city from bankruptcy, speeded the building of modern roads, improved real estate values, increased the township assessment rolls, taken a few hundred people off relief," and more.

Certainly, Ontarians recognized the good fortune embodied in these children. And given that the government treated the quintuplets as objects for profit, it followed naturally that the public also believed it had rights to the benefits the girls provided. As French-Canadian activists argued for the parents' custody to be restored, one Quebec politician proposed that his province invite the whole family to move there instead. Immediately, an editorial in the *Ottawa Journal* of May 14, 1936, responded cheekily that Ontario would go a long way to please Quebec, even so far as to hand over Premier Mitch Hepburn, but that "when they ask for our Quints ... a time has come to say No. We value the quintuplets

for several good and sufficient reasons. There is the senti-
mental point of view. There is the fact that no other such
family is known in all the world, nor in the pages of authentic
history. And there is the very practical consideration of the
quintuplets as a tourist asset." Five individual little girls had
become a single entity: Our Quints.

Not surprisingly, businessmen from North Bay rushed to cash
in on the booming site. On a paved plaza that had been the
roadway between the original homestead and the Dafoe Hospital
and Nursery, Philip Adams, who had a clothing store in town,
staked out his booth. Adams even hired Madame Lebel to staff
his "midwives" stand and sell her stamped autograph along with
his goods. His grandson, ten-year-old Murray Ruby, sold *Mail
and Empire* newspapers to tourists for three cents apiece;
Murray's uncle put himself through law school by snapping
pictures of people posed in front of a tepee with a hired Indian.
A small black bear cooped up in chicken wire was another lure.

One North Bay entrepreneur, Dan Saya, went into business with Oliva Dionne in the largest shop on site, notable for
its garish signs, which sold British woollens and souvenirs,
and drew tourists eager to see the world's most talked-about
father. Dionne, who had a second booth of his own, was criticized in the press for charging twenty-five cents for his autograph, and was wrongly assumed to be taking all the shop
profits himself. Only *he* drew harsh judgement with his
souvenir stand; he was maligned for trying to make money
from his children. It was an attitude that came naturally to a
public that had largely been fed negative stories about him. In
fact, he remained a figure of disdain for most journalists even

after the government's exploitation surpassed anything he could have imagined. The press reproach served only to alienate Dionne, who gruffly refused interviews for years, with rare exceptions, the most outstanding of which was an ongoing rapport with the supportive Lillian Barker.

Nevertheless, Philip Adams' son, Jack, now in his eighties, still believes that the quintuplets' fate would have been far worse had the government not intervened. Even after all he's heard about how their lives were harmed by this strange beginning, he holds to that view. "Otherwise they would have been freaks at the World's Fair if the government hadn't stepped in," he insists, ignoring what Quintland turned them into. "It didn't seem terrible at the time. The public felt sure [that] the kids couldn't see them through the screen, and that they were being raised as normally as possible. Later, I found it kind of shocking what happened. I thought someone was looking after their finances and that they were left much better off. A lot of money went through Quintland."

Many people shared this view. Everything the government arranged involving the quintuplets contributed to the impression that the children were living an exalted life. In May 1939, on the eve of their fifth birthday, the girls were brought to Toronto aboard a special train with the fanfare normally accorded visiting dignitaries. They were to meet King George VI and Queen Elizabeth as a special event of their majesties' royal tour. Contrary to the widespread belief that the children knew nothing of their role as performers, they blew kisses at the crowds that awaited their train.

Outfitted like miniature Elizabethan court ladies in ankle-length dresses of white organza, with matching poke-bonnets, white wrist-length gloves and black-patent slippers, the sisters were introduced to the royal couple, curtsied and, led by Cécile, each girl put her arms around the queen's neck and gave her a kiss. They then walked through the legislative building before an admiring audience of hundreds of MPPs and their guests "with immense dignity," said a nurse who accompanied them.

Even in the 1930s, the importance of family bonding and parental nurturing were well known, but for the Dionne quintuplets these basic needs were easily dismissed. Ironically, it was their former nurse Yvonne Leroux who, in a speech she wrote for a North American publicity tour she made when the sisters were five years old, openly called them "the five unluckiest children in the world." She spoke widely of the fact that the girls had no home, in the ordinary sense; in her speech, she said, "At the impressionable age the quins have now reached, they are missing the formative influences and contacts of family life."

In the *McCall's* articles upon which *We Were Five* was based, the sisters themselves said, "We knew there was a visitor whom the nurses taught us to call *Maman*, but it was not possible for her to mother us, so how could we miss her? The nurses—the loving ones—represented a kind of composite mother to us. When one of them left the nursery forever, we could not hold back the tears, because we loved all of them." Later on, they add, "The happiest, least complicated years of our lives were spent in the nursery. We had everything we wanted, everything within the limits of our imagination.... Above all else, we had one another, a gang of little girls, each geared to about the same speed and brought up in the same way."

But Leroux predicted that they were becoming "ominously interdependent" and losing the opportunity to develop individual initiative; and she said that their lives were so cosseted and unrealistic that, when they face the outside world, "there are likely to be shocks and disillusionment in store." Though Leroux's appearances were well-attended by the public and press, her words prompted no great outcry or investigation.

When the noted Viennese psychologist Dr. Alfred Adler warned that the girls' upbringing would prove harmful to them, he was pilloried in the press. He had written, in a March 1936 article in *Cosmopolitan* magazine, that "treating the quintuplets alike in every respect induces a uniformity which is not conducive to the development of the individual.... The quintuplets live like the inmates of a model orphanage.... Life in a glass house is not conducive to normal human development."

Years later, many who had been to Quintland to gape at the famed quintet felt defensive, as if they had invested in the fairy-tale myth. They had bought into the government-created fantasy that life in the Dafoe Hospital and Nursery was charmed, filled with play and laughter and loving care. Spectators believed they had taken part in something special, magical. Small scenes of amusing childish play, multiplied times five, seemed like hilariously entertaining skits put on solely for the audience's delight.

One hot day, Cécile and Yvonne, who had been sweeping the playground with two little brooms, took their toys right into their wading pool with them. When a nurse arrived to try to encourage them to take up some other activity, they dumped a pail of water on her. Immediately, Marie and Émilie appeared and began to wipe her off with their own little brooms. At that, the viewing gallery erupted in laughter, a noise so loud that it sounded like a thunderclap.

For the spectators, nothing could destroy that happy moment. Not even the truth of hindsight—the reality that exhibiting humans in Quintland was, after all, no different in its effect on the little girls than exhibiting them in Chicago would have been.

If anything further was needed to confirm the sisters' feelings that they were part of a sideshow, it was the fact that they were treated as laboratory specimens by scientists, with the government's blessing. The crusading psychologist Dr. William E. Blatz, with his controversial methods of rearing children, was given free rein to study the girls during a period of three years and use them as guinea pigs for his theories. He was permitted to bring teams of scientists, including two zoologists, to the nursery, and was allowed to enforce a rigid regime that included fifteen-minute play times and specific toilet times. And he barred the Dionne parents from interfering. Blatz had no place for a mother or a father in the lives of his star subjects.

In the quintuplets' case, Blatz had created a special research program far beyond what he offered at his school. He created an advisory board of enthusiastic academicians who designed tests of the girls in an atmosphere of experiment and curiosity, with an eye to future seminars and publication of their scientific papers. As well, these children, unlike his Toronto students, were kept in a confined space and subjected to unrelenting monitoring and charting of their every movement — including facial gestures — night and day.

A 1937 scientific paper that Blatz and his associates co-authored in *Collected Studies on the Dionne Quintuplets* for the University of Toronto openly enthuses that "for the first time in history five children are growing up in a restricted social atmosphere of multiple contemporary siblings." In its conclusions, the paper also points out fairly proudly that "for the past two years they have been on display almost daily."

Although Blatz is still revered by some as the father of child psychology in Canada, none of the tests he administered was necessary for the healthy development of the five little girls. The children received no counselling or treatment with regard to their unusual upbringing, or as a result of his findings.

Writing in the special 1994 edition on the Dionne quintuplets in the *Journal of Canadian Studies*, the sociologist Kari Dehli, who researched Blatz's involvement, notes that from March 1935 to March 1938, he "exercised a major influence in the Dionne nursery. He hired, trained and supervised the young nurses and teachers responsible for applying child-rearing methods to the Quintuplets." He had the Dafoe Hospital and Nursery remodelled to a school-like environment. And he oversaw the design of the public viewing gallery and the one-way screens (which resembled, by no coincidence, those used in psychological observation rooms).

Dehli also writes of the widespread interest of the larger scientific community. "At first the scientists were interested in the physical survival and health of the Quintuplets. As the girls miraculously lived through the first few days and weeks, however, psychologists and educators, as well as zoologists, biologists, forensic scientists and dentists, began to vie for an opportunity to study them for other reasons."

For Blatz, the obvious prize was the vast publicity and promotion he would get for the new science of child psychology and his controversial theories of child development. His ideas, which seem fairly benign from today's perspective, revolved around his central belief that traditional ways of handling children at home and in school were too strict and authoritarian. He believed in discipline, but not in the corporal type that was still common at the time. He thought children should be allowed to develop naturally, but to him this meant subjecting them from the earliest age to a strict routine based on their abilities. Parents and teachers, he insisted, should be studying the children in their care at all times, always watching for different stages of development and recording them.

At the time, those ideas—and the methods Blatz employed—were considered radical by the majority of parents. Still, he was attracting a small following among middle-class professionals and the academic community, who sent their children to his Toronto-based nursery school. But Dehli points out the now-obvious contradiction in the Dionnes' case: Blatz's theories of free and natural development were being applied to five little girls in an environment utterly confined and controlled.

Blatz and his main assistant tested each of the girls once a month for mental, social, physical, emotional, and speech development—even their bowel habits were monitored. Nurses recorded the girls' behaviour while awake and their physical movements while asleep. A single day's chart from May 1936 listed twenty-one activity periods from 6:30 a.m. to 6:45 p.m. These included directed play (music and stories) at 11:00; relaxation at 11:30; dinner at 11:40; toilet and dressing at 12:15; outdoor sleep at 12:30. At mealtime, food had to be eaten in a prescribed order. This military-like regimen was imposed on five two-year-old toddlers.

One room of the nursery was set aside for discipline (the scientists acknowledged in their papers that it was referred to by the press as "the jail"). If one of the youngsters was misbehaving, she would be removed and placed alone in that room. In one incident, one of the quintuplets—in this case, we don't know which one—plunked a hair ribbon into each of the five glasses of milk that were waiting for the girls on a table. When the nurses accused one sister, the other four all said they had done it so she would not be isolated. Although "time-out" punishment remains a choice of many parents today, the effect of it on these girls, raised as they were by a succession of hired nurses, some loving and some not, was devastating. They had learned very early that they had only themselves for comfort and affection. Being separated from the group and placed in a closed room was a terrible sentence. A further disciplinary method was the use of sleeping jackets, "which provided a measure of restraint without discomfort," the scientists reported.

The opportunity to conduct such experiments existed only because the children had been transformed, legally, into state property. If the government, as represented by the guardians, approved a study, a contract, a public appearance, the quintuplets had no choice but to take part. In the case of Blatz, the guardians never formally agreed to his presence. He was given initial access on the basis of a verbal agreement with Dafoe, then took command. Yet the guardians accepted that every aspect of the scientific experiment in child-rearing would be at the quintuplets' own expense: neither the government nor the university paid for this three-year project. The children's trust fund paid for Blatz's staff, travel expenses, and equipment.

By 1938, when Blatz was dismissed after he was caught in a dispute with Oliva Dionne over the firing of the sisters' francophone teacher, the guardianship arrangement had undergone a significant change. Croll had suddenly resigned from his duties the year before, after his handling of the quintuplets' financial affairs had been called into question in a letter to Premier Hepburn from Dr. Dafoe. Ontario's official guardian, Percy Wilson, another staunch Liberal, was immediately put in Croll's place. By April 1937, Croll had been fired from Cabinet, along with Attorney-General Arthur Roebuck, after both men broke ranks with Hepburn and his anti-union stance during a strike at the General Motors plant in Oshawa.

Unexpectedly, Croll refused to hand over his entire collection of guardianship records and quintuplet contracts from 1935 to 1937; he insisted they were "personal." Percy Wilson and others repeatedly requested the papers, but Croll held fast. He eventually did speak to Wilson privately about them, and even allowed the legal counsel for the guardianship to view some of them, but he wouldn't give them up. Croll is believed to have later burned all of these documents before he went away to war. Though he eventually returned to politics as widely respected senator, he always refused to explain his actions, leaving a mystery that will never be solved: Was he protecting himself or someone else?

❦

The Dionne fervour, which held ordinary people, the media, and government officials in its thrall, began to beat with a pulse of its own. That is one of the points made whenever questions are raised about how and why government control of the five sisters was perpetuated for so long. Hindsight, the argument goes, cannot be applied to events of sixty years past. Those events occurred in a time and a place too different and in circumstances too complex to be studied under a contemporary microscope. But there are many who see it differently.

Mariana Valverde, a University of Toronto criminologist, has studied what happened to the quintuplets and also wrote for the Dionne edition of the *Journal of Canadian Studies*. From her eighth-floor office in the university's Robarts Library, just a stone's throw from the province's seat of government, the mother of two young children says, "The Dionnes are an amazing story. These were children who were property for a long time, not of parents or nuns, but of the province."

Yet this was at a time when there was already a home-based child-welfare system in place to look after children who needed care. In fact, the Children's Aid Society, founded by John Joseph Kelso, a crusading journalist, as a philanthropic society to help kids at risk, had been around since 1891. Contrary to the widely held belief that child-rearing methods in 1934 were far different from those of today, Valverde says that by the 1920s the emphasis was on sending children in need to foster homes and farms. "By the 1920s there was an understanding of the importance of family-centred childhood. Still, the government takes over, and instead of giving the babies other parents, it puts them in a bizarre nursery and

61

deprives them of a mother figure, which was totally bizarre for them in terms of the psychology of the day. It was unheard of not to even try to find a family for newborns, and [to] put them instead into an institution."

But the government worked hard to maintain the public's perception that what was going on was for the good of the babies. After all, these were very special children, the politicians said, who therefore needed unusual measures taken to assure their care. Valverde says, "These had to be portrayed as not children, but as princesses, as scientific wonders. The emphasis was on high-tech solutions, the nursery with special things and sterile.... The government had an amazing public-relations campaign. The news clippings [of stories about the babies] are in contrast to the minutes of the guardians. Premier Hepburn says they're protecting the kids, but the minutes of the guardians show the government isn't spending any money at all. The Red Cross paid for the building of the $5000 nursery [supplemented by donations from the public, while the government claimed it footed a $20,000 bill for all of it]. Meanwhile, the many commercial endorsement deals signed by the guardians on behalf of the quintuplets built a considerable fortune from which the nursery and Quintland operating costs were paid."

Valverde says the public didn't grasp the crucial, legal difference between making the babies wards of the king and putting them under the protection of the Children's Aid Society. "CAS had social workers who visited, and other kids that were being looked after in the same way. But as wards of the king, a special law made the quintuplets the property of the provincial government. There were no social workers or child psychologists on the board of guardians." There was no one with the expertise to argue against what was going on.

Valverde also believes that the public accepted the notion of making the sisters royal wards because the girls were already famous. Children's aid societies had long been associated with the poor and with working parents who needed a temporary solution, and hence would have seemed to be beneath the quintuplets' status as celebrities.

During the course of her research, Valverde read some two hundred letters sent to Premier Hepburn at the time of the wardship, as well as old news reports from Toronto's three major papers. Only a few letter-writers said it wasn't right to take the babies from their parents, and not one journalist questioned why the existing child-welfare system wasn't involved. Nor did it seem to occur to anyone that while they were still in shaky health the babies could have been cared for in an established hospital that their parents could have visited, and with the understanding that they would be returned to their family when they were no longer at risk.

As for the distasteful freak-show element, it is too easy to fall into the trap of assuming that people were so very different then. Today's collective memory of bizarre circus sideshows harks back to human unfortunates like the Elephant Man and curiosities such as the fattest lady in the world, spectacles that were not uncommon in the late nineteenth century and first half of the twentieth century; indeed, these would seem to suggest that the public display of the quintuplets was not only accepted, but encouraged. But that memory of sideshows smacks of rationalization. Even that far back, children were considered a different matter.

Writing in a 1992 anthology of essays called *Regulating Womanhood*, Valverde noted that by the 1930s, live exhibitions of Siamese twins and the like were deemed incompatible with twentieth-century notions of innocent childhood. Public displays of children had by then assumed a mediated form, most notably in Hollywood musicals featuring Shirley Temple. But with a canny sense of what the market would bear, the Ontario government made exhibiting the quintuplets seem completely natural by turning them into charming starlets that were a must-see for travellers to Canada's rustic north.

Once the wardship law was passed, the money-making contracts and deals began to flow. The Ontario government effectively owned the children, as if they were a Crown corporation, and it happily sold rights to their image to Twentieth Century Fox, for example, for the films *The Country Doctor*, starring Jean Hersholt as Dr. Dafoe, *Reunion*, and *Five of a Kind*. The media quickly jumped in with photo and newsreel contracts, and endorsements were granted to every company that had a product that could be associated with the girls, from corn syrup to bread to chocolate bars (which Dr. Dafoe refused to let them eat).

On March 19, 1937, a special federal law, which was out of the ordinary framework of trade-mark legislation and ironically named the Act for the Protection of the Dionne Quintuplets, was passed to control the use, especially by competing U.S. companies, of the words "quintuplets," "quints," or "quins" to promote products. Ottawa then drew up a list of two hundred specific commercial articles that were acceptable for the babies to promote, including eyebrow pencils. Clearly, it was the lucrative profits that moved the federal government to get involved with this "provincial property," not any concern for the girls.

Just weeks prior, when David Croll had resigned from his duties as the quintuplets' special guardian, he was reported to have told the province's legislators, "Today, the quints have become big business." Thus, he said, the official guardian would be the logical choice to oversee the children's financial estates. Croll added that what the children needed most now was "a domestic normal life; association with their brothers and sisters, the love and discipline which their parents alone can completely provide. There is no substitute for a mother." Yet, it would be another six years before the children and their family would be brought together under one roof. By then, it would be impossible for the divided sides to fashion a normal life together.

The commercialization had turned the sisters into a flourishing industry instead of five members of a family. And it was all made possible by the unique legal structure the provincial government had set up to exploit the situation. "Once you turn the kids into a commercial property, all corporations will go in and take advantage. It was the government that did something unusual, not the cereal company," Valverde says. "The unusualness of what happened to the girls, of being put on the market to the highest bidder and [of] huge sums of money being offered, the unusual thing is from the government. And then what the others do is perfectly normal for business interests, for news companies and Hollywood studios."

Scientific wonders. Celebrities. Public exhibits. Crown property. Financial windfall. These unspoken labels for ever marked the sisters as objects, not individuals. Their future was also to be changed by the power struggle taking place between their father and Dr. Dafoe. To the girls, Papa Dionne, like their mother, Elzire, was only an occasional presence, and a sometimes disruptive one, while Dafoe appeared a lovable man who visited them almost every day. But in the public domain, Dionne was gaining ground. Some newspapers, always looking for new angles, eventually began publishing articles that questioned why healthy children were being kept from their parents. Well-connected Franco-Ontarian leaders and politicians raised the issue of the girls being taught in English instead of French. The savvy Hepburn was aware that Dionne was garnering francophone voters' support.

Meanwhile, Dafoe got caught in a fiasco. While being fêted in New York in 1939, he appeared, wearing a mortarboard and bathrobe, in a skit for the satirical Circus Saints and Sinners Club, during which he was given the degree of Doctor of Litters. The stage-show spoof ridiculed Oliva Dionne and featured five men dressed up as overgrown baby quintuplets. Dionne sued, and demanded an inquiry into Dafoe's advertising contracts; he wanted the money for all of Dafoe's endorsements that included the quintuplets to be put into the sisters' trust fund. By December 26, 1939, Hepburn ordered that Dafoe resign from the board of guardians, and that the matter be settled out of court, to avoid exposing all of the accounts. When Dafoe fell ill with cancer and had to be absent from the nursery, Dionne stepped up his efforts to estrange his daughters from the physician until the girls were no longer speaking to him.

❦

Just as journalists of the day had not questioned the guardianship arrangement, they did not question what happened to the money the quintuplets were bringing in, or how being raised in isolation was affecting the children. June Callwood, one of Canada's pre-eminent journalists, reflects, "There was no investigation done by the press in those days. Even when I started as a reporter in the 1940s, you were never asked to look beneath the surface. Even in magazines, the stories were one-dimensional."

Nevertheless, there were occasional glimpses that something had gone wrong. Nasty fissures in the girls' supposedly seamless and happy existence in the nursery became visible—and audible—in May 1941. Fittingly, it was a staged media event at which the sisters first revealed that all was not as it appeared in their tiny, perfect world.

On May 11, 1941, the quintuplets were supposed to perform on a Mother's Day radio show sponsored by the Ontario government. The show was to promote tourism from the U.S. and would be transmitted over the Columbia Broadcasting System (CBS) to eighteen states. But on the day of the broadcast, the youngsters refused to speak in English or sing the wartime booster "There'll Always Be an England," as planned. They pronounced their invitation to U.S. visitors to come see them that summer, along with special greetings to mothers, all in French. American listeners were outraged. Some even suggested that the children had been put up to sabotaging the war effort, since French-Canadians were largely opposed to conscription, unlike the rest of the population. Roughly four thousand letters of indignation were sent to Ontario's Tourist and Travel Bureau headquarters.

Two weeks later, on their seventh birthday, there was to be another CBS broadcast, this one with the popular news commentator Lowell Thomas—a friend of Premier Mitch Hepburn's—speaking with the girls in the Dafoe Hospital and Nursery. On this occasion, the children simply wouldn't talk at all, leaving Thomas sounding foolish in the void. Finally, they caved in and sang a short French song.

Following these two incidents, some members of the media finally started to ask penetrating questions about the whole Dionne affair. Canada's *Maclean's* magazine wrote, in July 1941, "So far as money is concerned, the Quints owe the province of Ontario nothing. They pay their own way. They have never been a public charge. Rather the shoe is on the other foot. Citizens of Ontario owe the Dionne sisters a debt that cannot accurately be measured in currency. Their presence in the province, their good looks, their gay reaction to public showings, have brought many thousands of visitors into Ontario during the past seven years, and many thousands of dollars into Ontario cash registers." The reporter, Frederick Edwards, added, "Public interest does not necessarily imply the right of public interference." At last, closer scrutiny was being brought to what was going on behind the locked and guarded gates of Quintland.

With the help of a French-Canadian lawyer and lobby groups, Dionne had heated up his language battle in the most public of ways: through the two radio broadcasts. The press fanned the controversy, warning of a potential French-English crisis; local businesses worried about loss of American tourists. In February 1942, Dionne convinced the guardians to give him sole control of his children, and to force Dafoe to resign as their physician, removing him completely from the girls' lives. Fifteen months later, Dafoe died of pneumonia at age sixty.

In nine years, Dafoe had gone from anonymity to fame and back to near-obscurity, but his name is for ever linked to the quintuplets' story. Years later, Pierre Berton and other writers would play up the view that the doctor's sudden popularity changed him completely. They would write that his fame went to his head, that he made money on the backs of the girls, and that his "humble country doctor" persona was something of a sham.

There is no question that Dafoe's life changed entirely. But it was the government that gave him *carte blanche* to take hold of the situation and carry his command across the road to a private ersatz hospital. As for contracts, the government clearly approved of them, since archival documents show that Twentieth Century Fox, for one, made Dafoe's three annual cheques payable to Welfare Minister David Croll, who in turn paid the doctor. By the time of the last payment, Croll was no longer in charge and there was a flurry of memoranda between government lawyers, Percy Wilson, and even the premier as to how to get the money to Dafoe without it appearing that Wilson had taken a direct payment. The government seemed to view Dafoe's extracurricular earnings as just part of the business of the quintuplets. What was really wrong in all of this was the official stamp of approval given to Dafoe's belief that he had more rights as regarded the five girls than did their real father and mother.

At the same time, the distractions of war were beginning to take their toll on tourism. The children were becoming less saleable because of the language issue—Twentieth Century Fox, for example, was considering a fourth movie but lost interest once the girls began speaking only in French—and because they were losing the baby-faced cuteness that had made them so appealing.

From the government's point of view, the quintuplets were no longer a profitable asset. In 1942 construction began on a new family home for the entire Dionne family, which had expanded to twelve children by then. Quintland was shut down in July 1943, and the family moved in together that November. A third guardianship act was passed by the Ontario legislature on March 20, 1944; this one named Oliva Dionne the sole guardian of the quintuplets until they reached twenty-one. For Yvonne, Annette, Cécile, Émilie, and Marie, the strange years of public display and government control were over.

The events of their childhood—which culminated in five little girls being put on daily view like prize fish in an aquarium, mostly to benefit government coffers—are almost impossible to grasp today. When the quintuplets' weird world was turned upside down nine years later, the government walked away unconcerned. The girls were reunited with a family that had never recovered from its public humiliation, and the occasional checks made by the province's official guardian were of the girls' money, not of their well-being. (This appointed official had a responsibility to determine the accuracy of the children's accounts, but no role to play in assuring their rights were protected.) When they moved with their family into the fortress-like mansion built from their trust fund, the five famous sisters still were kept isolated from the outside world. As young women, they emerged so devastated from the experience of their early years that each suffered terrible difficulties once on her own. To add insult to injury, the money they finally received from their trust fund was far less than had been widely believed, and could never make up for the pain wrought by their bizarre upbringing.

It was a tragedy brought about by the unprecedented actions of the provincial government—a failed experiment in human spectacle that damaged five helpless babies and an entire family. The government takeover allowed for all else that followed: power struggles over the children; exploitation by individuals, companies, and the guardians themselves; the media's manipulation of public opinion; and the benign acceptance by ordinary people of extraordinary actions that normally would have been considered unnatural and wrong.

Worst of all was the stunning irony that would perpetually haunt the girls: in the name of their own protection, they were turned into exhibits in a government-sanctioned freak show. As astonishing as all this was, the Dionne quintuplets' story would take many more shocking twists and turns in the years ahead.

4: CALLED TO ACCOUNT

B Y THE TIME THE quintuplets were returned to their
father's care, nine years had passed. During those years
they had been a tourism asset estimated to be worth half a
billion dollars to Ontario. Even after paying for all of
Quintland's expenses, they had put away close to $1 million—
an amount equal to roughly $10 million today—and everyone
assumed they would end up with even greater wealth at
twenty-one. It didn't turn out that way.

There was money in their trust fund, but not nearly the
sum that would have seemed logical, given the early reports
from the guardians. A tangled web of financial deals and
commercial exploitation had boosted their account, but
extravagant expenses and dubious billing practices had bled it
by half. In fact, the guardians were spending so freely that a
judge who saw the ledgers took them to task.

With the first guardianship arrangement, the children
became a legal business, which meant that the government
could make any commercial arrangement that it wished on
their behalf. Even a selected list of the contracts, salaries, and
spending activities of almost everyone involved is mind-
boggling. When the girls were only two months old, the
Toronto Daily Star had won through its photographer, Fred

Davis, initial exclusive rights to photograph the quintuplets. Davis took pictures every day for one year. He later was named the quintuplets' official photographer, and he eventually married Yvonne Leroux, the babies' first nurse.

The *Star* sold off world rights to the photos to the American syndicate Newspaper Enterprises of America (NEA). Once the guardians were on the scene in 1935, however, a bidding war took place for exclusive access to the youngsters, and this time NEA took over, paying $10,000 a year for the first twenty-one months after the sisters became official wards. The company renewed the contract for $50,000 for another year at the end of 1936, and paid $25,000 for two more years after that. In total, their contract was worth $117,000, or $1.17 million in today's dollars. (The records of royalties received from revenue-generating contracts from 1934 to 1956 show that NEA paid $100,599.38 into the trust fund.)

NEA hired Fred Davis and sold Canadian distribution rights to the *Star*'s syndicate operation, Star News Service. The syndicate was the only money-making department of the newspaper during the Depression. According to a later syndicate director, publisher Joseph Atkinson and managing editor Harry Hindmarsh insisted that the money be donated back to the quintuplets' trust fund. Records of that donation cannot be found, however, and were perhaps lost when Welfare Minister David Croll destroyed the guardianship documents from 1935–37. Available records show only the *Star*'s original, short-term contract, which brought in royalties of $1598. Nevertheless, a 1938 *Harper's* magazine article bears testimony to the paper's intention. In describing the sale of photo rights, the magazine states, "They were bought by the *Toronto*

Star, less for commercial reasons than to provide the five tiny premature babies with the funds that were so desperately needed at that time."

These photo contracts alone altered the five little girls' lives permanently. The guardians agreed in the NEA deal "to do all in their power to see that no pictures are taken of the said infants except by or on behalf of the Company and that they will take what steps are possible to prevent any such unauthorized pictures being taken." This was interpreted by their guardians to mean that the girls could never leave the nursery compound, never go to a public school, never be outside on their own to play—all for fear that someone would snap a picture of them, leaving the guardians and the government open to a lawsuit.

A separate contract negotiated by Oliva and Elzire Dionne with the *New York Daily News* in the spring of 1935 gave the paper similar exclusive rights to photograph the couple and their other five children. That deal added another dimension to what was becoming one of the strangest family situations in history, because it meant that the quintuplets and the rest of their family members could not be photographed together for a number of years. Once again, the children's great celebrity widened the gap between them and their parents and siblings.

NEA's virtual hold over the quintuplets' lives helped turn the girls into unwitting performers on an international stage. In 1938 the company had the sisters pose, with props, stage settings, and scripts, as elaborately costumed characters from a series of fairy tales and nursery rhymes. Cinderella alone, with Yvonne in the starring role, included seventeen scenes that were reproduced in publications around the world for five days running. Other photo stories included Old King Cole, with Yvonne as the king, Marie as the page, and the other girls as fiddlers; Mary, Mary, Quite Contrary; and Hickory, Dickory, Dock. NEA sold the series to some fifty newspapers, according to a former nurse who was on the scene.

With millions of photos and newsreels flashing the sisters' captivating images around the world, it took no special leap of imagination for advertisers and entrepreneurs to see the promotional opportunities, and the guardians, besieged with contract proposals, took easily to deal-making. For its part, the government loudly boasted that the various product endorsements were bringing in dazzling sums for those Depression years. The money, the government insisted, would insure a rich, secure future for the famous quintuplets—just what the public wanted for the children who had made their world feel brighter and more hopeful.

By the end of March 1937, when the girls were almost three years old, total cash receipts on their behalf came to well over $500,000—which would be the same as $5 million today. But that was peanuts compared with the provincial government's take: an estimated $20 to $25 million a year in American tourist traffic alone, according to Canadian tourist bureau statistics.

The astounding range of contracts can be seen in an Ontario government archival document that includes details of the following receipts:

• From the Alexander Doll Company, in the second year of its contract, $27,828.27, or five percent of quintuplet product sales.

- From Brown and Bigelow, a calendar company that used the girls' image on annual calendars sold to dozens of companies, $61,911.92, or 7.5 percent of sales. That contract was renewed every few years and continued past the end of the government wardship and through the years when Oliva Dionne was sole guardian.
- From Colgate Palmolive Peet, $10,250 for using the quintuplets in ads for Colgate Ribbon Dental Cream. Another $8333.32 was received from Karo corn syrup; and $10,416.71 came from Tiny Town Togs for the manufacture and sale of children's dresses promoted with the quintuplets' name.

Added to this was the most lucrative one-shot deal of them all: a total of $350,000 from Twentieth Century Fox for the three full-length feature films based on the lives of the popular youngsters. The quintuplets were described in one magazine article as "the greatest audience-drawing combine in the history of motion pictures."

The first movie deal, for *The Country Doctor,* was signed when the babies were only eighteen months old. (Although they were the stars of the film, they appear only during the final ten minutes.) It was shot at the nursery in August 1936, and filming was allowed for only one hour each day, between eleven and twelve in the morning. All the crew members were obliged by Dafoe to wear face masks and white lab coats to prevent them from passing on germs to the babies, and everyone had to have their noses and throats sprayed with a special antiseptic. Even the camera was dressed in a sanitary gown. The original screenplay was written by Charlie Blake of the

Chicago American, and although the story was fictionalized, Oliva Dionne was portrayed as a buffoon who bragged of his baby-making prowess. Dafoe, on the other hand, was portrayed as a noble and unassuming hero who refuses money and contracts sent to him on behalf of the quintuplets.

Of course, the public was never told that money was pouring out of the children's fund as swiftly as it went into it. For instance, all expenses for the Dafoe Hospital and Nursery, which the government proudly pointed to as its creation, were paid for by the youngsters. Even the land the government appropriated from the Dionnes' neighbours was paid for from the quintuplets' account. Perhaps most disturbing of all, in at least one year the sisters were charged for their own birthday gift: a pony that their father later that same day gave to one of their brothers.

Further costs were also being paid out of the income that was supposed to be set aside for the girls' future. A sample of these included all staff salaries at the nursery and Quintland, a tennis court for the nurses' use, transportation costs for staff to go to church, construction costs for the building of a staff house and the spectators' viewing gallery, maintenance bills, postage stamps for Dafoe's correspondence, and lunch bills for visiting government officials. The provincial treasurer even billed the girls' account $5.36 for telephone calls and telegrams for the month of February 1937. No expense was too small to be charged to the quintuplets.

Under normal accounting practices, the money taken in by the province through tourism should have paid for the day-to-day running and upkeep of tourist facilities, which is what Quintland was. And the government, acting in the place of the parents, also should have paid for the children's basic necessities, including housing, food, and clothing. Indeed, a trust fund is usually set up as a way of assuring that children will have money set aside for their own needs as they go through life. The government's own statements, trumpeted in the press, gave the impression that this is exactly what they were doing. Shortly after the girls' first birthday, a public invitation to visit them in Callander was issued under Welfare Minister David Croll's name. It was accompanied by a pitch to buy a photograph of the five "exceptionally beautiful children," as a contribution to their trust fund. This fund, Croll wrote, "is being administered without cost of any kind by the Ontario Government."

But the lists of monthly disbursements, approved at regular meetings of the guardians, are most illustrative of what was really going on. They reveal that the five girls even had to pay the costs of being treated like scientific specimens and incarcerated by guards. Some of the items they paid for included:

• A bill from Dr. W.E. Blatz on September 17, 1937, for expenses incurred during his studies of the quintuplets—some described as "mental tests"—since March 1935, including twenty-six return train trips from Toronto to North Bay, secretarial expenses, and incidental costs, for a total of $1384.39. His rental of a camera, tripod, and film to photograph the girls on September 20, 1935, is also billed to them at $50.50. The guardianship records show other Blatz bills, such as travelling expenses of $202.50; materials from the University of Toronto's department of biology, $76.78; slides and graphs for Blatz's scientific conference, $126; and research and consultation expenses, $157.95.

- A monthly salary for Dr. Allan Brown, pediatrician and consultant to Dr. Dafoe, of $121.35. Dafoe's monthly salary was $210, and he got an additional stamp allowance, which came to $18 in January 1938.
- A monthly allowance for the Dionne parents of $100. This was bumped to $300 on March 1, 1938. Dionne also had some legal bills paid by his five daughters' fund, including one for $500 in July 1940.
- A monthly salary for Quintland's guards—three in the winter, six in summer—of around $100 each.
- A salary for Keith Munro, a former *Toronto Star* political reporter who had befriended Hepburn and later Dafoe and was appointed business manager of the quintuplets' trust fund. He received $500 a month, plus telephone costs and travel expenses, which covered frequent trips to New York, where he later moved and started a Madison Avenue public-relations business. Munro's expense notes were handwritten and usually submitted without receipts.

In July 1938 alone, there were some sixteen people being paid a regular salary from the trust account, and the fund was also paying extra labour costs and operating expenses. For the period between May 1935 and March 1937, for example, operating costs for the hospital and nursery were an astonishing $58,173.55. Additional construction took another $55,088.06 from the girls' account.

From the same fund, Oliva Dionne was granted ongoing school costs for his older children. Ernest, Thérèse and Rose-Marie, for example, were awarded $838.93 in August 1938 and an additional $329.50 in November of that year. In fact, bills from the other children's schools showed that the quintuplets paid for their siblings' tuition, private lessons, dentists, school trips, travel, even their cod liver oil. That same November, Dionne himself received, in addition to his regular $300 salary, $1500 as an "allowance on passing accounts." All of the guardians granted themselves this yearly sum. (They originally got $2500 each, but Judge J.A.S. Plouffe of the Nipissing District Court, who was assigned to examine the girls' account from time to time, said it was too high. Judge Plouffe also revealed that the annual cost of running the hospital, Quintland, and the fund itself had swelled to a third of the total amount earned in a year by the quintuplets; in 1938–39, the amount of money going out came closer to half of the children's revenues.)

Under the guardianship agreement, the fund's remaining monies were invested largely in Province of Ontario bonds, Hydro Electric Power bonds, Temiskaming and Northern Ontario Railway bonds, and Dominion of Canada bonds. Yet again, the investments, mostly at three and four percent yields, all benefited the government.

There were also donations to charities. In the children's names, the guardians gave $1750 to the Canadian Red Cross Society to buy an ambulance; in another instance, Chicago's medical officer of health was given money to distribute a speech of Dr. Dafoe's to all Chicago physicians, because the guardians agreed "this was a philanthropic work and a good thing for the Quintuplets to do." The minutes of the guardians' meetings are sprinkled with pious sentiments like these. In 1940, business manager Keith Munro was recorded as saying that "it was the duty of the Quintuplets to do war work," a belief that led the guardians to give away $5000 of the youngsters' money to pay for booklets to help sell war savings certificates. Though these causes all may have been worthy, no other citizens were conscripted to be the government's own public-relations ambassadors—while having to pay for every promotion themselves.

Being raised by a government-appointed committee with an eye on maximum capital return meant years of micro-management down to the smallest detail. A separate file was even kept by the official guardian on the children's hair. (Records reveal an ongoing battle between Elzire Dionne and both Keith Munro and Percy Wilson over transforming the girls' naturally straight hair, which Elzire favoured, into trendy moppet curls like those of Shirley Temple, which American audiences were said to prefer.)

That the children were considered a business asset rather than five individuals is made clear in a telegram sent to Ontario premier Mitch Hepburn on September 14, 1938, by the mayor of Parry Sound, a town en route to North Bay. The latter had heard rumours that the guardians had been asked by Dr. Dafoe to consider moving the girls to a new site at Trout Lake for health reasons. The doctor had said the water quality of the Quintland site was worrisome. He had stressed that the light topsoil in the district was not heavy enough to absorb all the sewage from the many tourist camps.

Mayor W.M. Ketcheson's telegram read:

> Understand movement on foot to move residence
> of quints from birthplace at Callander. Town of
> Parry Sound urges that you will do everything in

your power to prevent such move as we believe
they with parents should be kept at birthplace.
Any change in location would greatly lessen their
value as attraction for tourists who are very much
interested in original house in which quintuplets
were born and in everything connected with
actual place of birth.

Similar telegrams were sent by the Callander Businessmen's
Association and the Parry Sound Board of Trade. As a result of
this pressure, Quintland was not moved and a later home for
the sisters and their family was built just up the road. Hepburn
had caved in quickly to the concerns of local business.

When they were only four years old, Cécile, Annette, Yvonne,
Marie, and Émilie had brought a whopping $1.8 million to their
trust fund, according to a 1938 report by Judge Plouffe. The
figure was staggering for the times. Yet somehow the amount
they received when they turned twenty-one was far less.

Despite the reckless spending of the guardians, some
opportunities for a significant infusion of capital were
rejected. The New York World's Fair, for example, had negotiated with the quintuplets' guardians to exhibit the girls
during its 1939 season. Fair organizers promised a full repro-
duction of the nursery, complete with its playground and
spectators' gallery. They also promised better conditions—
soundproofing and air conditioning—and offered to bring the
nursery staff and all members of the Dionne family to New
York. Full measures would be taken to protect the girls against
kidnapping. The deal was worth at least $500,000, and

included a percentage of receipts that could have brought the total close to $1 million.

But the government and local businessmen feared a loss of tourism revenue to Ontario, and the province worried it would lose jurisdictional control of the sisters; members of the press took their side. As they had done with the Chicago World's Fair when the girls were born, all three factions maintained that the issue was one of not turning the children into sideshow freaks. Even though Quintland had been open for five years, no one seemed to realize that the quintuplets were already being displayed as objects of curiosity. And of course, no one worried about what turning down the offer would cost the girls' trust fund. Joseph Sedgwick, who was then acting as the fair's agent and had once been David Croll's deputy minister, well knew the circumstances of the girls' account and the spending habits of the guardians. He pointed out that the sisters would need at least $1 million to support themselves and their entourage as they grew up. This hefty infusion might have made a huge difference to the quintuplets' future security. But the offer was declined. Moves like this, when combined with the extravagant spending by the guardians, reduced the trust fund as if the money were going through a sieve.

Even as Oliva Dionne gained control of the quintuplets and their finances, the government set up conditions that meant expenses would continue to be paid from the children's funds. In a meeting on September 24, 1941, for example, it was agreed that "Mr. Dionne be paid by the Guardians a fixed monthly sum to meet all the expenses of the home including the salaries of the nurses, teachers, guards and other personnel."

At the same meeting, it was decided that a new home

would be built to accommodate the entire family, at a total cost of $50,000. That figure had almost doubled by the time the house was completed. In December 1942, Judge Valin approved a limit of $15,000 for furnishings alone, a lavish figure for the war years, when most people spent conservatively. It was also agreed that the nursery quarters, formerly the hospital, would be converted once again, this time to a school for the quintuplets and their siblings, and that the staff house would be converted for teachers. All building costs would be borne, of course, by the five girls.

By June 30, 1944, when Oliva Dionne was given full custody of his five daughters, the account had shrunk from $1.8 million to $945,000. Somehow, nearly $900,000—the equivalent of $9 million today—had been used up over six years, despite the fact that money was coming in all the time from endorsements and other deals.

In his report of April 16, 1942, Judge Plouffe had some strong things to say about the careless spending he uncovered during the fifteen months from February 1940 to June 1941. Though the judge ultimately approved the accounts, he said he could not refrain from noting that "the cost of administration, the travelling expenses, the legal fees paid to solicitors both in Ontario and the United States are out of proportion with the yearly revenues of the Estate." The fees paid to auditors and both sets of lawyers, plus a manager and a secretary, totalled $17,591.49, he said, though the work of all those persons could well have been done by "one lawyer of average experience and competence" for $5000.

He went on to compare income and outlay from 1935 to 1940. For the year ending March 31, 1935, he pointed out, the fund took in \$106,297.44 and paid out \$8,825. Four years later, the account received \$147,909.25 and paid out \$61,320.70. Administration costs had soared to far more than one-third of what was coming in. Judge Plouffe concluded that for the years 1940 and 1941, the expenses were "not justified neither by the amount of capital to be administered neither by the work done."

The judge also expressed annoyance that no one had informed him that Dr. Dafoe was receiving financial benefits from commercial contracts he had signed—he mentioned as an example three payments of \$1000 from the Woodstock Rubber Company. Because he had not known this, Judge Plouffe had previously granted a high annual compensation payment to Dr. Dafoe beyond his monthly salary for looking after the children. Out of fairness, he had also granted all of the guardians the same payment.

If nothing else, Judge Plouffe's report clearly showed that the fund that was to ensure the financial security of the famous quintuplets was being depleted by waste and the free-spending attitude of those who were in charge. Yet even after the judge's reprimand, business manager Keith Munro wrote, on June 17, to the special guardian, Percy Wilson (whom he familiarly called by his nickname, Wicky), a letter that ended as follows: "I suppose you'll be up [in North Bay] for the passing [of accounts]. I'm a bit scared of it, I can tell you. Sincerely, Keith." Whatever financial shenanigans might have been erased through the disappearance of Croll's guardianship records, there were clearly internal concerns over how the handling of affairs would be perceived long after Croll was out of the picture and others were in charge.

After Oliva Dionne was granted control of the quintuplets' finances, his projected expenses had to be approved by a master of the Ontario court. According to this guardianship act, the province's official guardian, Percy Wilson, was to be notified of this amount in advance. The surviving Dionne sisters say that Wilson became a close friend of their father's, that he visited their home, and that their parents had once remarked that their friendship with him was the best thing that had happened to the family. Dionne never had to produce receipts to show how he spent the approximately $40,000 a year that he charged to the fund. It is well known that he purchased a new car at least every two years. (Yvonne's recollection is that the purchase was made every year, on Oliva's birthday. "Dad got a new car every year," she remembers. "Mom would tell us on August 27 that Dad was going out to get his birthday gift, and she would laugh and we would wonder why, and it was a new Cadillac.") And he bought a cottage on Lake Nipissing. Annette also recalls many expenses for their siblings. "All the brothers had a car," she says. "Everybody had a good education. The brothers went to a special college in Ottawa. Thérèse and Pauline went to Eastview convent, which is a very good education. They had so many opportunities to be well educated but we were cut off from those good schools and it was our money that paid for them." Under Dionne's management, the fund brought in $57,282 in 1945 and paid out $37,440 in expenses; in 1954, close to the end of his guardianship, revenues were $31,815 but expenses were higher, at $43,328.

After Dionne took over, Wilson continued to receive a small annual salary from the trust. According to Mariana

Valverde, Wilson also became very close to the business manager, Keith Munro, and the two made frequent trips to New York on behalf of the quintuplets. Writing in *Regulating Womanhood*, Valverde notes, "Wilson charged every plate of fish and chips eaten in North Bay hotels to the quints' trust fund, not his own government department, and towards the end of the guardianship he even collected payments of eight hundred dollars per year [on top of his salary] for the regular administration of the fund."

In February 1998, as news spread that the surviving three quintuplets were living in poverty, CTV's investigative current-affairs program, W5, hired a forensic accountant, Frank Vettese, to probe their finances. He dug into fifty boxes of Ontario archive files on the girls' guardianship. While Vettese was not given the time or the money to do exhaustive research, his study of contracts, government correspondence, and ledgers proved that much of the quintuplets' trust fund had gone towards the running of Quintland, and that the children had been exploited.

Vettese estimated that the province owed the women $2 to $3 million just in costs they were charged for a tourist attraction that brought Ontario revenue. He added an estimated $1 million for the loss of the New York World's Fair contract, which the government had rejected. When he translated these amounts into today's dollars, he conservatively calculated that they were owed a total of $22 million.

Ironically, the five babies were turned into money-making machines but were never allowed to handle real cash. Their pretty purses were only for show. Says Annette Dionne today,

"I didn't know a nickel from a quarter until I left home for the first time at eighteen." At convent college, the two-dollar allowance they received from their father each month kept them paupers compared with the other students. Believing it was their father's money, they begged the Mother Superior to ask for more on their behalf. The quintuplets had no knowledge that all of their expenses and those of their siblings came from their own trust fund.

At twenty-one, Yvonne, Annette, Marie, and Cécile signed an agreement with their father that transferred their money into separate accounts with the Guaranty Trust Company of Canada. Though they were not aware of the huge industry they had spawned, records would later show that from 1934 to 1957, their trust fund had accumulated a total of $2,086,747 but had paid out $1,114,033. The house, its land, and the cottage were valued at $171,981, and there were bonds worth $169,867.

When Émilie died at age twenty, her share of the fund was parcelled out to her parents and all of her siblings in fourteen equal portions. The four surviving quintuplets first learned that they had any money at all when they read a newspaper account of Émilie's death that gave details about her share of their trust fund. By then, the total left for the four sisters was $630,866, plus the bonds and other assets. The family home later sold for half of its original cost, a deal that ate up huge amounts in legal fees because of complications between the sisters and their father. Somehow the cottage never came into their hands.

In the end, each sister received $133,951.38 in cash, plus her share of the bonds. According to the Consumer Price Index of 1955, that amount was equivalent to approximately $850,000 in today's dollars. But the money did not flow directly into the women's own hands, and their father continued to charge some expenses to them.

The trust company agreement was written in English, a language that was no longer familiar to the girls, particularly in official documents. At first they refused to sign, and insisted that they needed a translation. But they were exhorted by their mother to sign anyway because, she told them, their father had taken ill and was dying (he lived for another twenty-four years).

As adults, the women received regular interest payments that began at $500 a month and lowered as they withdrew capital. The only designated times for lump-sum payouts, according to the agreement, were when they turned thirty-one, thirty-six, and forty-five. The arrangements were complex. At thirty-one, each sister was entitled to withdraw fifteen percent of her account; at thirty-nine, each could get twenty-five percent of the balance; and at forty-five, fifty percent could be taken. But the account always had to maintain a balance of more than $30,000, which would presumably pass on to any heirs.

The women believe that their father instituted the controlled payouts because he thought they wouldn't live long lives, and therefore that the rest of their siblings could inherit from them, as had happened in Émilie's case. Indeed, the agreement read much like a will, and stated what would happen if any of the four remaining quintuplets died. If there were no children to inherit, then their parents and all of their other siblings would each receive an equal share, even though the money had been accumulated on behalf of the quintuplets.

The agreement came with other conditions. Half the monies had to be invested in mortgages in the North Bay area—a peculiar choice, since the women lived in Montreal and North Bay property was not a booming commodity in 1955—twenty-five percent had to be invested in federal, provincial, or municipal government bonds; and the remaining twenty-five percent in preferred and common stocks. Finally, the sisters were subject "to a life interest in [their] father and mother." They were to pay Oliva Dionne $1250 a year to cover the carrying charges and maintenance of the family home so long as either parent occupied it.

At the time, Larry M. Edwards of Guaranty Trust said in an interview, "The trust agreement entered into after their twenty-first birthday gives generous treatment to the parents. It provides for really more than the Quints can afford. The agreement simply formalized what had been going on before the girls attained their majority. If anything, the parents are a little better off than before."

The trust company was to provide payouts to the parents, as well as to the individual quintuplets, and their spouses or children, if the advisory committee okayed it. The committee was made up of Oliva Dionne, his lawyer, Richard Donnelly, and the general manager of Guaranty Trust. When Dionne later resigned from the trust in the 1960s, he chose his son-in-law, Maurice Girouard, as his successor. The quintuplets weren't asked their opinion and were given the papers to sign, agreeing to the change in committee members, as a *fait accompli*.

At times, expenses appeared on the women's accounts that had been approved by their father without his discussing it with them. The sisters have said publicly that the fees for the detectives their father hired to follow them when they lived in Montreal were paid out of their own trust accounts, for instance.

✺

Owing in large measure to mismanagement and unsound financial decisions by the guardians, and the restrictiveness of the agreement with Guaranty Trust, the adult lives of the four women turned out to be far from glamorous. They each started out at twenty-one with a trust account of $169,800. That amount came from a one-fifth interest in bonds worth $167,000; a one-fifth interest in $632,000, which was sitting in cash with the accountant of the Supreme Court of Ontario; and a one-fourteenth interest in the $140,000 estate of Émilie Dionne. Other assets, such as the family home and cottage, were out of their hands for years.

Though each woman's share was a solid amount for the times, unexpected circumstances in their personal lives and a conservative investment approach dictated by their trust agreement forced them to live from event to event, payout to payout. The costs of buying and running a house, raising children, helping each other through difficulties—all ate into their funds. The depletion process was hastened by their childlike lack of knowledge about money and their inability to take charge of their own affairs. Cécile, who experienced the most financial difficulties because of her early divorce, many illnesses, and four children, was down to $16,000 when she turned forty-five.

When Oliva Dionne died in 1979, his will specifically excluded the quintuplets from inheriting anything. His estate passed on in trust to maintain his wife in their family home, and upon her death was to be divided into equal shares for his other children. In a final paragraph, he added the following: "... and I further declare that I have made no provision in this my Will for my daughters, ANNETTE ALLARD, CÉCILE LANGLOIS and YVONNE DIONNE, by reason of the possession by them of their own adequate means." By the time of his death, Dionne surely would have known through Guaranty Trust and his son-in-law's involvement on the advisory board that Cécile was struggling to make ends meet, that Annette was raising children on her own, and that Yvonne lived modestly. But he left nothing to them, though he had lived for many years in comfort thanks solely to their trust accounts. Elzire's will, written a year after her husband's death, included the same clause. She died in 1986, leaving whatever she owned to her other children and nothing to the surviving quintuplets.

When Guaranty Trust merged with another company in the late 1980s, its officials informed clients that they would receive what was left in their accounts. Cécile, who had used up the most money, received $6000. At the time, she had only $100 in her bank account.

5: LIFE IN THE BIG HOUSE

A T THE AGE OF NINE and a half, Yvonne, Émilie, Marie, Annette, and Cécile, each clutching a large Shirley Temple doll in one hand and a suitcase in the other, walked the hundred metres from the nursery that had been their home to the new house they would occupy with their family. For the Dionne quintuplets, the idea of family, by then, was a foreign concept.

As if torn from their parents and siblings by war, these girls had never known the warm protection of a family unit. Their parents had not been allowed to even touch them as infants, except for a few rare photographed seconds. For years, their brothers and sisters could look at them only through a fence. Unlike babies who are adopted or put in foster homes, these children did not join a new family of any kind. Yet they were not orphans, either.

They were public children. Hired nurses cared for them, though in a misguided effort to protect the children, all were discouraged by Dr. Dafoe from showing affection. Some were fired for getting emotionally attached; others left after a year without even saying goodbye. Dafoe's own fondness for them was evident, and he was rewarded with their giggles of delight whenever he visited. But the doctor spent only an hour or so with the girls on his regular visits to the nursery, and some days didn't show up at all. He did not tuck the five sisters into bed at night, read them bedtime stories, teach them to count, or do anything that a father does for his daughters.

In some confused way, the quintuplets did come to know that their real father and mother lived only a stone's throw away and visited them briefly, at times more frequently than others. Unfortunately, the visits were often associated with the stress of the constant tug-of-war between Elzire and the nurses, and between Oliva and Dafoe. The parents were not allowed to do normal things like bathe and cuddle their children, and although various caregivers told the girls to love their parents, the meaning of the word and how to show it was unclear to little girls who were rarely hugged, or kissed, or told that they were loved.

The quintuplets themselves were the only constants in their isolated world. They developed speech later than average, communicating with each other with just a glance and a secret language of their own invention, not uncommon to twins and other multiples. They relied on gestures, communicating, as Dr. Blatz put it, "as a flock of birds may do." For example, Blatz wrote, "A child called by the wrong name would thump herself vigorously on the chest, shake her head from side to side and, with evident exasperation, point to the appropriate sister." Nurse Yvonne Leroux, in a public speech she gave about her experiences with the quintuplets, said, "By keeping the quintuplets from free association with brothers and sisters, their dependence on sign language and their own private code of wordless sounds was prolonged. They could only teach each other to talk volubly in quin-language—and they did. The months went by without example or incentive for acquiring French or English, beyond a few simple words and phrases." As well, the only periods of separation the girls knew occurred when one of them misbehaved and was placed in the isolation room. Each girl found it painful to be apart from the others. Unintentionally, their doctors and nurses were teaching them not only to try to please others, but also to retreat to each other for comfort.

When the little girls saw their brothers and sisters, it was usually during one of the tension-fraught visits from their mother, who was at odds with their nurses. They had no daily contact with the rest of their family until age seven, when Oliva Dionne forced the guardians to agree to a family reunion. At that point, the girls began to eat Sunday dinner in the Dionne farmhouse in a gathering that was awkward for everyone. Soon after, in a move meant to show he was gaining the upper hand, Oliva Dionne, his wife, and their seven other children—Ernest, Rose-Marie, Thérèse, Daniel, Pauline, Oliva Jr., and Victor—crowded into the nursery along with the quintuplets and lived there uncomfortably for more than a year under the gaze of staff and the guardians, who were still officially in charge. During that time, the lengthy and costly construction of a mansion said to be one of the most lavish homes in northern Ontario was under way. In fact, archival documents show that the government deliberately hid the details and costs of the venture from the press. On November 17, 1943, they all moved into the new house, on their own for the first time since that fateful day in May 1934. Another brother, Claude, was born there three years later.

The strained, restrictive atmosphere of their new home was best exemplified by its nickname: the Big House. An eighteen-room, gated, Georgian-style manor home, it was built and decorated with money from the children's trust fund. With its ten bedrooms, five bathrooms, ten-metre living room, playroom, music room, and red-carpeted library with leather couches, it stood out in the farming village because of its extravagant size, sumptuous furnishings, and tight security. The irony of the name was apparent—"the Big House" is a common North American slang term, popularized in countless movies, for a prison. The quintuplets would one day speak of both Quintland and the Big House as places in which they were locked away from the world.

Sadly, the Dionne family reunion had been doomed from the start. The events that quickly followed the quintuplets' birth had left the parents so deeply scarred that they and their other children for ever blamed the girls for having turned their world upside down. They went from living a private existence to being criticized all over the globe. They were embarrassed even in their own community—where respect was a family's only currency—by a press that made them an example of the "primitive French-Canadian race," as it was then described.

At the time, anti-French sentiment in Ontario had been heightened by the introduction of a provocative education policy called Regulation 17. In 1912, French instruction was virtually banned in Ontario schools, a move that was supposedly made to improve students' overall fluency in English. French Canadians, of course, viewed Regulation 17 as an assault on their very existence in much the same way that today's French-speaking Quebec nationalists equate language with culture. But English Ontarians accepted that its purpose was to raise literacy levels, and believed that allowing the coexistence of two languages was divisive. The issue of family size separated the two populations further. In those times, large families were common in rural areas because children could be useful on the farm. In Corbeil, they were also a matter of pride. But English Protestants favoured small families, and couched racist attitudes in their ridicule of Elzire Dionne for having produced "a litter" like a lowly sow.

The University of Ottawa's David Welch, a professor of social work writing in the Dionne edition of the *Journal of Canadian Studies*, argues that Franco-Ontarian activist groups became involved in the Dionnes' custody fight after the provincial government made the quintuplets permanent Crown wards in March 1935. Until then, it had been generally accepted by the French, Welch writes, that "in order to survive, the Quints needed special medical treatment, a need that might include being isolated from other family members for a number of months. It was assumed that the Quints would be reunited with their family as soon as it was medically sound."

That time seemed never to come, despite the fact that the girls were obviously fit and robust by the time they were toddlers. When the quintuplets were almost two years old, Charlie Blake of the *Chicago American* wrote two stories that ran side by side—one quoting doctors and a dentist who had treated the girls and said they were getting the finest care in the world; the other an interview with Oliva Dionne, who said the children missed the normal benefits of a mother's care, and of growing up with their sisters and brothers. Dionne said he and Elzire were lonely for their daughters and called the children's hospital "their jail." Blake wrote another article on the girls' second birthday, in which he described them as he saw them emerging from their bath: "Strong sturdy arms and legs. Great big beautiful, clear, wide, jet-black eyes. Oceans of curling dark brown, lustrous hair…. Those Dionne quintuplets are the healthiest, strongest, smartest children any one will ever care to see." It's a compelling word picture. But nowhere in it did Blake ask why such healthy youngsters, free of the dangers they initially faced when born so fragile, needed to remain under government control.

By the time the Dionnes were finally reunited, the sisters were as different from the rest of their family as night is from day. Although in their youngest years they had heard English from some anglophone nurses, from Dr. Dafoe, and from Dr. Blatz and his staff, they were eventually schooled only in French, thanks to their father's protests. When they moved into the Big House, they were no longer familiar with English. Meanwhile, their siblings slipped easily from one language to another, just as their father did. Also, the quintuplets had for nine years experienced none of the normal give and take that occurs within a family of different ages and sexes, and they knew nothing of the farming lifestyle. By the time they were five, they had been outside the artificial world of the nursery and its playground-on-display on only one occasion.

In the nursery, the girls were never physically punished. The nurses were not even allowed to raise their voices or show anger in any way. The quintuplets had never encountered the roughhousing that normally occurs between siblings, and they had no preparation whatever for dealing with the excesses of a parent's frustration. As one of their nurses put it, while they were in the nursery the girls were treated "as children in a royal household," with staff to minister to their every need. Yet it was the reverse in the Big House. There, the only signs of wealth and privilege could be found on the building itself: a formidable two-storey entrance with oak-panelled walls and a sweeping staircase that circled the upper floor, archways into rooms, vast bay windows, and bedrooms with built-in bureaus and adjoining bathrooms between them. But the quintuplets' fairy-tale existence was over.

For decades, controversy has raged between the two sides of the divided Dionne family—the parents and siblings and the tightly bonded quintuplets—over what went on in the Big House. In the book *We Were Five*, written in 1963, Annette, Yvonne, Cécile, and Marie hinted at physically and sexually abusive treatment from both their parents, and jealousy and meanness from their brothers and sisters. The allegations were made much more explicit in a second book, *Family Secrets*, published in 1995.

According to the sisters, the household atmosphere was tense from the beginning. Their father was beset with excruciating migraine headaches that made everyone wary of upsetting him. Even without the headaches, he was an authoritarian man not to be crossed. As the girls became teenagers, their problems at home only increased. In *Family Secrets*, the three surviving women described sexual advances made by their father. All three say he repeatedly tried to touch their breasts, using driving lessons in his car as an opportunity to sit close to and try to fondle them. On one occasion, he French-kissed Cécile and asked her to become his mistress; on another, he drove Yvonne alone to a cottage, where he ordered her to have sex with him. The sisters also allege that two of their brothers sexually harassed them. As for their mother, they say that she was given to irrational outbursts and physical assaults, once knocking Yvonne unconscious.

The five surviving siblings—Thérèse, Oliva Jr., Pauline, Victor, and Claude—deny every charge. They say that their parents were not capable of such behaviour, and that the incidents detailed are not only false but a terrible insult to their parents' memory and their own family name. Thérèse Callahan, their oldest living sibling and a retired high-school music teacher, has long been the most outspoken and has publicly disputed most of their allegations. She spoke out most strongly on television and through an extensive interview with a Quebec French-language magazine after the publication of *Family Secrets*.

In spite of all the accusations, what is indisputable is that there were vast differences in the two camps of children. The years of family union would later be described by both groups in stories so conflicting it was as if they had lived in separate houses. And in a way, they had. Observers confirm that the five girls were treated by their parents as a group apart from the rest of the Dionne children and in a manner quite different from them. For example, the quintuplets were suddenly expected to perform household chores demanded by Elzire. Though she may have been trying to adjust the girls to life as ordinary kids, the change in their treatment was shocking and frightening for them. After being raised in a hothouse environment, the girls felt that being made to scrub toilets and wash floors was a punishment. Though their siblings also had work to do, the sisters say the bulk of the menial tasks fell to them. "For big events, we had a cook and housekeepers come, otherwise Mom did all the cooking and washing. We five did all the cleaning and sometimes Pauline, too. Thérèse worked on the farm," Annette says.

And, of course, in most other ways, the quintuplets were not like regular local kids. They were not free to play with others and go about on their own, and their contacts with outsiders were restricted. The Big House was surrounded by a chain-link fence topped with barbed wire, the gate padlocked and guarded by watchdogs. Even as teenagers, the five sisters were allowed out only in groups, always accompanied by their father and often by a uniformed policeman. Their siblings, however, went to movies and parties without his supervision.

The quintuplets could not help noticing, as well, the wealth that was being showered on their siblings but not on them. They were not yet aware that it was their own trust fund paying for these items. Looking back, Annette says, "So many things came into the Big House after we moved there, from our money. A brand-new tractor, cars for the boys. We were the first to have television, new clothes for Dad. At each birthday, the others got lots of gifts like clothes; for us, chocolates. They think we don't need anything because at twenty-one we'll get a fortune."

They weren't allowed to go to the local Catholic school or later to established boarding schools, as their older siblings had done. The Sisters of Assumption of the Sainted Virgin, a French-Catholic order that had a convent in North Bay,

103

suggested to Dionne that he allow them to set up a formal secondary school in the old nursery, and that ten other girls of the same age be invited to attend at a minimal charge. Dionne agreed. He created his own private school, under the supervision of the ministry of education, and had the nursery rebuilt with proper classrooms and a dormitory upstairs. He was not ready to let his world-famous daughters out of his control, although as always he blamed his overprotectiveness on a fear of the girls being abducted.

The high school, which opened in 1947, was named Villa Notre Dame, and its operating costs—$72,000 a year—came out of the quintuplets' trust fund, as did the tuition fees for the other Dionne children's boarding schools. Still, it was the first chance the quintuplets had to be on an equal footing with other teenage girls and to form normal friendships, some of which have held to this day. The quintuplets happily assumed the nicknames their friends and teachers used for them: "Netta" for Annette, "Cis" for Cécile, "Ivy" for Yvonne, "Peewee" for Marie, and "Em" for Émilie. The surviving three women sometimes still use those names when speaking together.

For the first year, the entire class lived together in the dormitory during the week. The Dionne girls delighted in the new camaraderie. They loved to hear stories about the other girls' lives but shared little about their own family, whom they rejoined in the Big House every weekend. The following year, only Émilie was allowed to sleep in the dormitory with the visiting students, largely because she had begun to have frequent epileptic attacks after the move to the Big House. In those days, the convulsive seizures caused by epilepsy evoked superstition and fear and were even associated with the Devil, particularly in unworldly communities like Corbeil. Certainly, the disorder was little understood by the Dionne family. Émilie's attacks disturbed her parents, who left helping her to the rest of the quintuplets and their teachers. Eventually, Oliva Dionne decided to leave Émilie in the school dorm but made the other four sisters return home each night. He had become distrusting of the nuns, afraid that they were becoming too close to his daughters, and that the quintuplets were confiding in them.

Sister Rachel Martel was a teacher at the Villa Notre Dame high school. She remembers how happy the quintuplets were when they were at school, and how unhappy they seemed to be at home. "We knew they had difficulties at home. It showed in their sad faces. But they didn't talk or explain their sufferings to me. They kept everything in their hearts. They are not liars, they had good hearts." She says she and the other nuns often discussed the situation facing the girls at home. "We talked among ourselves. It was a very special case. We tried to keep peace between them and the family. Mr. Dionne was controlling everything. I wanted the girls to be sent to a different convent, but he wanted a special school there to keep them at home. The other girls [the quintuplets' sisters] went to other boarding schools and convents. The quints wanted the same privilege to go out and find the world. But they had to obey. He was strict."

Sister Claire Tremblay has written a book, *People Who Walk by the Star*, about the work of the Sisters of Assumption of the Sainted Virgin. One chapter is devoted to the work of the nuns in their missions, including the Villa Notre Dame.

Sister Tremblay interviewed a number of the nuns who taught at the school, although they were unwilling to be named in either her book or this one. These elderly nuns had spent a lifetime avoiding disputes, and some still feared an angry backlash from the quintuplets' siblings, especially if they still lived nearby. Sister Tremblay says, "These sisters, the nuns, lived through hell in there. They saw what the family did to the quints and couldn't do anything about it, or they would make it worse. They knew about the abuse, and saw a lot with their own eyes. They said everything in the French book [*Family Secrets*] was true and they said it was much worse."

Tremblay went on to say, "The Sisters [the nuns] were aware of the sexual abuse. I wondered why the Sisters didn't do anything. I learned that they would have been fired, and it would be worse at home for the girls. Life was terrible for the nuns. They couldn't show any affection to the girls [in front of the parents]. They had to have two faces. The first group of Sisters that went there were kicked out by Mr. Dionne at the end of the first year."

Today, teachers and health-care workers are urged to speak out if they suspect that children are being abused or mistreated, but in those days looking the other way was the recommended course of action. Corbeil was a small village, and people got along best if they minded their own business. As for the nuns, they would never have dared talk back to a man with authority, such as Oliva Dionne.

During the course of writing her book, Sister Tremblay studied documents at the Centre for Research in French Canadian Culture at the University of Ottawa and read archival papers from the Association canadienne-française, the organization that had helped Dionne regain custody of his daughters. In reading written reports from the teachers to their order's base in Quebec, Sister Tremblay found harsh descriptions by the nuns of the other members of the Dionne family. According to the teachers, Elzire was given to wild mood swings, Oliva was suspicious of the clergy if they appeared too sympathetic to the girls, and the other siblings spoke vulgarly to the nuns.

Another observer who worked closely with the quintuplets confirmed that "life was miserable for the girls. They were not well treated at home. The rest of the family was envious of them.... The girls worked hard at home. They scrubbed the floors and did all kinds of menial work. Their mother would let her other kids buy or order clothes and put it on a bill, but the quints could not. All the other children ganged up on the five."

This source, who still prefers to go unnamed, also says that Émilie understood that she had to stay in the dormitory because the family didn't want to deal with her illness. One teacher at the school learned to take care of her, and Émilie confided to that teacher that her mother didn't really love her and that she was a burden to the family. Yvonne once told the same teacher that her father loved her only "when interested for other reasons." Though the quote is elliptical, it reflects a time when no one, least of all nuns and their young students, talked openly about sex. Yvonne also confided that she wanted to run away because her report card was so good that she was sure her mother would react negatively. In the past, Elzire had criticized her for being too smart.

Yet all the girls, save for Émilie, were careful about how much they told the nuns. For one thing, their siblings appeared to be reporting to their father any overt closeness between the quintuplets and their teachers. Also, the four who lived at home feared evoking their father's wrath if they disobeyed his order to reveal nothing of their home life to outsiders. Nevertheless, Sister Tremblay acknowledges that the passive girls were disappointed in the nuns for not speaking out in their defence, and for telling them instead to pray when they got upset.

There were some happy times in the family home, of course. Occasionally, the girls and some of their siblings performed before visiting priests and family friends. Sometimes boyfriends of Thérèse and Rose-Marie were allowed to visit and watch a movie or dance to records with the rest of the family. But ever since the sisters' two books revealed the overriding problems in the home, both sides of the family remember even pleasant occasions as being darkened by their profound differences. The quintuplets say that they were constantly being taught songs, dances, and drills by their mother and their teachers, as if they were to be ready at any given moment to put on a show. And when local young people came to their home and danced and sang, "they were always parties for the others and their friends, we were always apart," Yvonne recalls. The siblings, meanwhile, claim the girls stuck to themselves, and blame them for not trying to be part of the family.

Sadly for the women, most of their early memories have been tainted by their later recognition of how unnatural their lives were. In the nursery, for example, the girls were described by the scientists as a joyful sisterhood, playing boisterously in the playground; singing French folk tunes; banging noisily on drums, tom-toms, cymbals, and bells in their Dionne Quintuplet Orchestra; and marching vigorously to recorded music. Thousands of photographs were taken of the youngsters in these merry moods. Yet the adult women can look back only in hurt amazement, crushed that no one saw how empty that childhood was of normal family love. As Yvonne says, "We didn't know at that time that the whole way of life in which we were raised wasn't good for us. It left us with a lack of learning how to live normally." In *We Were Five*, the sisters had put it this way: "There was so much more money than love in our existence. It took a long time to realize what it did to us all."

Still, in ways that would not become clear until many years later, some of the quintuplets' experiences as children and teenagers would play a positive role in shaping their character. They learned to be gracious in public, and developed inner strength that helped them when things appeared to go wrong. The government of the day had forced them to become young performers; a later government would find itself facing poised and dignified adversaries.

In 1952, the time finally came when the quintuplets could no longer pursue their education in Corbeil. After completing grade twelve, their last year of high school, a decision had to be made about where they would go to further their studies and what courses they would take. Again, the choice was not theirs to make; the girls were never asked what they wanted for their future. But when their father told them that he had enrolled them at Nicolet, a Catholic college for girls in Quebec, they were overjoyed. Freedom at last, they thought, though it didn't quite turn out that way.

The long train ride to the beautiful campus, which was situated between Trois-Rivières and Quebec City, was thrilling to the quintuplets, as was the chance to widen their circle of friends. Once there, however, they learned they'd been arbitrarily enrolled by their parents into the Institute in Family Studies. They were dismayed to discover that, although the school had other excellent courses to offer, they were restricted to taking classes in domestic skills. A friend of Annette's from the time remembers, "I saw the parents one time in Nicolet. The girls were taking a French diction course. Their mother came in like a great wind to take them out of the course because she said they were there for domestic studies." They knew that their courses in knitting, weaving, petit point, and embroidery could hardly prepare them to be able to earn their own livings one day. They were given the strong impression that their parents expected them eventually to move back home with them or to devote themselves to the church.

Their father also saw to it that they were not allowed off the premises, and had his daughters locked in a classroom during free time on Sunday afternoons. Though their school fees and spending money came from their own trust fund, they were given only two dollars a month each as an allowance, far less than other students got.

On the quintuplets' nineteenth birthday, Elzire and Oliva made a rare visit to Nicolet. During the family's get-together, Marie stunned them all with the surprise announcement that she had decided not to return to the college the following year. Instead, she would enter a cloistered convent removed from the everyday world and devote herself to constant prayer.

This announcement was shocking because never before had any of the quintuplets been permitted to follow a plan of their own devising. Yet Elzire was delighted. A devout Catholic, she had always believed that she had been chosen to bear these miracle children and had had to endure so much since their birth because at least one of the quintuplets would eventually serve God.

Marie left home the next fall for Quebec City, where she would begin her life with a strict order of nuns, the Servants of the Very Holy Sacrament. Yvonne had also decided to strike out on her own, and left for Montreal to study art at the Collège Marguerite-Bourgeois. Émilie, Cécile, and Annette returned to Nicolet. It was the first time the five girls had ever lived apart. And, tragically, it presaged a permanent split.

6: ÉMILIE: FROM LAUGHTER TO TEARS

EPILEPSY IS SAID TO be the most common neurological disorder after migraine headaches. Yet to this day, it is stigmatized by the superstitions and ignorance of the past. In ancient times, as far back as 1067 B.C., it was wrongly thought to be the work of evil spirits and witches; later it was confused with leprosy and lunacy—all with horrible results for its sufferers. The International Bureau for Epilepsy recently reported that in one Western European country (which it discreetly left unnamed), it is still accepted practice to beat an epileptic child after a fit in an attempt to discourage him or her from having more attacks. Laws barring some epileptic patients from marrying were in place until the 1970s and 1980s in North America and the United Kingdom.

In sixteenth-century Europe, people with epilepsy were tortured and burned, and in some places, a hot iron was applied to the head. By the nineteenth century, epilepsy had been lumped in with other illnesses that early psychologists blamed on masturbation; some male patients were circumcised as a potential cure. But by the early 1900s, drug treatment had begun, and knowledge of epilepsy moved speedily ahead. Nevertheless, in Corbeil in the mid-1940s, when Émilie first exhibited its strange symptoms, the condition was still considered shameful. Fear and misunderstanding persisted in rural communities, while in Montreal, not very far away, great strides in the study and treatment of the condition were under way.

Émilie had her first seizure at age ten, early one morning. She and Yvonne had been assigned a shared bedroom in the Big House, which they'd moved into only months before. All of the sisters had approached this new phase in their lives with apprehension. Before the permanent reunion, they had never been away from the familiar setting of the nursery for even one day. And their tightly bonded unit had never before been divided into separate bedrooms. All of a sudden, here was Émilie, crying out in her bed, her muscles twitching involuntarily, her face frighteningly drained of colour. The sisters rushed her to their father and lay her across his knees. He acted helpless. Dr. Ildor Joyal, whom Oliva Dionne had chosen to replace Dr. Dafoe, was called and came to the house from North Bay. Cécile recalls that he said it was nothing, and linked Émilie's "faint"—he was not told of her other symptoms—to her having just started to menstruate. After the incident, the four sisters kept close watch on Émilie at all times.

Oliva Dionne was clearly worried that if the public found out about Émilie's illness, it could harm the entire family's reputation and the quintuplets' celebrity. The sisters were warned never to mention the epilepsy to outsiders, and as far as they know, Émilie was given no regular medication for her condition for years after it took hold, even though there were modern drugs that could have prevented her seizures. Joyal later claimed that he had "never seen Émilie in an epileptic seizure, but that there was much hearsay about such attacks."

When he finally acknowledged Émilie's disorder, Oliva Dionne told a different story than his daughters. A May 1955 article in the U.S. magazine *Redbook* included an interview with him in which the subject was raised. He said that he had taken his afflicted daughter to a child specialist in Ottawa, and that when she was fifteen she had been examined in Montreal by the respected neurosurgeon Dr. Wilder Penfield of the Montreal Neurological Institute. (Penfield had been honoured internationally for having developed a surgical procedure for treating epilepsy, but Émilie did not have that operation. Cécile does recall that when Émilie saw Penfield, she was given medication, but it was clearly not strong enough to curb the convulsions and there was no follow-up.) Dionne insisted that through all the years of her illness, Émilie had been given the latest drugs to help control it. In fact, newspaper reports years after the fact did say that Émilie was diagnosed in 1946 by an Ottawa specialist, but there was no mention of any treatment and the sisters saw no evidence of any at that time. The *Redbook* article noted that she was admitted to the hospital under the name Miss Michaud so that her epilepsy would remain a well-kept secret.

Former teachers report that Émilie regularly suffered attacks in the Villa Notre Dame high school, and that her classmates and visiting priests were all aware of the problem. Her convulsions occurred so frequently that her father had her continue to board at the school overnight so she could be constantly attended.

From all descriptions of Émilie's condition, it's evident that she suffered what are called grand mal seizures (now known as "tonic clonic" seizures, a reference to the sequence of stiffening and jerking). In these episodes, most of the nerve cells of the brain are firing at the same time, so consciousness is lost. Usually, the person's muscles stiffen, causing them to fall down; the back arches, the eyes roll back, and the limbs extend. Breathing is difficult and the skin turns bluish-grey. Then, the limbs, body, and head begin to jerk rhythmically, saliva builds up in the mouth, and the tongue is sometimes bitten. At the end of the seizure the body is limp, the person usually confused, sleepy, and headachy. This matches descriptions of what occurred during many of Émilie's epileptic attacks.

In 1950, Oliva Dionne and senior clergy members arranged for the girls to appear at a much-publicized event in New York. An illustrious memorial dinner was being held to honour Alfred E. Smith, the late state governor. He had been the first Roman Catholic to run for president of the United States, but had lost to Herbert Hoover in 1928. The quintuplets and their schoolmates were invited to sing for the huge gathering, but Émilie disappeared for part of the program due to an alleged headache. Only her sisters and a nurse, whom Elzire had requested go along, knew the truth. There was always a familiar warning symptom, or aura, before an epileptic attack—in her case, it was often a feeling of irritability—so Émilie, aware that it was about to happen, hastily left the party. As frightening as these episodes must have been for her, there was always at least one quintuplet who watched over Émilie whenever possible.

Annette, Marie, Cécile, Émilie and Yvonne, around age three. This photo was one of the items sent to then Premier of Ontario Bob Rae to indicate the sentiment of Cécile's son, Bertrand Dionne, that the quintuplets had been robbed of a normal childhood and much of their trust fund money.

Annette, Cécile and Yvonne making an appeal to Premier Mike Harris at a press conference at Queen's Park, on February 26, 1998. — Ron Bull, *Toronto Star*

Dr. Allan Roy Dafoe, the country doctor who became famous as the physician who helped deliver the quintuplets and kept them alive despite enormous odds.

The Dionne homestead which was in Corbeil, a French-Canadian farming village 12 kilometres from North Bay, the closest city and 3 kilometres from Callander, the town that became the site of Quintland, where the quintuplets were displayed. Now the Dionne Quint Museum, it was moved to a North Bay site in the 1980s. —Vian Ewart

The five girls in a publicity photo with their parents. From left to right, Marie, Oliva, Yvonne, Émilie, Annette, Elzire, and Cécile. The children were still living apart from their parents.

Oliva Dionne's large souvenir stand at Quintland, where he sold Quintuplet and local souvenirs, woollens, snacks — and his own autograph.

Quintland. Crowds line up to get into the U-shaped observatory, in front of the Dafoe Hospital and Nursery.

A 1936 billboard indicating the time of two daily half-hour shows throughout the spring, summer and early fall months.

Annette, Yvonne, Cécile, Marie, and Émilie, at age 6 during a publicity shoot, leaning against a 1940 La Salle.

"CROWN BRAND" JOUE SON RÔLE
dans la famille Dionne

LES CINQ PREMIERS ENFANTS DIONNE ELEVES AU
SIROP DE BLÉ-D'INDE (MAIS) "CROWN BRAND"

Partout le Canada LES MÉDECINS DE CAMPAGNE
recommandent ce célèbre aliment producteur d'énergie

Dans le temps où les maintenant célèbres parents Dionne n'avaient à s'occuper que d'élever et de nourrir leurs bébés, et que la nécessité les obligeait à se procurer à un coût aussi modique que possible l'aliment le plus nourrissant — leur choix s'arrêta sur le "CROWN BRAND".

Alors nous pouvons dire en toute justice que ce fameux produit non seulement contribua au bien-être de ces cinq enfants — mais aussi à la santé de leurs célèbres parents.

"CROWN BRAND" est le premier sirop de blé-d'inde (Maïs) et celui qui se vend le plus au Canada.

Ecoutez l'émission "SYRUP SYMPHONIES" radiodiffusée tous les lundis soirs de 8 heures à 8 heures 30, sur un réseau de postes canadiens, comprenant CKAC et CFCF.

SIROP de BLÉ-D'INDE (MAÏS)
EDWARDSBURG
CROWN BRAND

Un produit de
The CANADA STARCH COMPANY Limited

Oliva Dionne arranged a promotion contract for his other children, the five siblings born before the quintuplets. Clockwise, Ernest, Daniel, Rose-Marie, Pauline, and Thérèse.

Oliva Dionne with his daughters, age nine, after the parents, other siblings and the quintuplets moved together on their own for the first time. From left to right, Annette, Yvonne, Oliva, Marie, Émilie, and Cécile.

The Dionne quintuplets in New York, age 16, to sing at the Alfred E. Smith Memorial Dinner in the presence of Cardinal Spellman. Left to right, Émilie, Marie, Cécile, Elzire, Yvonne, Annette.

In New York, age 16, sightseeing, and followed by huge crowds. Left to right, Yvonne, Cécile, Émilie, Marie and Annette.

Nipissing Manor, in 1988, the nursing home that was formerly the Dionne family home known as the Big House, just 100 yards across from the farmhouse where the quintuplets were born. The 18-room mansion, built in 1943, cost some $100,000 to build and furnish, paid for from the girls' money.

The entire Dionne family in the Big House. From left to right, standing in back row, Pauline, Thérèse, Elzire, Rose-Marie, Ernest, Daniel, Oliva Jr., Victor. Front row, from left to right, Annette (leaning on couch arm), Émilie, Marie, Cécile, Yvonne (resting on couch back), baby Claude and Oliva.

Faye and Jimmy Rodolfos, and their dog, in July 1998 in the living room of their Woburn, Massachusetts home, where they display their enormous collection of Dionne memorabilia. —Kevin Jacobus, Woburn Advocate

When they shared a bedroom in the Big House, Yvonne had taken responsibility for Émilie. When the five teenagers all went off together to study at Nicolet in Quebec, Cécile took charge of her. It was never revealed beyond the college that Émilie suffered too many convulsive attacks to even attend classes there. Once, while they were living in the dormitory, Émilie had a seizure in the students' bathroom and Cécile had to crawl under the locked toilet door to get to her.

She had "a lot of crises, seizures," Cécile remembers unhappily. "I brought her food every night. Why didn't I bring her to see a doctor? Sometimes I reproach myself. One night she had seizure after seizure. They called Father, but he didn't do anything. She had no medical examination, no blood samples taken while at the school."

The image of Émilie as a stressed young woman besieged by rampant epileptic attacks is in stark contrast to the image of the playful child of Quintland days. Yet there is a certain sad fit between Émilie as the comic extrovert and the worried teenager she later became. It was as if Émilie had an inner barometer that could gauge the extreme changes in the quintuplets' unusual environments. The controlled atmosphere of the nursery, with its constant routines, overseers, and public shows, sparked pranks from Émilie the youngster, while the volatility of the Big House raised anxiety in Émilie the teen.

Though she was born almost as frail and vulnerable as her mirror twin, Marie, Émilie grew into a chatterbox and an outgoing child star. "She posed on the top bar of the playground gym like a circus acrobat," Annette remembers. Wherever they were—at home or on the road—Émilie would

117

play to the crowds. When the celebrity children were presented to King George VI and Queen Elizabeth, newspaper reports said that Émilie wanted to stand on her head instead of curtsy. Louise Corriveau, a nurse who accompanied the girls, later wrote of Émilie that she was the one who was curious about mechanical things or gadgets, and so boldly touched and examined the buckle on the belt of the king's uniform. To his amusement, the youngster said that it was just like the one worn by a member of their nursery police guard. As the youngsters walked through the legislative chamber, Émilie, always the crowd pleaser, threw a kiss with her hand to the audience, which broke into applause.

How did this mirthful, outgoing young girl end up withdrawing to a secluded, church-run hospice? The answer lies in the years between the nursery and the convent, and is tempered by her epilepsy and how it was handled.

The terrifying episodes grew more frequent and were exacerbated by Émilie's menstrual periods, when a seizure always occurred. Sometimes they happened several times a week. The situation was made worse by the actions of Elzire Dionne, who, the three surviving quintuplets say, took out her frustrations by hitting them. Émilie and Marie, they say, were her most frequent targets because they were the weakest. Émilie, the child who had once seen life through laughing eyes, became fearful.

Then there was the added stress of what the sisters describe in *Family Secrets* as Oliva Dionne's sexual abuse. Annette tells of an incident that happened when the girls were in their teens. She walked past her father's study one day and caught sight of him and Émilie sitting together in the dark with the door partially closed. "There were no lights on. He was talking to her. Later she told me that he asked her to show him her breasts," she reports with a pained look on her face.

The trigger for Émilie's convulsions was usually tension. "An argument in the family, any stormy scene that she could not escape, was usually followed by the telltale giddiness and then unconsciousness," the sisters reported in *We Were Five*. "When adolescence began, she had a seizure regular as the calendar, month by month. We learned how to treat her ourselves, most of the time, with a spoon in her mouth to prevent the teeth clenching on the tongue, watching to be sure she did not hurt herself unknowingly. The cry from her bedroom and then Yvonne slipping in to summon us—this was part of life, too."

Not only did the Dionnes keep Émilie's epilepsy a secret, they also kept quiet about her decision at nineteen to become a nun, perhaps believing that any attention drawn to her would expose her condition. Émilie had been influenced in her decision by a priest who visited the house in Corbeil. A recruiter for a special order, the Oblates of Mary Immaculate, Father Louis-Marie Parent had founded a rest home for ageing clergy. It was a rambling white hostel in Quebec's picturesque Laurentian Mountains, near the popular ski resort town of Ste-Agathe. A small group of nuns cared for about a dozen clergy members there, and Émilie was to join them and then become a postulant, the first step towards eventually taking her vows.

Soon after Émilie joined the Oblates, Father Parent was enlisted to retrieve Marie from her Quebec City order, whose arduous regime had proved too much for her. He drove Marie to another Oblate convent in the town of Richelieu and, at her request, called Émilie and asked her to join her sister for comfort.

Regrettably, he did not take into account that Émilie had never been on a bus on her own, or that she did not know her way around the busy, downtown streets of Montreal, where she would have to transfer to a second bus. He did not realize that she had minimal experience handling money, or that she'd never even been to a candy store alone. And he did not know—how could he?—that the bewildering journey, the cars with their horns blaring, and the crowds of people would send Émilie into a state of near panic and set off a series of epileptic attacks.

Baffling stories appeared in newspapers around the world on July 16, 1954. They reported that Émilie had been found wandering the streets of Montreal at night, dazed by the bright lights and traffic, and had been picked up by police in a patrol car. At first, they had been unable to learn what she was doing in the city. Mortified, she refused for a while to tell them even her name, not wanting anyone to know she was a famous Dionne and fearful of her father's reaction to any negative publicity. She finally gave in and told the police who she was, on the promise that they would not tell the press. No chance. Cécile recalls that Émilie later told her, "They [the police] said I was stupid. I did not want to tell them my name. Then I made them promise first that they would not let anyone know if I told them I was a quintuplet, but they broke their promise. They were very rude." An officer leaked the story, and it made front-page news.

In the meantime Émilie had spent the night in the police station—a fact that the press never figured out and that was covered up by false reports that she was taken to her sister Rose-Marie Girouard's home in a nearby town. The next day, once her identity was known, she was taken to the archbishop of Montreal's palace. From there, she was driven back to the convent in Ste-Agathe. She never got to see Marie.

Elzire Dionne, acting on Oliva's direction, went to the convent with Cécile to bring Émilie home. Says Cécile, "I didn't want Émilie to go back home and be alone with Mom and Dad. Mom was afraid of her seizures." After Elzire spoke privately to the nuns in charge, somehow it was decided that Émilie would remain at the convent. Cécile was shocked to hear the nuns later say that they weren't told about the epilepsy. At the time, according to the 1954 register of specialists of the Quebec College of Physicians and Surgeons, the greater Montreal region was home to as many as twenty-one neuropsychiatrists and eleven psychiatrists involved in the treatment of epilepsy. But Émilie, who then lived close to that city, was getting no treatment at all for her illness.

Émilie died as a result of an epileptic seizure on August 6, 1954. She was just twenty years old.

The world learned the news in bold, shocking headlines. Toronto's *Globe and Mail*, accepting Oliva Dionne's explanation, ran the words "Quint Dies of Stroke" across its full eight-column front page. The attached story began, "The fairy-tale world of the Dionne quintuplets crumbled today...."

Newspaper reporters the world over were scrambling to come up with the whole story. Though they'd written millions of words about the quintuplets over two decades, they had never before found out that one of them had epilepsy. But word got out when one newspaper quoted Rose-Marie as saying, in error, that Émilie had had polio at age three, and that ever since then she'd had "fainting spells from epilepsy." (In fact, Émilie had taken very ill with a high fever at age three; years later, Yvonne recalls, "Mom told us they had thought it was polio, but they were never sure." There was no evidence after she recovered that it had been polio.)

The quintuplets gave their own account of Émilie's death years later. As they told it, there had been repeated seizures, up to twenty a day, during the three weeks after Émilie returned from her harrowing night in Montreal. The day before her fatal episode, she was helping out at a picnic given for the elderly residents on the hostel's grounds. Struck by a seizure, she fell and broke her ankle, but for some reason she was not taken to a doctor. Fearing more attacks, she asked that someone stay with her all night. Her sisters had always made sure that she was not alone during her epileptic state, and she knew she needed to be watched. She had three more attacks in the night and refused food. Tragically, the nun who had stayed by her side all night went to Mass with the others, leaving Émilie alone. When she returned, Émilie was dead.

The coroner said death was the result of suffocation, an accident. Émilie was found asphyxiated, face down on her pillow; her teeth had bitten into her tongue. The nuns said afterwards that they had never been told that their young postulant had epilepsy. There was no explanation of what they thought was causing Émilie's seizures.

∽о◡

Émilie's body was driven the five hundred kilometres back to Corbeil in a black hearse. Photographs taken at the house show Cécile, Marie, Yvonne, and Annette keeping vigil beside her open coffin, standing in a row at her side as a final barrier against the suffering she had known in life. Their faces reflect more than sadness: they look weary beyond their years. In contrast, Émilie's face, above a black-and-gold shroud, is childlike, at peace.

The padlocked gate of the Dionne mansion was thrown open to the public, as was the front door. Thousands came to pay their respects. Hundreds more arrived the next day and followed the funeral procession to the little church in Corbeil. There was no eulogy, no sermon. The Dionne parents were public about Émilie's death but allowed no summary of her life.

Yvonne recently described her mother's first reaction: "At the time of Émilie's death, Mom came to my room and said to me quite simply, like this, 'Fortunately, Émilie did not die here because there would have been a whole inquiry.' I was completely surprised to hear this, and I stood open-mouthed."

More crowds gathered at the small village cemetery, three-quarters of a kilometre away down a country dirt road. There, Émilie was buried in the Dionne family area of the graveyard, which sits in the corner of a farmer's field. After her death, her sisters left home and returned less and less over the years. But whenever they return, to this day, they visit that weedy cemetery and pray at the grave of their beloved sister.

It is no surprise that despite the overwhelming grief they felt when Émilie died, Yvonne, Annette, and Cécile admit they were also relieved that their sister would be troubled no longer. Still, Cécile says it was very hard to let go of her grief. "Inside, there's a voice that said, 'You should have done this or that.' It took a long time to get over it." Unsurprisingly, Annette and Yvonne also described the loss of their sensitive Émilie in terms of relief mixed with persistent grief.

They were no longer five.

7: MARIE: AGAINST ALL ODDS

ÉMILIE'S DEATH WAS AN overwhelming blow for Marie. The two had formed a separate pair bond within the group of five, and were protected by their other sisters because of their weaker constitutions. Their parents had treated them differently as well—though rather than singling them out for protection, they sometimes targeted the two vulnerable young girls in less caring ways.

Marie, weighing only 1 lb., 8½oz., was born the smallest of them all; Émilie was hardly bigger. Both newborns repeatedly turned blue and needed reviving with Dr. Dafoe's proven rum-based stimulant. Both were close to death for days during that much-publicized struggle to survive. At one point, Marie's heart almost stopped.

The two sisters, described by scientific experts as mirror twins, displayed opposite personalities in their nursery years. While Émilie was outgoing, Marie was passive. A nurse who cared for the children wrote of seven-year-old Marie, "[She] is sweet, loveable and easily influenced. She lets herself be ordered around by her sisters and except for rare outbursts will take what's left over after the others have chosen.... She is easily tired and likes to be babied, has occasional outbursts of temper, but on the whole Marie is the most pliable of the quints."

Yet in contrast to her sisters, who became more reticent when they moved to the Big House, Marie became more outspoken. She astonished the others by daring to talk back to their father when she felt his demands were unjust. But she did not win those fights. Cécile remembers, "Dad was the authority. We were afraid of him, that he would hit [us]. We saw him hit the others. He threw Daniel down the stairs. He was hard on Marie; she talked back. Once he made her kneel down until suppertime. Once I saw him climbing the stairs and going after her, and she was going to throw herself down the stairs."

At the Big House, as it had been in the nursery, Marie was closest to and played most with Émilie. Worried that any heavy household chores would overstress her sister and set off convulsions, Marie surprised everyone with her energy and did the work of two. Unfortunately, the girls' closeness caused both parents to lump Marie and Émilie together as the weak pair. The two had to sit in the back of the car, for example, when Oliva was teaching the others to drive. Marie was also singled out and told by her mother that she couldn't go certain places or do various things because of her poor vision. It was thought that flash bulbs containing magnesium and sometimes exploded close to the infants by eager photographers had injured Marie's eyes soon after she was born. She had strabismus, or what's commonly referred to as a lazy eye. The right eye was extremely weak and turned in; she had to wear thick-lensed glasses to correct her vision. She even underwent a cataract operation in her early twenties, far younger than is common.

As a baby, Marie also had surgery to remove a benign tumour from her leg. The operation, performed by a surgeon at no cost, was reported in breathless detail around the world. Her delicate health and petite size had made her a favourite with countless adoring fans. Even Dr. Dafoe never hesitated to show that he also considered Marie to be the most special. Years later, the Marie doll is still one of the most cherished by Dionne collectors.

Though Marie was the frailest of the quintuplets at birth, she emerged as the one who fought the most dramatic battle for independence. Bolder than her whisper of a figure suggested, she was the quintuplet most likely to risk her father's formidable anger by stating her own opinions. She also had the courage to be the first to strike out on her own and leave her sisters, and the daring to enter the unknown world of business by setting up a florist shop in Montreal.

The fact that none of these moves brought her lasting success has in the past left people with a sad, tragic view of Marie that pains her sisters and her daughters and is at odds with much of her real life. It neglects the feisty spirit of this tiny woman—she was, at 4' 11", the shortest of the diminutive sisters—who battled all of the odds against her.

She continually chose to test herself in difficult territory. On the quintuplets' nineteenth birthday, their parents came to see them at Nicolet and the family spent some hours together at a private cottage on the property. As was usual for the sisters, the occasion was a staged photo opportunity. (By the time they moved to the Big House, they were no longer subjected to the daily photography sessions agreed to by their government-appointed guardians, but there were still publicity shoots arranged by their father.) When the photographs had all been taken and the Dionnes were alone as a family, Marie made the dramatic announcement that she planned to become a nun. She had been on a recent retreat to a cloistered convent with her sister Pauline and had become convinced that it was the right place for her. She told her family, "I am going to enter a convent and serve God. I have thought of it for a long time. I have prayed, and I have decided. I care nothing for the things of the world. I feel I belong in a convent. It is the only place where I can be happy."

Oliva Dionne was so taken aback that he did not announce Marie's plan to the press for three months. In typical fashion, however, he managed to convey the message that although one quintuplet was going off on her own, he was still in control. "For several years now, little Marie has been developing an idea which she did not dare discuss with her mother and father in case they would object," he said. "As I have always done in the past, every decision was made for the girls' own benefit. Therefore, once more I don't feel I should interfere with Marie's intimate desire." But the victory was still Marie's; she had won over her father, who had never let the sisters do anything he hadn't pre-approved.

In the fall of 1953, she entered one of the strictest orders, the Servants of the Very Holy Sacrament, based in a convent in Quebec City. She would spend a six-month trial period as a postulant before becoming a novice. A life of religious devotion was nothing new to the five sisters, who had been taught and supervised by nuns for years, and often saw members of the clergy come to Corbeil to visit the family. And they had been brought up, like nuns, with a strict schedule governing when they would wake, wash, eat, learn, say prayers, and sleep. But Marie's choice of an extremely disciplined order that barred public contact worried her sisters, especially in light of Marie's previous history of fragile health.

The closed order's regime dictated that all of its members would take part in continuous, twenty-four-hour prayer. Each nun would have to kneel for several hours at a time, speaking only after the midday and suppertime meals. They slept on straw mats on the floor and were required to forsake all worldly goods. Every moment of their day was governed by a book called *The Holy Rule*. As a postulant, Marie was required to wear a white veil that covered her from the tip of her head to below her waist at all times. And as Sister Marie-Rachel, she was sequestered behind a grilled wooden door that afforded a glimpse of the outside world, but closed the convent off from it.

After less than a year, however, Marie had become too ill and weak from the exhausting convent life to carry on. Father Parent went to Quebec City to retrieve Marie and took her to a different convent for rest. On her suggestion, he called Émilie and asked her to visit. That call prompted the fateful journey that ultimately led to Émilie's death.

For Marie, the loss of Émilie was a turning point. Twice, she would attempt to bring life back to the name Émilie. She fell short with her brief ownership of a flower shop, Salon Émilie, when she had to close it, but succeeded joyously when she named her first-born daughter for the sister she had loved so dearly.

After Émilie's funeral, the four surviving sisters left Corbeil for Montreal. While Cécile and Yvonne trained to be nurses and lived at the busy Hôpital Notre Dame de l'Espérance, Marie and Annette enrolled at the Collège Marguerite-Bourgeois in the upscale Westmount area. Its relaxed rules meant the girls could leave the grounds whenever they pleased. From that time, Marie became closest with Annette, though all of her sisters agree she still kept a great deal of her thoughts to herself.

At the college, Marie took a general course in literature and, with her pleasant soprano voice, studied singing. She and Annette had their own rooms close to each other, and slowly Marie started to get past Émilie's death and find some happiness. But when she and Annette went home for a visit in November 1954, Marie was pressured by her mother to remain in Corbeil. She was needed by her parents, she was told.

Annette and Cécile both recall that when they next saw Marie, in May 1955, there was no light in her eyes. She appeared hopeless and worn down. Annette remembers, "Mom insisted that Marie stay. Marie told me that Mom needed her because there was so much work to do. Mom had a very strong will." Cécile agrees. "Something had changed. She was not smiling, she was feeling very low. Émilie was gone. Marie was very discouraged; she seemed disconnected. She had no expression on her face."

The next fall, she and Annette were back at their former school, Nicolet, where they had decided to spend another year, this time choosing their own courses. After just a few weeks back, Marie insisted that she was strong enough to return to the rigorous routine of the convent in Quebec City. Annette accompanied her, sad over her decision and concerned because Marie still seemed to lack energy. Shortly after her arrival, she collapsed, suffering from frequent chest pains thought to be angina. By December, it was decided that she would be unable to take her vows.

Rejoining her sisters in Montreal, Marie was hospitalized in Notre Dame de l'Espérance. At that point Marie was in a deep depression. At a course on psychiatric patients, however, Cécile had learned that she could snap Marie out of a collapse by slapping her face to bring her back to reality. The method seemed to work, but Annette, who was in Marie's company more often, was reluctant to do it.

When she left the hospital, Marie joined Annette in a Montreal apartment. There she at last began to enjoy the freedom her sisters had been experiencing for some time — having fun, friendships and social outings on their own. Annette and Cécile both had boyfriends; Yvonne and Cécile would soon have professions. Encouraged, Marie set about finding her own path, and revived her strong will.

Marie had long dreamed of owning her own business, and she pursued this dream by attending a course on how to buy, sell, and care for flowers. She took the course in Sorel, a town east of Montreal, where Annette's boyfriend, Germain Allard, had a cousin who was a florist. On Mother's Day in 1956, when she was just twenty-two, she proudly opened the doors of her flower boutique at the bustling Montreal intersection of St. Urbain Street and Pine Avenue. It was a time of great excitement for Marie, who had spent months planning, shopping, and preparing for the store — a remarkably ambitious venture for someone so young and so previously sheltered from anything having to do with commerce.

The flower shop was to be her material salvation. She enlisted Philippe Langlois, who was by then Cécile's fiancé, to help her set up and run the business. The two enjoyed the hectic period of organizing the project. But in *We Were Five*, on which Marie collaborated, her fruitless efforts to get some start-up money out of her trust fund are described. Oliva Dionne, who was on the advisory board that controlled the accounts, was against the venture; when Marie asked for a release of funds, she was turned down flat. But her determination prevailed. "Whatever happens, I will open my shop," she said. "I will not be stopped now."

The sisters agreed on a plan. According to the agreement they had been urged to sign, their father was receiving $500 a month from their trust fund for the care of the Big House, where he and Elzire still lived. But Elzire had complained that the sum was too little, and had prevailed on the sisters to give them an additional allowance of $300 monthly. To try to please her, the four surviving quintuplets had asked the trust company to decrease their own monthly allotment by that amount and send it to their parents. Now, they diverted the $300 per month into Salon Émilie.

Unfortunately, the quintuplets' unusual upbringing had left Marie unsuited to the hard exchanges of business, and she was given no opportunity in her young life to learn. It was natural for the kind-hearted Marie to give flowers away to friends and to churches, and to take money from the cash register to help out nuns who sought donations for a cause. Soon, far more money was going out of the shop than coming in. Marie again approached the trust company for an advance to sustain the shop, but was again refused. It took until

Christmas, only seven months, for Marie to be forced to close the store. It had ended up a financial disaster. Recalls Annette, "She was very discouraged, dispirited. She lost a lot of money from her trust allowance." (Ironically, her instincts were right even if her business acumen was not. There is still a flower shop in the same Montreal location.)

According to Pierre Berton's *The Dionne Years*, Marie lost $42,000 in total on the venture. Thousands of dollars had been spent on everything from store counters to engraved stationery, which she blithely charged at Eaton's department store, knowing that those bills would go directly to Guaranty Trust and that the company would have no choice but to pay them from her account. A new station wagon was bought on credit. She also rented an apartment over the store, where she lived during its operation.

After she closed Salon Émilie, Marie worked for a while in another florist's shop under an assumed name, Denise Mousseaux, to avoid recognition. With her thick glasses and her deliberate style of dressing plainly, no one realized who she was. But she and her sisters were aware that they were all being watched closely by their father. Bills for the fees of the detectives who followed Marie showed up on her trust fund statements.

A bout of depression took hold. Marie lost weight and would often dramatically fold onto the floor, as in a faint, without warning. She suffered a nervous breakdown, was in and out of hospital under a fictitious name, and had an operation on her right eye. Meanwhile, her sisters were moving forward. Annette and Cécile both married that year, and

Yvonne was working as a nurse. After Marie was discharged from hospital, she appeared restless and dissatisfied with her life. She was beset by moodiness whenever she visited the Allard home, where she often stayed. Annette recalls that Marie felt ready for marriage and children, and wanted it to happen soon.

Florian Houle, who was unknown to Annette and Germain Allard, somehow managed to attend their small, private wedding. He seemed to be there on his own. The sisters later learned that he had met Marie while she was using a false name and did not detect at first that she was one of the famous Dionnes. They had begun to date.

When Marie introduced him to the others, her sisters were surprised that she had chosen a man twenty-one years older than her and very conservative in manner. Houle was a civil servant who worked as an inspector in the sales-tax department of the Quebec government. "With us, he was kind but very reserved. I always remember him wearing a hat," says Annette. Marie later confided that he was authoritarian and tried to control her.

The couple married on August 13, 1958, in a wedding so private that none of Marie's sisters was even told when it would take place. This was by choice. Marie had initially planned a ceremony with her sisters as guests, but she was unnerved by a disturbing message she had received from a clergyman who informed her that she was surrounded by people who wanted to hurt her.

In truth, it was Cécile who, concerned when Marie announced she would marry Houle, had called the priest. She believed that Marie was not emotionally strong, and that having children would be more than she could handle. Cécile, like Yvonne, had felt personally responsible for the well-being of the two most vulnerable sisters, Émilie and Marie, when the five young girls lived in the Big House. But her call to the priest, whom she thought might be able to counsel Marie about her plans, turned out to be poorly placed. He saw Cécile's act as threatening to Marie and issued the warning. As a result, Marie moved up the wedding date and told no one of the change.

Annette still keeps a memento of her sister's original preparations, which included a celebratory dinner at the Montreal restaurant C'est Si Bon. The wedding menu had already been printed: champagne, chicken, strawberry shortcake. But that dinner for relatives and friends was cancelled, and the ceremony took place two days earlier than scheduled in the Sacred Heart Chapel of the Church of Notre Dame, an imposing Montreal landmark. Two altar boys served as witnesses. Marie sent a letter to her father telling him the news, but timed it to arrive after the wedding. The couple drove off for a ten-day honeymoon throughout Quebec.

Marie never complained to Cécile about her intervention, and the sisters, in turn, accepted Houle as her husband. The couple visited the Allards in Saint-Bruno whenever they were able; Yvonne was present at these gatherings whenever possible; and Annette and Marie kept in touch by phone between visits. Though Cécile, who was living in Quebec City, didn't see Marie often, she spoke to her from time to time.

After the death of Émilie, Oliva Dionne had taken public relations into his own hands. In a two-part series in *Redbook* magazine, which ran in its April and May 1955 issues—just before Yvonne, Cécile, Annette, and Marie reached age twenty-one and independence—Dionne told writer William Peters of "outsiders" who, he said, were trying to drive a wedge between the quintuplets and the rest of the family. He also described how he and his wife had had difficulties with their five daughters when they rejoined their family. He said the girls didn't like to mingle with their siblings and could not take any discipline without running off to someone, often the nuns at their school, for solace. He painted a picture of two parents who were, according to Peters, almost in awe of their own children.

Peters concluded his articles by saying that the most poignant aspect of the quintuplets' story was the girls themselves. "If they are something less than well-adjusted adults today, it is not their fault. Perhaps all of us in this curiosity ridden, easy-money-seeking world are somehow to blame."

Cécile denies all of her father's charges. "We always [made] a big effort to mingle with the family," she says today. When she, Marie, and Annette were being interviewed for the 1963 *McCall's* magazine articles that formed the book *We Were Five*, they told, for the first time, how they saw those same events—their siblings' cold reception, their parents' harshness, and their father's unwarranted suspicion of anyone who came in contact with them. They described the Big House as "the saddest home we ever knew." Immediately, their father was interviewed and quoted as saying that their revelations were "a tissue of lies."

The women also gave the public a selective glimpse at their first years of marriage, stressing what was positive in their adult lives. The three acknowledged that it was Marie who was the most eager to prove the early experts wrong: the quintuplets were perfectly capable of becoming pregnant and bearing children. After two miscarriages, which did not deter her, Marie gave birth to Émilie in 1960 and to Monic in 1962.

In the opening article of the series, published in October 1963, there is a photograph of a charmed gathering of the three married sisters and their children taken by the famed Canadian portrait photographer Yousuf Karsh. He captured the women at age twenty-nine, smiling widely and glowing with vitality, in a lovely outdoor summer setting. A relaxed, robust Marie, in a sleeveless floral dress and bold big-button earrings, is holding her youngest while her elder daughter leans against her aunt Annette. Both girls are wearing identical gauzy dresses with puffed sleeves and lace-edged collars, as if dressed for a festive occasion. Marie's smile is at once proud and happy.

The idyllic scene was not to last. Marie separated from Houle in 1964, when the girls were three and less than two. In fact, it had been obvious to the sisters during the *McCall's* interviews that something was wrong between the couple. When Houle learned what was being revealed for *We Were Five*, he called the Dionne parents to disclaim any part in it and urged Marie to withdraw from the meetings. She did, but approved the draft of the book as it was written instead of deleting the parts Houle didn't like. And while the couple was still together, Marie's fainting spells continued. Yvonne recalls a birthday party at Annette's house when they had to pick up Marie and lie her down in a quiet bedroom after she fell in a heap on the floor. Allard and Houle were so unmoved that they did not even interrupt their conversation to inquire about Marie's condition. It is a testament to Marie's strength of spirit, however, that she left Houle and took the children, fleeing what she knew was a bad marriage, despite the pressures of the times and the church's dictum that wives remain with their husbands.

Eighteen months after the separation, Marie was hospitalized once again because of her low emotional state, this time in the psychiatric hospital of Hippolite La Fontaine. There, she received shock therapy. In Marie's case, the therapy was said to be unsuccessful. That is only one part of her story, of course, though it is the part the press would periodically sniff out and report. She also underwent intensive psychotherapy that clearly helped her, since over the next five years Marie enjoyed periods when she was feeling energetic and joyful. She rented a two-bedroom Montreal apartment, which she shared with her beloved animals, a dog named Lassie and two cats, to the delight of the youngsters. She also wanted to own a parakeet, and took the girls on numerous visits to pet stores in search of one to buy. She was playful and full of laughter with her children. On frequent outings to a nearby park, she would roll down the hill like a rolling pin right alongside them. Both daughters remember her from these times as happy and affectionate. There was also a love affair in Marie's life for some time: the man was her doctor and the two were dating. He sometimes visited them all on the weekend, and it was evident to Marie's older daughter that the two were close.

In spite of these happy occasions, Marie's sisters believed she was lonely when her daughters were not there. Concerned, Annette got into the habit of calling her every day. One

Monday in February 1970, there was no answer when she called. Perhaps she has gone out, Annette thought. No answer on Tuesday, either. Nor Wednesday. Annette became alarmed. On Thursday, she called Marie's doctor, whom Marie had confided she had been seeing, and he said he would look in on her. He called back that same day and said the dreaded words: "It's over. That's it." Marie was dead. He had found her on her bed, and she had been dead for several days.

An autopsy was performed on February 28, 1970, and put the cause of death as "undetermined." No cause could be pinpointed since four days had passed before she was found. But the press reported that Marie had died of "an apparent blood clot." The phrase is said to have come from Florian Houle, who was besieged by reporters immediately after news broke of Marie's tragic end. Though he was separated from Marie, he felt a responsibility to her and to their children to come up with a response that would stop speculation. There was already sensational talk. Houle told reporters that she had died of "an embolism," or blood clot, in the brain.

Cécile hurried to Montreal when she heard the news; she went to the morgue first, then to the apartment, accompanied by Houle and the two young girls. She still recalls the scene vividly. An emptied bowl of cereal, with dried crumbs at the bottom and a used spoon resting within, sat on Marie's bedside table. Nearby stood several bottles of pills for her bouts of depression and fragile health, medications that had swelled her weight to a reported 130 pounds. A shopping list was stuck on the fridge door. Houle told her to leave everything untouched, because the police would be investigating the death. To Cécile, however, these details signalled that

139

Marie had been sitting on her bed having a small meal. Annette says, "She loved to live and was full of life."

There was a brief time after her separation when Marie tried to escape her blue periods by drinking, and this caused some erroneous reports that she drank heavily, an allegation the press has repeated through the years. At her well-attended funeral in Saint-Bruno, the mourners included her parents, Elzire and Oliva, the quintuplets' siblings, and other family and friends.

The silence of the surviving quintuplets, who spent almost thirty years after Marie's death rigorously avoiding the press and living without public notice, was, they say, partly out of respect for Marie's privacy and the tragedy of her early death. All three now say they regret that their own personal circumstances prevented them from taking in Marie's daughters. Annette says, "I think Florian was shocked and disappointed that I wouldn't take them. It was not easy for him to look after them alone. He was too old."

As a result, Marie's innocent children were left motherless. The two girls, who were nine and seven when Marie died, have shied away from publicity all their lives and wish only to note that their memory of their mother is fond and enduring. They say they remember their times with her as "filled with love and laughter."

8: ANNETTE: LIGHT
IN A GREY SKY

LIFE CHANGED DRAMATICALLY for all of the quintuplets after Émilie died. Each of the sisters became determined to find her own identity, and Annette wanted to pursue her lifelong interest in music. She was musically talented, as were many in the Dionne family, particularly on her mother's side. Even as a child, she could play any tune by ear. She had listened to soothing classical works like Beethoven's "Moonlight Sonata" and Puccini's operas on the record player in the nursery (under Dr. Dafoe's orders, only classical music was permitted while the little girls rested), but in the Big House, where there were three pianos, Elzire sometimes barred Annette from practice time, though she encouraged her older daughter Thérèse, who went on to study at the Royal Conservatory in Toronto. "I had to practice for my music exam, but Mom wouldn't let me," remembers Annette. "She wanted me to help her outside. I went to Pauline, and she persuaded Mom to let me practice." After she graduated from Nicolet, Annette attended Montreal's Collège Marguerite-Bourgeois to learn how to teach music—a pursuit Elzire accepted. Originally, Annette had wanted to be a nurse, like her sisters Cécile and Yvonne, but when she summoned up courage to tell her mother the plan she had for her future, Elzire said flatly that it was out of the question. She had had enough of that profession. It was not going to be, not for Annette, the daughter who had so compliantly scrubbed toilets and floors in that vast mansion. It was a refusal Annette would never forget. She had been accepted into the nursing course and encouraged by the head nurse, who said she had the right qualities for the profession. Yet she gave up on the spot. "I was the girl [who] easily obeyed. I was always looking for Mom's approval," she later said.

Nevertheless, a life in music seemed an acceptable alternative, and the Collège Marguerite-Bourgeois, situated amid rolling acreage on the heights of the rich, English-dominated Westmount district, brought back the cherished world of Mozart, Chopin, and other classical composers Annette had known as a child. Recently, she visited the school again and saw her former piano and music-theory teacher, Sister Marcelle Corneille, for the first time in forty years. They recognized each other immediately. Sister Corneille said of Annette, "She was very serious and attentive. She was confiding in me. When she was here, she was being observed. I had the impression that at nursing school someone was also watching Yvonne and Cécile." Annette confirmed her belief that some clergy members, as well as private investigators, were spying on the girls for her parents. She said of Sister Corneille, "Though I only confided a few details in those days, she was very sweet in her advice."

Back then, just descending the hill to Sherbrooke Street to buy an ice cream alongside her schoolmates felt like a step towards independence. Slowly, however, Annette began to imagine that she could have a life other than that which had been laid out for the quintuplets by others. The message had always been clear: they were different; they could never date and marry like normal girls, never have babies. Their destiny was either to serve God in the church, or to serve their parents at home. In spite of this, the natural spirit of the four surviving quintuplets was surging forward to challenge the dictates of the past. Surprisingly, Annette turned out to be the most optimistic among them.

Germain Allard was a philosophy student in Montreal, and Annette had known his sister at Villa Notre Dame. Cécile and Yvonne met him when he visited his brother at the hospital where they were training. A meeting with Annette was arranged, with Cécile acting as matchmaker now that she had a boyfriend of her own.

Annette was shy to speak when she first met Allard, or to trust her own feelings as they began to date. She had long been afraid of men, a fear that had its origins in haunting incidents with her father. "Once in the car, Dad was trying to show me how to drive. He put his finger into my blouse. I was thirteen; it was 1947. I froze, unable to speak. He said, 'You don't like that, eh?' After that, for two years, I was hating men. I was always wearing a turtleneck, or something tight up to my neck, in summer as well as winter. I was a virgin before my marriage. I never thought, I will meet a man who will love me." But she fell in love with Allard and believed that he loved her too.

Nevertheless, Annette did not rush into marriage. Allard had a university course in commerce, finance, and administration to complete before he could make a living. After spending one year in Montreal, Annette returned to Nicolet and continued her music studies there for another year.

The move was partly a retreat from a worrisome question that was plaguing her: Was marriage right for her? "I saw so many quarrels about money at home and that scared me very much," she later recalled. To try to come to terms with her past and move into the future together, she and Allard talked to a priest, who was their spiritual adviser. "We went to see him often. I wanted to do the good thing. The problems with my parents were preoccupying me. It was always the same advice from the priest: 'Try to forget, try to like them.'"

Annette and Allard got back together after her year at Nicolet, and she began to confide in him about her past. He first met her parents on an overnight visit to Corbeil, shortly after Christmas 1956. In an interview, Allard later recalled, "It was not a happy home at all." To Annette, Allard seemed a protector. She left school in June 1957 when she was twenty-three and, despite advice from the nuns to marry herself to the church, put herself in the arms of this man instead.

Normalcy in marriage and motherhood was what Annette dreamed of when she agreed to marry Allard. They married in Montreal in a private ceremony with the church's front doors locked to keep out curious onlookers. They chose the parish church near the apartment Annette was then sharing with her sister Marie. She says she loved the modern 1950s architecture of Notre-Dame de la Salette, which was named for a French Alpine town where an apparition of the Virgin Mary was believed to have appeared 150 years ago. With its bright-coloured mosaic mural, its chapel and pews in the round, and a marble altar in its centre, the church seemed to Annette to be beautiful and refreshingly modern. It's strange to learn, then, that she never went back there for more than forty years. In July 1998, she made a nostalgic visit to several important places in her life. Despite all that had gone wrong in the years since, she returned to the site of her wedding with a warm smile. She walked quietly down the aisle she had travelled as a bride and stopped at the marble railing bordering the altar. Then she knelt in a silent prayer, her face bathed in the light streaming through the stained-glass windows.

The couple married on October 11, 1957, at 10 a.m. Both wore coordinated brown suits; Annette's was chicly fitted to her wisp of a shapely, five-foot figure. She wore a beige hat and gloves and carried a beige purse. Her father walked her down the aisle in a smart charcoal suit, while her mother was dressed in a simple cotton coat that she kept on over her dress. Annette remembers feeling sorry that her mother seemed no longer to care about her appearance. But for herself, she felt nothing but joy.

She describes herself now as someone who always tried to put a bright face on things. "I would like to put light in the darkness of everybody. I work very hard to be positive, to see beauty in a grey sky." Indeed, "hard work" could well be the sum description of her marriage, though it began with both Annette and Allard apparently in love.

The couple split the cost of their wedding, the reception in the church basement, and their honeymoon visiting Allard's relatives around Quebec. But soon the major expenses were being dropped into Annette's lap. At first, she didn't think much about it. After all, the quintuplets were used to having their trust fund cover the cost of running things—the nursery,

Quintland, the Big House. They had somehow come to accept that their role was to both perform and pay.

Annette and Allard started their life together in a modest apartment in northeast Montreal, where they had their first son, Jean-François, in 1958. Allard paid the rent out of a common budget that he shared with Annette, and to which she contributed half of her $500 monthly allowance. At that time, Allard was earning $10,000 a year as a branch manager for Beneficial Canada, a finance and loans company.

Shortly thereafter, a friend of Allard's helped them find a three-bedroom family home, a ranch-style bungalow with a big backyard, in quiet, suburban Saint-Bruno, an ideal neighbourhood for their growing family. Their move was typical of the new breed of white-collar managers leaving behind grittier Montreal streets for the clean, open spaces of outlying areas on the south shore of the St. Lawrence River. She raised their children while Allard, who had turned into a weekday workaholic and a weekend *bon vivant*, worked and stayed out late.

Allard had become part of Quebec's aspiring new middle class, which emerged in the 1950s as the children of working-class parents were educated in affordable technical and business schools, and got jobs in banks and offices.

In the words of author William Weintraub in *City Unique*, his book about Montreal in the 1940s and 1950s, "This new bourgeoisie wanted better things in every realm," and Allard was no exception. Annette was expected to provide the down payment on the $19,500 house from her Guaranty Trust account. She shared the $264 monthly payments with Allard out of their joint budget for thirteen years, until he left the family. (She carried the mortgage payments alone after that, and finally paid off the final $6000 when she received her last bit of cash from the trust at age forty-five.) She bought all the furniture and paid many of the household bills, she says. Indeed, she paid for much of a lifestyle in which she hardly took part.

On the surface, Annette was living the so-called suburban dream. In reality, she spent almost two decades continuously cleaning and caring for their three-bedroom house and weekend chalet. How did her dream turn so sour?

Annette's second son, Charles, was born in Saint-Bruno in 1961, and Eric was born in 1962. In the early years, Annette was so busy with three little boys, and her husband worked late so often, that she called on Yvonne to come over whenever a child got sick or the demands of the house and kids became too much. After five years and three children, she and Allard had grown so far apart that they hardly saw each other, by day or by night.

So inexperienced in the ways of the world were all the sisters that Annette did not question why she and Allard never got a babysitter and went out on their own. It was not in her nature to rock the boat. She had once been the quintuplet whom behavioural scientists had described as the most aggressive in making contact with others. But her later experiences at home and in school had turned her quiet and submissive.

Allard, meanwhile, took holidays, went hunting, attended wine courses, and enjoyed at least one lover. His and Annette's only outings as a couple were to a dinner held every two months for Beneficial Canada employees. Annette started to see a therapist to learn to express her feelings more openly to Allard, but the breach between them had become too wide.

147

They never told each other how they were feeling—instead they shared their home and children like two sentinels guarding the same property but never speaking. Once, at a company event, a man told Annette she looked lovely. The comment stuck in her mind. She could not remember the last time she had heard that from her husband.

In his defence, Allard says his wife "had no initiative, made no decisions on her own." On one occasion, he asked her to phone a movie house to find out when a film began. She dialled the number then handed over the phone, saying that he was more used to handling such things. That incident, which was indicative of how timid and insecure she had become, annoyed him.

Allard didn't understand how much Annette feared looking incompetent. She was scarred by Oliva Dionne's insistence that she was not as intelligent as his other children. Of the quintuplets, only Yvonne was considered smart. That feeling of inadequacy stayed with Annette for years and kept her a submissive woman all that time.

Her passive nature also made it impossible for her to ask the bigger question: Why did Allard no longer make love to her after Eric's birth, just five years after they were married? "I remember being very naïve about sex," she says today. "Gerry did not have the character to be tender. I was timid. He was not stroking me. I was not used to doing things. In the early years I was very reserved." More than forty years after their wedding, she still speaks in clipped phrases on the subject, guarding her sense of delicacy. Still, the admission is staggering: A couple who started off in love lived together for eleven years without having sex.

She tried to improve the relationship by getting sex counselling. "I went frequently. I followed the advice to speak more and express my feelings." But it didn't work. As she puts it, "When a man has no more feelings.... He came home so late. I was asleep in bed."

Naturally, there is more to the story on both sides. In an interview, Allard told it this way: "Annette didn't want to have any more children," and true to her Catholic upbringing, she wouldn't use birth control. One must remember that all of the Dionnes grew up in an era when priests frequently used the pulpit to denounce the evils of birth control, masturbation, and divorce, even going so far as to say that a woman would burn in hell if she resisted her husband and to interrogate women in the confessional on their sexual practices.

By the time Annette had married, however, Quebec's French-Canadian Catholics, like Catholics elsewhere, were beginning to feel the stirrings of a change in attitude towards their religion. By the mid-1960s, a veritable revolution was taking place, as the II Vatican Council, begun in 1962 under Pope John XXIII, brought massive changes to church policy. But during the period that she was having children, the influence of the clergy on Annette's life was still strong, even though it sometimes troubled her. "Once, when I was saying confession," she recalled, "the priest asked how old my child was. When I said one and a half years, he asked, 'Why are you waiting to have another?' It frosted me so much that not having a baby each year was a sin.

"After three children, I realized that giving [Allard] another child was not a way to win him back. I would have liked to have had sex but I was turned off." She says she knew nothing in those days about condoms, nor did Allard suggest using them. She couldn't trust the rhythm method because her periods were irregular. She regrets that Allard didn't choose to discuss sex with her, and says now, in an admonishing tone, "He could have talked openly to me."

Still, Annette wasn't keen on divorce, and she wanted to make the marriage work for the sake of the children, so she took her therapist's advice and recommended to her husband that the couple go out together once a week. He agreed, but insisted she pay him $50 each time. She was shocked. "After it happened twice, I didn't ask him again. If he was going out with other women, then he was no more interested in going with me."

In telling her story, Annette tries to minimize her husband's reliance on her money. She is not a bitter woman by nature, and rather than being angry, she seems embarrassed by it all, as if she was foolish for not recognizing that something was wrong. Allard was equally embarrassed about the $50 charge when reminded of it, and he claimed that it was simply a matter of needing to increase their joint budget if they were to add the cost of going out together.

No matter whose version of events is accepted, the union was clearly an unusual and unsatisfying one. Allard later reflected that Annette's strange upbringing left her "not prepared for marriage, in an extreme way. Living in such a closed atmosphere in the nursery—where even if the girls had to go to the washroom, there was someone waiting in the corridor to take care of them—there was no chance to develop any initiative at all." And Annette's later experiences under her parents' care, he says, also had a negative effect on their marriage. "She was afraid of intimacy; she was scared to undress fully."

Annette agrees that she lacked confidence then, but says firmly, "I learned as the years went by. I always looked after the house and children by myself."

In 1963, as their marriage continued to quietly disintegrate, Allard encouraged Annette to be interviewed for *We Were Five*. The project was embraced by Annette, who was trying to gain confidence from marriage and motherhood and wanted to liberate herself from her past. Cécile was also eager, though primarily because she needed the money that would come from the book's royalties. Yvonne also agreed to the book, but was living away in a convent in New Brunswick and so didn't take an active part. Allard handled the negotiations, making a deal with the publisher for $110,000. It seemed a huge amount at the time, but after the agent took ten percent and the writer got half, the four sisters were left with around $11,000 each.

The book was the first time the quintuplets revealed the unhappiness they felt when united with their family in Corbeil. Typically, they, and Annette especially, diluted their stories in the belief they were still being respectful of their parents. The family thought otherwise and reacted angrily; Oliva Dionne immediately denounced the book publicly. But it hardly mattered. Most readers missed the vague references to sexual abuse.

One chapter, also typical of Annette's rosy outlook, describes her marriage to Allard as though she'd been carried off from darkness into domestic bliss. But reality was beginning to take a more visible toll, and Annette spent the next years devoting herself to the care of two homes with a vigour beyond duty or need. "I wasn't angry in my speaking. I took it out in the housework. The children say they knew about it. They say that it was too much for me. At the chalet it was always crowded. In my daily life, in my marriage, I was like an innkeeper," she says with remembered annoyance.

She could have been a model for those mindless ads of the 1960s, in which women were seen only as consumers of detergents and appliances. As William Weintraub has written, the role Annette was living had been the church-proscribed regime for Quebec women throughout the 1940s and 1950s. One Montreal priest even gave frequent lectures on how sinful it was not to be a perfect housewife. But though other women began to assert their rights in the 1960s, Annette was left trapped in an outmoded belief, reinforced by Allard, that her lot in life was only to serve her husband and children.

Every weekend the family went to the chalet near Drummondville, Quebec, and Allard's relatives and friends piled in to join them. Allard had bought the land for the chalet from his father and paid to have the house built himself. As with everything in their Saint-Bruno residence, however, it was up to Annette to pay for whatever else was needed. She wrote all the cheques for the special built-ins, the chimney and the brick fireplace, the chairs and table around which so many guests gathered.

Though the house was close by a river, Annette was too busy cleaning up after all the guests to go in the water and enjoy the outdoors. "I never had a single minute with Gerry. It's like in the beginning, when I was being raised by many people." She says all this with a shrug of self-recrimination. At the time, she believed she was doing the right thing by staying in the background as Allard wanted.

In the country, Allard kept up his nights-out habit, saying that he had new, rich friends in the area and that his life was changing. Annette later learned that he was having an affair, an indiscretion Allard now admits to. "I cannot say no to my having had an affair. It did happen."

During this period of increasing isolation from her husband, Annette also had to face another tragedy. In February 1970, Marie died from an indeterminate cause. Her funeral was one of the rare times that Annette, Cécile, and Yvonne were together with their parents since they'd left home.

That year, remembered for ever by the sisters as the year of Marie's death, marked the beginning of more than two and a half decades of retreat from public life. Yet that same year was a pivotal one in Quebec's history; it brought to a climax the separatist feelings that had begun to be stirred with the Quiet Revolution a decade earlier.

On October 5, 1970, members of an extreme nationalist group, the Front de libération du Québec (FLQ), kidnapped British diplomat James Cross in Montreal, and then, on October 10, snatched Quebec's labour minister, Pierre Laporte. One week later, Laporte's body was found in a car trunk. In December, the FLQ cell holding Cross was discovered and his release was negotiated. The group responsible for Laporte's death was later located and arrested, its members convicted of kidnapping and murder.

Prime Minister Pierre Trudeau took a tough stance and proclaimed a state of "apprehended insurrection" under the

War Measures Act, which suspended normal liberties throughout October and November of that year. The army was called
in to boost local police, and more than 450 people were
detained in Quebec, most without charges. The move galva-
nized public opinion in both French and English Canada and
was vigorously debated, especially in Quebec.

But for Annette and her sisters, who had once been pawns
of the Ontario government and of several Franco-Ontarian
lobby groups, politics had no place in their lives. Annette
recalls, "At that time we were not political at all. Life had
been so insular at home when we were with our parents."
Their adult lives turned out to be similarly insular, preoccupied as they were with family, marital, and financial concerns
over which they had little control. "It's very hard to learn
things [about our trust account] after so many years. It hurts
me and makes me feel strange that we had no control over our
own lives." But Annette quickly adds, in a remark that testifies
to her desire to have her opinions as an individual taken seri-
ously, "Today we know what is going on."

The following year, 1971, Annette plunged into a new
round of counselling to try to make sense of her marriage and
her life as a whole. She thought that the sessions were helping,
and that she was at last beginning to take some steps in the
right direction. But without warning her, Allard had a court
document asking for a divorce sent to her in the summer of
1973. Annette was shocked. Divorce was not common then in
the traditional Catholic world she inhabited, and despite
Marie's separation from Florian Houle, it was something she
never really contemplated for herself and Allard.

When Pierre Berton's *The Dionne Years* was published a few

years later, Annette read for the first time her ex-husband's public explanation for their marital split. He said that when Cécile and Yvonne were both living nearby in Saint-Bruno, they interfered in the household and he'd been forced to ask his wife to choose between them and him. When she couldn't, he left. Annette never told her version of events. Though Berton wrote to Annette requesting an interview with her and her sisters, the three women preferred to protect their privacy as best they could and declined to meet him. As a result, Berton had to turn to some sources who had once been close to them but were no longer, such as Germain Allard and Florian Houle.

In a recent interview, Allard repeated the same explanation for the marriage breakup, but then acknowledged that he had not told the whole story, and that during their union he was rarely at home and often left Annette on her own. He said he knew when he gave her the ultimatum that his wife would never agree to sell their house and move away from her sisters. He now recognizes his own role in the marriage breakdown: "I was working all the time, day and night. I didn't realize what was going on. I do realize it's really, for a big part, it's my fault." Annette adds, "I realized he didn't accept my sisters. He was jealous of them. He always had to have control."

Allard had never discussed finances with Annette during all the years that she paid for furnishing and maintaining both houses. When they separated, the support money he offered her, and that she accepted, was $40 a week, which had to cover all the food, household bills, and clothing for three sons, aged fifteen, twelve, and eleven. He says now that he had no idea how poor Annette later became.

During their marriage, Annette felt that Allard resented that the house was in her name, even though she had paid the down payment and a share of the monthly mortgage payments. Once they separated, his contribution was so small that even young Eric began to wonder if they had enough money for food.

Though Allard had a large family, Annette never heard from or saw any of them again save for one brother, who picked up the kids each weekend to take them to the chalet, where their father would join them. Her former brother-in-law regularly parked outside and waited for her sons to come out, but never knocked on Annette's door or visited with her. Allard also did not contact Annette after he left. When his brother was dying, he asked his sons to tell Annette that if she wished to go to the hospital, she should go at a time when Allard would not be there.

Annette's closest friend is a former classmate named Hélène Gauthier. A handsome woman who became a professor of literature and ran a bookstore in northern Rimouski, she has lived in Montreal since 1995. Of the situation with Allard, Gauthier says, "Annette has never complained about her husband. Her schooling at Nicolet taught her that a good woman is a good housekeeper. She thought it was her duty.

"After her divorce, Gerry was taking advantage of the situation financially. Annette had looked after everything in the chalet. His colleagues from Beneficial Canada were always there. She was always cooking and cleaning. She was working so hard, and she's not very healthy. She was very elegant in this divorce, and with her three sons. She had the courage to take care of them alone."

Devotion to the three boys carried Annette through the hard times. She found that despite her difficulty expressing her inner feelings to Allard, she had no problem being affectionate as a mother. There was some irony in this, as Annette had never been able to mend her relationship with her own mother. In fact, she had no more contact with her parents after she and Allard split. Elzire Dionne died without Annette having the chance to say any final words to her. "I felt badly when Mom died, that we'd had no opportunity to straighten things out." But like her sisters, Annette insists, "She was always saying what went wrong was our fault. They had twisted minds very long ago."

It is a metaphor for Annette's determinedly sunny outlook in the face of all this anguish that after she separated, she took dancing lessons in the local community. She had tap-danced to everyone else's tunes all her life. Now she wanted the uplifting feel of dancing as a free individual. She also became a part-time aide at the Saint-Bruno library, where she had volunteered before the breakup, and was later paid two dollars an hour to start. She worked there for fifteen years. With her low wages and the $500 a month from her trust fund, she was able to just manage. She sold her wedding ring for cash when things got tougher.

She dated and had a warm, two-year romance with one man, though he lived too far away to see often. He would come for one-week visits to Saint-Bruno, then she would travel to his home in turn. But the obstacles of long-distance courtship, not to mention the costs, cooled her interest. "I have a good memory of him," she says today. "We still phone [each other] often."

157

Several times over the years the sisters sought legal advice about how to get at their trust money. But the Quebec lawyers they met said they couldn't help them, since the money was with a company based in Ontario, and the sisters didn't have the money to travel to Toronto and hire a lawyer there. Annette didn't have time to pursue the problem either. Her children needed her. They were dealing with the divorce, the change in their financial circumstances, and at times, the Dionne factor.

As the youngest son, Eric, tells it, "After the divorce, things changed. At thirteen, I had become the one to get the groceries. We had no car and I walked or biked a mile to the store. I became much more responsible for taking care of the backyard and the house. I remember one time during the summer, I cut the grass, trimmed the trees, worked all day around the house. At the end of the day I asked for two dollars and Annette said no. I realized she was really worried about money and I saw that there was very little."

His oldest brother, Jean-François, or Francis, as his mother calls him, often told Annette that one day he'd make a lot of money and help her. But those were the airy words of a dreamer, and eventually were put aside in favour of his love for skiing. He left school at eighteen, moved to Mont Ste-Anne, near Quebec City, and spent eleven years working on ski-hill maintenance and as part of the emergency team. In summer he lived off unemployment insurance. For a couple of years, he didn't work at all. In the late 1990s, however, his life took a different direction. After completing a course in how to operate forestry machinery, Francis began working in the logging industry. He now gets to visit his mother in Saint-Bruno only infrequently. A few years ago, however, when

Annette was booked into the hospital and had to stay up for hours before an early morning test for epilepsy, Francis offered to sit up with her and the two talked the sun awake.

Charles, the middle son, drew closer to his father after the split. He missed him so much that on one occasion, soon after Allard left, the boy stayed at school crying rather than come home. When he was in his teens and still a student, he moved into his father's apartment in Montreal, where Allard still worked. Father and son lived there together for ten years.

After graduating from university, Charles worked as a soil engineer in Africa and made enough money to live independently when he returned to Canada. At thirty-seven, he's an environmental consultant, lives with his common-law wife, and has a six-year-old son from a previous union. Annette missed Charles when he left to live with his father, and she is grateful they can still connect closely on occasion.

The third son, Eric, was aware early of the Dionne legacy. He remembers at age five being told by teachers that his mother was famous because her birth was so unique. One time, a nurse conducting a blood clinic at his school walked into his classroom in the middle of a lesson to tell him she knew his mother and aunts. The attention created an embarrassing scene for the boy.

When he was around ten years old, he was dismayed to learn from Annette that the birthday pictures he saw of the quintuplets at age two were staged. The photography shoot had been held weeks ahead of their real birthday in order to meet magazine and newsreel deadlines. Even the cake was fake. "I realized it was cheap for her to have everything done only for appearances. The people around her were cheating her," Eric says.

159

Although he didn't ask too many questions, fearing they would bother her, he often wondered how the sisters could have been so popular once and yet have become so poor. That thought hit home when, as a teenager, he saw the National Film Board/CBC documentary on the Dionnes, which showed soap, cereal, and syrup among the many, many products that used the five girls' endorsement. "Everyone made money off their backs," he says today.

Eric talked easily of the past in an interview at the modest Montreal duplex owned by his fiancée. They live in the same northeast middle-class area of the city where his parents had their first apartment. Relaxed even in the midst of renovating, he says his mother's story taught him that life is unpredictable and that he should take enjoyment when he can. He rejects the workaholism of his father, which left Annette raising her children alone during their marriage. He says, "She got cheated again."

Even as a boy, he understood that his father made a good salary and that the $40 a week he gave Annette didn't half pay for the groceries and other expenses. He told his father it wasn't enough. But when his brother Charles left home, even that support money was stopped. "It was shocking. He [Allard] left my mother without resources, and I knew the trust [would] run out shortly."

From the age of sixteen, Eric worked summer jobs to pay for his own clothes and entertainment. Though his father had paid for a private French school for a while, Eric had to seek government bursaries for a course in hotel and restaurant management and for his university studies. He was approved for them because of his mother's low income. With a degree in administration, he got jobs in accounting and worked for eleven years as a project manager, most recently for Bell Canada.

Luck has not been with him financially, though he was always a steady earner. With fifteen thousand other Quebecers, he invested in a research and development program that was deemed a tax shelter from 1988 to 1993. He raised the money to invest by borrowing from the bank. But in 1993, the federal and provincial governments ended that tax shelter retroactively; people who had been getting tax rebates had to pay them back.

Eric was on the spot for both the bank loan and the taxes. He turned to Annette, who permitted him to take out a $30,000 mortgage on her house, which he would pay off through his Bell salary. But in 1998, he was laid off. A few months later he started a one-year computer course to improve his job chances. Today, along with others who made the same ill-fated tax-shelter investment, he's part of a court action to get his money back.

By the 1990s, Annette's own funds had dwindled to a monthly pension of $320.52 from her years of working at the library and a Quebec pension that started at age sixty. Eric gave her $4000 for house repairs, a new front door, and dental bills. He felt it was all he could do on his $30,000 salary. Charles and Jean-François pitched in with him to fix the roof of the house where they grew up.

After Cécile was forced to give up her own Saint-Bruno apartment and moved in with Annette because of poor health and lack of money, Annette's financial situation also became desperate. Cécile couldn't help at all to support them, since she received a pittance of only $27.41 a month from the Quebec government and nothing from her years of working as a nurse in hospitals that had no pension plan. "Cécile had no place to go and it was making her sick. I put myself in her place and I just couldn't refuse her. She lost her home just a few blocks away." Annette's friend Hélène Gauthier says, "She's very generous to her sisters. Annette is always at the point of her family to help everyone. Besides all her troubles, she's very balanced, very stable."

When Yvonne asked to move in with them after her hip operations, her $399 pension brought their monthly stake to $746. The poverty and the new living arrangements changed Annette's lifestyle radically. She went out less, rarely saw her friends, put on unwanted pounds that added to her unhappiness. The only light moments for all of the women in those dark days seemed to come from the antics of their four cats — Annette had two, and Cécile and Yvonne each brought one of their own. The three women share a love of animals, a holdover from their teenage years in farm country, when animals freely roamed their property. In the nursery, however, Dr. Dafoe would allow no pets in case they carried germs to the precious, protected girls.

As the three sisters were adjusting to living together under strained circumstances, Annette was the first to learn that she had epilepsy. She was told that it was a form of petit mal, and that her seizures would follow a pattern: she would sense a strange odour, the same one every time, then black out. The episodes last at least three hours. One day in 1993, she had several. Petit mal epilepsy is also known as "absence seizures" because patients lose awareness, become unresponsive, and appear blank or spaced out.

The diagnosis frightened Annette at first. The quintuplets had seen epilepsy's overwhelming effects on their sister Émilie. How could Annette forget that this condition, though milder in her case, had ultimately caused Émilie's death? It took time for her to feel secure that daily medication would control her illness.

While she was trying to come to terms with all of this, Jean-Yves Soucy published *Family Secrets*. The Quebec press jumped on the book's explicit allegations of sexual abuse, and on the other siblings' denials that it had ever happened. The brouhaha lasted for weeks and got to Annette's nerves. But she and her sisters stuck to their story. "About that subject [abuse], we can't lie," she says pointedly.

At the same time, Cécile was in a heavy state of depression from all that had happened to her, past and present. Yvonne was weak and having trouble walking after her double hip operation. The entire household was beset with worries and growing despair.

By the time they began pleading their case for compensation before the public and press in 1998, the house itself was worn shabby, so drafty from insulation that had long since lost its usefulness that the three women wore heavy sweaters and scarves inside in winter. The floorboards were thin and splitting, the paint peeling, the living-room furniture sagging, the dining room cluttered with papers and books belonging to all three. Yvonne had to pay for all their food and medications, since none of the three women had insurance for prescriptions.

Despite this enervating atmosphere, it would be a mistake to think that Annette entered the battle for a settlement from the Ontario government any less determined than Cécile, who acted as the sisters' spokesperson. Though Annette's demeanour is quiet and her appearance is made delicate by a

163

taste for softly feminine clothing, she was firm in her conviction that the three had to go public. She had no doubt that there was ample evidence to prove that the quintuplets had been exploited by numerous government officials, who cleared a path for others to follow. She believed fully that she and her sisters were owed something in return. "The press conference was our only chance or hope. On $2000 a month [the pension that Premier Harris first offered] we couldn't live apart, we couldn't afford to live with security. I don't want to be avaricious, but for all the trouble we had, which was caused by the government, the amount wasn't fair."

9: YVONNE: YEARNING FOR PEACE

YVONNE DIONNE WATCHES intently out the window as the car follows the highway along the St. Lawrence River's north shore past stately Quebec City, and, nearby, spectacularly cascading Montmorency Falls. Farther north, past neat houses clustered in a tiny village, she admires the imposing, twin-spired basilica of Sainte-Anne-de-Beaupré, famous as the site of more than a million pilgrimages a year. At last, the road veers off into an alpine valley golden with fall foliage that wraps the town of Baie-Saint-Paul like a jewel. Yvonne's face lights up. She has come home.

The convent in this far-flung place was her spiritual home. The eighteen months she spent here as a postulant and novitiate in her quest to become a nun were central to her development as an adult. "It shaped me," she says simply during a visit in late 1998.

The nuns who remember her from their time together in the early 1960s greet her with warm laughter and hugs, which she shyly returns. For them, life has continued as before—the same duties and devotions practised daily by the Little Franciscans of

Mary. They live, pray, nurse, teach, help the elderly and the poor—all within their order's commitment to poverty, charity, simplicity, chastity, and obedience. For these women in their simple brown dresses, some with the traditional white veil covering their hair, it would be unthinkable to have to face the public exposure that the surviving Dionne quintuplets have endured. A childhood raised by strangers, the carnival of Quintland, the divided family, the revelations of abuse—all belong to a world the nuns left behind in favour of the quiet protection of convent life. Yvonne had longed for the same retreat from chaos, and she still holds this place dear.

Yvonne has no lack of talents and skills. She has been a nurse, an artist, a world traveller, a library worker, a major help to Annette and Cécile in raising their children. The first born of the quintuplets, she often played protector to them in their childhood and picked up the responsibility again when the three surviving sisters were older. When she was at her strongest, she could fix car motors, cut trees, cross-country and downhill ski, cycle, play sports. But the scope of her past interests and activities is surprising when one considers the quiet, frail Yvonne of today. Surgery in 1993 to replace both deteriorated hips has left her with a halting walk and arthritic pain. She has been so strictly warned not to gain weight (which could weaken her bones) that she has become notice-ably thin, even for her small frame. She's a woman of contrasts, however, who still chooses sporty clothes that would look suitable at the golf club.

Although the hurts of the past have made her wary and often sombre of expression, she can be the most playful of her sisters. She sat at a recent dinner in a Montreal restaurant eating sparsely and rolling the wine bottle's cork across the table to another guest as a child would do, laughing at the distraction from serious talk.

But serious is the only way to describe her childhood. She was portrayed in early stories about the quintuplets as the leader among the five young girls, almost as a mother to them. Whenever they had problems, the other four came to her. Scientists who studied the quintuplets reported dryly that Yvonne was "sought after by the other children, perhaps because she is willing to respond and thus prolongs the social contact." And she was outgoing. Once, when the sisters were caught in the rain in the playground at Quintland, Yvonne waved her hand at the people she knew were in the viewing gallery and called in French, "Do go home, ladies and gentlemen! Don't you see it's raining?"

At age five, the three surviving sisters recount, it was Yvonne who boldly took hold of King George VI's hand when the girls were presented to the king and queen. Annette still describes her as coquettish with men, and both she and Cécile say that Yvonne was their father's favourite, and that his preference annoyed their mother. Yvonne believes his favouritism was based in the belief, reported by the scientists, that she was the most intelligent of the quintuplets, and that he compared her favourably with himself. "He was always telling us how intelligent he was," she recalls with a shake of her head to disagree. Yvonne, however, had no such pride in her own abilities. "During the time we were at school in Villa Notre Dame, our studies were very hard for us because there was too much tension at home. That made it difficult for me to believe that I was intelligent." The tension started when the family moved into the Big House together, she adds. "We didn't know the family. We were scared to say anything because we weren't sure of their reaction."

There is an incident detailed in *Family Secrets* in which the teenaged Yvonne witnessed Elzire repeatedly slapping Marie and Émilie, who were cowering in fear. Yvonne yelled at her mother to stop, and in response Elzire knocked her unconscious with a blow to her head. That unrestrained whack left a permanent mark on the girl's mind. According to Nurse Leroux, there had been a period when, as a child, Yvonne had been drawn to her mother, running to her rather than to her father whenever the couple visited the nursery. This brutal incident, however, taught her that there was little maternal warmth in return. In fact, Elzire accused her of falling to the ground on purpose. "She hated me," Yvonne says now. "I think sometimes she didn't realize what she was doing. She had to take it out on somebody. Dad seemed to have a preference for me. After me, it was Cécile."

Like Annette and Cécile, Yvonne alleged in *Family Secrets* that their father sexually abused them. The worst incident occurred when she was fifteen and Dionne drove her alone to the family's summer cottage on the shore of Lake Nipissing. He told her that he had heard from her mother that she was sneaking into her brothers' rooms at night, the implication being that she had had sex with them. He then ordered her to go inside the cottage and lie down on a bed, where he would eventually join her. If she could do it with her brothers, she could do it with him, he said. Yvonne refused. She hurled back the statement that her mother had lied, then fled from the car and ran down to the lake, where she stood rooted with despair at the enormity of both parents' betrayal. Eventually Dionne turned the car around, honked for her to get in, and drove her back home in brooding silence. At all other times, she says, she was able to avoid her father's advances. "I always saw when something was coming."

In this, as in all other matters, Yvonne's first instinct was to protect her sisters. In June 1947, the entire Dionne family was invited to participate in the celebrations marking the hundredth anniversary of the founding of the Catholic diocese of Ottawa. Annette recalls that it was Yvonne who had the courage to speak to a high-placed nun about two of their brothers, who were trying to sexually assault them, pinning them down on the floor, fondling them, and trying to remove their panties. Not long after that, the Sisters of Assumption of the Sainted Virgin convinced Oliva Dionne to allow them to run a school for the quintuplets. Although it is not certain that this plan came about as a result of Yvonne's plea for help, the quintuplets have always believed that it was her intervention that led to the creation of a convent school that would separate the girls from their brothers. (Yvonne dislikes taking credit for speaking out, though the story of abuse by the brothers has been told publicly by the surviving quintuplets.)

Over the years, unfortunately, Yvonne's independent streak was repressed by fear. And often it was Elzire who was the embodiment of that fear. Once, she snatched away the quintuplets' cherished Shirley Temple dolls, suddenly and arbitrarily, an incident that shattered the young Yvonne because of its callousness. The dolls had been given to the sisters when they were five, and were fascinating to Yvonne.

She couldn't believe that the dolls had been reproduced identically, just as she and her sisters were exactly alike, but that unlike the sets of five quint dolls, each Shirley Temple doll reproduced only one individual. Years later, their mother's harsh gesture would appear even crueller when the quintuplets learned through books and documentaries that Elzire had had a collection of dolls so beloved that she wouldn't give them up even when she married. In Yvonne's own words, "We were apprehensive about leaving the nursery for the Big House [in the first place]. The proximity [of everyone living together] was painful. Clearly we were too much for them and we were not on the same wavelength. On our arrival, our beautiful Shirley Temple dolls vanished as if by magic, as well as other gifts we received from strangers … a rosary, a medallion, jewellery, a necklace…. No one ever said a word. We were docile and wounded by fear."

Events in the house felt like a mockery of the fairy tale Yvonne had played out as a four-year-old in the nursery. Sadly, in the Big House, there was no fairy godmother to rescue her or her sisters. Yvonne said recently, speaking of her parents, "We were living in a situation where we were caught in a vicious circle. We were apart from them, something was wrong. They didn't love us." Still, she went home to Corbeil several times as an adult, to try to keep a sense of family. But her attempts failed. "I tried to go home and make peace, to maintain a link. But it was useless to try, a waste of time. They were always so cold," she says. "The family was always saying that it was our fault about what went wrong. It's strange that our siblings are so angry with us, because they had so many advantages growing up with our money. When we were living

170

in the Big House, the older ones were often away from home, except for Claude. They were going to good schools."

Claire Morin, a friend from Yvonne's nursing school days, accompanied her once on the sixteen-hour drive to Corbeil from Baie-Saint-Paul, and she recalls that Yvonne was nervous throughout the visit. The Dionnes were polite to Morin, but she says that they spoke to Yvonne mostly in English so that Morin would understand little of their conversation. Though some of the siblings lived in the area, none came around to see Yvonne, she recalls.

Along with her sisters, Yvonne left home at eighteen for college at Nicolet; her stay there did not last long, though she loved the convent and its school. "They saved us. They were so good to us," Yvonne says of the nuns. When the five shy teenagers arrived, Yvonne was the most popular, the most sought after by other students. And it was at Nicolet that she discovered her interest in art. Though Oliva Dionne had restricted his daughters to a course in home economics, Yvonne was able to join a drawing class when her other studies were done. It was this class that awakened her interest, and as a result, Yvonne decided that after she completed her first year, she would go elsewhere and study art. "I needed a change. I asked to leave," she said.

She turned out to be the quintuplet with the tenacity to make it on her own, away from their tightly bonded unit. She moved to Montreal to attend the Collège Marguerite-Bourgeois and focus on her art studies. After years of being surrounded by four others exactly like her, going it alone was "scary. It was a big shock, but I had to do it." She wrote to her

171

sisters often, travelling to Nicolet to see them and looking forward to visits from them in return.

But there had been too little encouragement in her life for Yvonne to have confidence in her art as anything other than a hobby. When it came time to choose a profession, she decided, like Cécile, to become a nurse. For Yvonne, as for the others, Émilie's death had been a shock. And though she threw herself into her training at Montreal's Hôpital Notre Dame de l'Espérance, she was tormented by the thought that she might have been able to save Émilie, as well as by the disturbing events of her younger years. It was during this period, Yvonne says, that she learned about parts of her background that made her feel that the quintuplets' history was "a veritable puzzle, because all the most important pieces were missing." As an example, she says, "It was only during my nursing course in 1954 that I found out that Dad had taken steps to sell us to the Chicago Circus [the World's Fair]. It was a patient who was reading *Paris Match* while I was preparing her medication [who told me]." For a young woman of twenty—a woman who, along with her sisters, had been kept in the dark about much of her unusual upbringing—this new information was stunning and hurtful.

Nevertheless, Yvonne was determined to try to overcome her past. Although the three years of nurses' training were hard, and included stages of intense study in pediatrics, obstetrics, and psychiatry, it was also a heady period of young womanhood and the independence that came at age twenty-one. Time away from the hospital was made more fun by the added presence of her sisters' beaus, Cécile's Philippe Langlois and Annette's Germain Allard. Yvonne was often invited to go along with the couples to movies and for walks. Later, Marie, who had left her convent, took an apartment with Annette, so for a time all four sisters were together in Montreal. It was a treat for them to go out without the constant supervision they had always known. Little things like shopping in stores for clothes and giggling at the cosmetics counter were new, delightful experiences, though the young women often donned sunglasses to avoid being recognized and pestered.

Yvonne remembers how different it was for them to be in vibrant Montreal, which was the world's second-largest French city, and to live among Quebecers. Compared with the minority Franco-Ontarians, who tended to be conservative and somewhat embittered, the Quebec francophones, who were the majority population in that province, were far more expressive and joyful. Yvonne acknowledges that it took her and her sisters some time to get used to their more outgoing manner.

This was a happy time in Yvonne's life. She was devoted to her patients, especially those who were children. The year after she graduated, she worked at a summer camp near Montreal for children with disabilities, the same camp where Annette had worked as an aide in the summers. During the rest of the year, she took private nursing jobs in people's homes, starting with the dying father of a friend. She felt glad that her profession gave her the opportunity to be truly helpful to others, though the work itself was demanding. But something else was tugging at Yvonne, suggesting that her future lay elsewhere.

For a while, she returned to her art in a serious manner. She moved for a number of months to Saint-Jean-Port-Joli, an artists' haven on the south shore of the St. Lawrence River some three hundred kilometres from Montreal. There, she was brought into the circle of a master sculptor, Jean-Julien Bourgault, and his family of artists, who were famous for their church statuary; Yvonne was taught by Bourgault's son, Gil. The work seemed to combine the creative and spiritual forces that were both pulling at Yvonne. Her former teacher remembers her as being "anxious to learn. She had some aptitude but studied only for some months.... [She was] so quiet, and very bashful, having no confidence in herself." Looking back, Yvonne says unequivocally, "I don't think I was ever good enough as a sculptor to become professional. My desire to be a nun became much stronger."

Perhaps she had been inspired by the kindness of some of the nuns and clergy whom she'd known during the difficult years in the Big House. Sister Ruth, for example, who taught music at the Villa Notre Dame, had been "like an angel to me," Yvonne said, and was someone so trustworthy that Émilie had felt free to confide in her. Father Gustave Sauvé, who visited the house on occasion, often brought movie reels for the children to watch. "He was always kind," she says, and never said a critical word about their parents, though Oliva was suspicious of him because the girls liked him.

At twenty-five, Yvonne decided that she would become a nun. She could still bring her nursing skills to bear to help the sick, but first she would complete six months as a postulant and two years as a novitiate, and then finally take her vows. A few years after that, the Mother Superior would decide what her long-term role as a nun would be. Yvonne could only hope and pray that she would be permitted one day to combine her two dedications.

She chose a convent in the charmed setting of Baie-Saint-Paul, a secluded town that is 650 kilometres north of Montreal but whose beauty has drawn artists and craftspeople for decades. It nestles in an ancient land formation and historic region known as the Charlevoix, which stretches from east of Quebec City to the Saguenay River fjord, where white beluga whales abound. In a book on the hundred-year history of the convent's congregation in Baie-Saint-Paul, the area is aptly described: "Framed by the Laurentian Mountains that open an immense window on the Saint Lawrence, the village looks up at the hills and out to the sea." Yvonne's artist's sensibility was stimulated by the striking landscape and the welcoming atmosphere she found there.

Yvonne first went to Baie-Saint-Paul to visit her friend Claire Morin, who had joined the convent. Morin was the centre of a group of friends that included other nurses who were going to enter the same convent.

One would think that the daily routine of a convent would be too rigid for a young woman so recently liberated from a life heavily controlled by others. The schedule never varies: wake at 5:00 a.m., meditation in the chapel from 5:30 to 6:00 a.m., prayers, breakfast at 7:30 a.m. The work, for postulants and novitiates alike, includes cleaning and cooking for what's called the Mother House. In Baie-Saint-Paul, this is a large three-storey brick house with wood floors and banisters that require frequent polishing. In Yvonne's time there in the early 1960s, there were more than five hundred nuns living and taking their meals in the building, which meant a lot of food preparation and housework.

Training to be a nun, however, was a labour of love for Yvonne. She took easily to the simple dormitory life—after all, she had grown up in a roomful of five girls. She slept in a large, sparsely furnished room with some twenty others; each kept her clothing in a locker, and personal items like clocks or radios were banned. Yvonne accepted it all. She appreciated the long periods of Grand Silence for reflection, and the opportunity to be alone within herself while still among friends. The required meditation period each morning before Mass, when all the nuns gathered in the chapel and entered into silent contemplation, left a lasting influence, and she has meditated ever since.

Yvonne had been one of eleven novitiates; eight of them are still nuns today. As the importance of religion to people's lives has lessened, the convent population has dwindled to 150. Most of the remaining nuns are in their senior years. Convent life is no longer the draw to young women it once was, and there have been no new entrants in more than seven years.

Yet the beautiful Chapel of the Sacred Heart, which is open to the community, is carefully maintained. It is the awe-inspiring, architecturally lavish structure—with its cupolas, gold candles, gilt-edged sculpture, and elaborately carved columns—that evokes the most pride in Yvonne for having been part of this sacred place. During her visit, the nuns switched on all 1254 tiny lights in the chapel's vaulted ceiling and arches, something that is done so rarely that Yvonne was delighted and very moved.

The convent library houses photos, artifacts, and documents

related to its history. The founders were four nuns of the Little Franciscans of Mary based in Worcester, Massachusetts, who in 1898 were asked by the priest in this remote Quebec mission to come and tend to the elderly. On display there is a photograph, taken on November 9, 1961, of those four women being reburied in a special ceremony on the birthday of Saint Francis of Assisi. Yvonne is in that photo, wearing her novice veil, a tiny figure who is otherwise no different from the other nuns in the chapel.

It came as a great surprise, then, when she was denied the opportunity to take her vows. But she was given no reason why. In those days, the Mother Superior decided, and if the decision was no, there was no recourse available. Yvonne was simply told she was not suited to the life she loved; a few other women were told the same thing. "They just tell you it's not your place," she says matter-of-factly. "What could I do? I didn't understand it, but there was nothing I could do about it. I was hurt. I thought I had the vocation, the calling. I thought I'd be happy there. I would have liked to stay, but that's life. I didn't want to become sick over it." All this is said with a characteristic shrug that indicates there's nothing more to be discussed.

Unlike Cécile and Annette, Yvonne never took to therapy courses or individual counselling. She's not an overly reflective woman, and meditation and work have long been her way of dealing with her feelings. She carries her internal struggle in her guarded gaze, her careful thoughts. Still, both of her remaining sisters have said of Yvonne that although she talks the least, she is the most profound. Her former brother-in-law Germain Allard concurs. He says simply, "Yvonne is mysterious, but she is very smart."

177

And determined. When her time at Baie-Saint-Paul was over, she decided to try to become a nun at the Convent of the Sacred Heart in the port city of Moncton, New Brunswick, 1125 kilometres away from Montreal. The distance made it impossible for her to see her sisters, save one occasion during the writing of *We Were Five*, when Annette, Cécile, and Marie visited her along with Yousuf Karsh, who took photographs for the book.

Yvonne spent five years in Moncton, so dedicated to her chosen vocation that she never left the convent grounds in all that time. She followed a regime similar to that at Baie-Saint-Paul, one of prayer and the housekeeping duties of first a postulant, then a novice. She waited patiently for the time when she would be permitted to use her nursing skills at the new hospital that was to be built nearby, but after being stalled for more than two years, she was finally told, once again, that she would not be allowed to take her vows.

In today's assertive age, it's hard to comprehend that such pronouncements were accepted without question, that, in spite of all her efforts, Yvonne was given almost no explanation and did not insist on one. The student revolutions of the 1960s had not spread from mainstream liberal universities to young women in remote, strict convents. All Yvonne was told was that she had "high ideals"—faint praise, since her ideals seemed to be interfering with her goals.

Yvonne, like a woman rejected in love, felt the losses keenly, though she had learned much from the convent experience. She would meditate for the rest of her life, be firmly guided by self-discipline, and take comfort in periods of silence during occasional visits to convents for reflective retreats. "I worked a lot on myself, watching myself and trying not to hurt anyone. I was happier living that way. Work helped me a lot, and faith."

These might seem superficial responses to the trauma of being turned away from what she felt was her life's calling. But the reality goes deeper. Yvonne kept her dream alive within herself through a daily connection with spiritual thought. When she meditates, she reflects on the larger aspects of religion and life. When possible, she walks during these reflective periods, alone in her thoughts. Other times, she simply sits in a quiet spot at a moment in the day when she feels fresh and not tired. "You go inside yourself, you take a vast subject and you meditate on it. It's very spiritual. Then you try to empty your mind to nothing. It doesn't take too long, but it helps me." But with her characteristic humility, she adds, "I'm not a saint. It's easier now to meditate than it was when I was in the convent where you have to be all together in the chapel. Today, you can meditate everywhere." She says she still feels strongly religious, but not in the same way as she did in her younger years, when she followed every church dictate. "I take what I need and I let the rest go by. Just like someone needs food to go on, I need the spirituality to go through all the things I face, to live."

Yvonne was in her early thirties when she realized, after nearly a decade of religious seclusion, that she had to get on with her more worldly life. To the amazement of her sisters, she took off on a six-week international tour.

A friend she knew from her nursing days, Jeanne-Aimée Richard, had been living in Bombay. She was working for the

Peace Corps, teaching student nurses. Yvonne, who describes Richard as "a strong woman who made me believe in myself," joined her there. They spent some time in Bombay among Richard's friends, then the two women set off travelling, staying in inexpensive hostels and spending their days sight-seeing—Madras, Calcutta, Delhi, Jerusalem, Bethlehem, Rome, Venice, Florence, Frankfurt, Brussels, Paris, and London. Yvonne lists the cities with a smile of accomplishment just for having been there. It was the trip of a lifetime for anyone, but for someone who had been enclosed behind fences and locked gates, and in isolated retreats for so many years, the foreign stamps in her passport were symbols of freedom. A photograph of Yvonne in an airport at the time shows her with a short, urchin haircut and cat-eyed sunglasses, in the impish style of movie star Audrey Hepburn, who was popular at the time.

On her return, Yvonne savoured the exhilaration of choice. French Montreal, which prided itself on having a finer sensibility than the hard-headed English business interests, offered a feast of artistic and intellectual pursuits. After years of living simply in convents, she had enough money saved from her $500-a-month trust fund interest to pay for the education she had always wanted. She took courses at the University of Montreal in art history, music history, and literature.

The cosmopolitan city was then in its prime, having just hosted the wildly successful World's Fair, Expo 67. Indeed, at the time Montreal was the cultural and entertainment centre of Canada, and it was lauded for its stimulating, colourful nightlife and a *joie de vivre* that left Toronto dour by comparison. As William Weintraub wrote in *City Unique*, Montreal had already drawn international attention in the 1950s through its writers and poets, including Mavis Gallant, Mordecai Richler, Brian Moore, Irving Layton, and Leonard Cohen. Toronto novelist Morley Callaghan had described Montreal in 1958 as "the continent's most flavourful city." And it was close to scenic mountain getaways, fresh lakes, and picturesque towns that lured recreation-seekers as well as the artistic-minded.

But the year of Expo also signalled political trouble, as a separatist group established its own Parti Québécois. In July 1967, France's president, Charles de Gaulle, who was visiting the fair, shouted from the balcony of Montreal's City Hall the separatist slogan, *"Vive le Québec libre,"* an exhortation for the province to secede from Canada. Political instability and mounting separatist sentiment took their toll, and Montreal's reign as one of the world's great cities lasted only until the mid-1970s. After René Lévesque was elected as the first separatist premier in 1976, the city declined in an atmosphere of political uncertainty; its lifeblood was drained by the flight from the province of anglophone head offices and 200,000 anglophone residents, mostly to Toronto.

Yvonne had enjoyed her life in Montreal during its heyday. But in truth, she did not fully partake of the city's vitality. She says with frank self-appraisal, "I was living more quiet, and reserved. My courses were at night so I couldn't go out much; I had a few friends, and my sisters." Always in her mind was her interest in her sisters. If Cécile needed her, she would travel to Quebec City and take her some money. Cécile recalls, "Yvonne was my parent for me. She was always there, bringing gifts; she bought things for the children." Yvonne would also drive to suburban Saint-Bruno to help Annette look after her three sons when they came home from school, and she even took over their care when they were sick. She kept in touch with, and occasionally visited, Marie, who by the mid-1960s was a single mother. Remembering the shock of Marie's sudden death can still make Yvonne go silent with sorrow nearly thirty years later. She regrets that she was not always around while Marie was on her own, and that she wasn't in frequent contact with her during the time preceding her death.

In the end, Yvonne's practical side took hold. She was working in the early 1970s at a day care in the town of Beloeil, not far from Montreal, and studying ceramics there. She had shown such considerable talent that some friends hoped she would make her artistry a serious, lifetime pursuit. But by 1973, Cécile had moved closer to Annette, and both women were raising children on their own and struggling financially. Yvonne saw that her future was in Saint-Bruno, where she could help them. From her savings, she bought a small one-bedroom house with a backyard she could tend. According to one friend, the house was decorated by Yvonne "with a few well-chosen pieces of furniture, and ceramic and craft pieces. She has very good taste." She soon secured a job at the library where Annette was already working; Yvonne would work there for the next twenty years and four months. Looking back on that period, Yvonne says, "It happened so quick when I started there at the library, when I heard they needed more people. I worked full time for no money for two years because I wanted the job. I loved it, though I had no time to read myself.

Sometimes I worked nights, and I'd be so tired after work that I went straight to bed."

There has been no special man in her life, no failed romance. While she enjoyed a social life with colleagues from time to time, Yvonne was not given to constant companionship and often preferred to be on her own. "I think I am too selective," she offers. "I was used to working with men, laughing and joking with them in a group. I went to the movies often with men, but always in a group. And I like to dance. So many things have happened in my life that I have no time to think about why I'm not married."

Remaining unmarried has traditionally been common for some women in large French-Canadian families. Some were former nuns or, like Yvonne, were drawn to that vocation but for various reasons left the convent. Yvonne's sister Pauline, just a year older than the quintuplets, also never married. People close to her are convinced that Yvonne was too independent-minded for marriage, that she feared the controlling nature she had seen in her father and was discouraged by the outcomes of her sisters' unions.

But these things, like the events of her bizarre childhood, are in the past, and Yvonne no longer dwells on that past, saying emphatically, "That's quite over." At age fifty, when Yvonne was contacted by the *Toronto Star* for a brief interview, she spoke beseechingly: "We just want to be happy. Most of all, we value our privacy.... It's still hard to make a normal life. We try not to discuss any more the way we grew up, even with each other." Though she went to see Elzire in the hospital before she died, Yvonne expected no final resolution of their differences. Unlike her sisters, who regretted not having some last, forgiving words with their mother, Yvonne says, "I would have liked that she asked for us. But she didn't. I saw the reality and I accepted it."

The circumstances of Yvonne's life have turned her into a private, reclusive person. Today, apart from her sisters, she does not see many people. "Real friends are very rare. I have some that live far away, like my teachers. Some are from the convent, and some are schoolmates." One close friend is Patricia Minn, a ceramic artist who now lives in California and is the cousin of the woman who travelled with Yvonne in the 1960s. Minn says, "Yvonne confided in me about her family life twenty years ago. It was the same information as they wrote about. They have a hard time [learning] to trust other people. I know how separated she was from normal life. There was no occasion to meet any men when they were young, and they were too timid about the unknown. She had no therapy about her father. Yvonne didn't learn to deal with her emotions. She doesn't express herself. It is hard for them to believe that someone could love them."

Minn says it hasn't been easy to keep up her friendship with Yvonne through correspondence alone. Typically, Yvonne, who is so careful in choosing her words, writes little about herself or what she's doing—often just a line at the end of a standard message included in a greeting card. Yet although Yvonne is guarded and has never had many friends, says Minn, "She's faithful to the few she had."

Since she never married and didn't spend much money during her twenties, Yvonne was the one surviving quintuplet who had no financial troubles. Yet she, too, was made insecure by the restrictive arrangement with Guaranty Trust, and by the sense that she had no control over her own finances. "Very often I asked for money from the trust. I wanted to invest it myself to be more secure. They never wanted to give it to me." Once she asked for $10,000 to invest on her own. She had been working steadily for years by then, and thought the firm's officials would see that she was responsible. Instead they asked her to prove why she needed the money and then refused her request.

She believes that the contract with the trust firm was made deliberately restrictive because her father and his advisers assumed that the quintuplets would not live long. If they died, the money would go to their parents and siblings, as had been the case with Émilie. She spoke to several Quebec lawyers about the contract over the years, but "they always said the damage was already done."

On a recent visit to the Saint-Bruno public library, with its soft green décor and friendly atmosphere, Yvonne was a popular guest. Former workmates greeted her warmly, just as the nuns had done at Baie-Saint-Paul. Tucked in an administrative office, away from the general public, was the desk where she had worked so diligently, preparing books for rebinding, cataloguing them, doing work that would be far too solitary for many but suited her perfectly.

During Yvonne's long period working and living in the mixed French and English town, Quebec was experiencing a political atmosphere fraught with passion and controversy. Premier Lévesque and his government were determined to separate the province from the rest of Canada in order to preserve its French language and culture and finally bring to fruition the 1962 election promise of former Liberal premier Jean Lesage, who vowed that Quebecers would become *"maîtres chez nous,"* or "masters in our own house." Some likened the divisive fight between the federalist No forces and the sovereignist Yes group to the American Civil War. In a referendum on May 20, 1980, the No supporters won with sixty percent of the vote; but that still meant some 1.5 million Quebecers were dissatisfied with the current federal–provincial arrangements. Even after he lost the referendum, Lévesque signalled that the dream of an independent Quebec was not dead.

Yvonne listened to the heated discussions that took place among the library staff, though she didn't say much herself. "I tried to learn more about it," she explains. "At home, they never talked about politics, except when it was time to vote. Then, Dad always voted Liberal. I often wondered why it was always the same [choice], but I didn't dare ask. The only thing I thought about the referendum was to stay together, and it would make it all [Quebec and Canada] stronger." Like her sisters, she always voted but never got involved in politics. The women had come to realize that most of their troubles from birth onward had started as a result of political opportunism in Ontario, and this realization made them wary of the political arena. They concentrated, instead, on getting on with their lives; in Yvonne's case, she immersed herself in her library job, and would have worked there longer had her hip problems and subsequent surgeries not weakened her to the point that she could barely walk.

The first operation was performed on November 11, 1993, the second on November 22. She was in hospital for several weeks, then went directly to Annette's home. Though she had lived independently for years, she no longer had the confidence to be alone even after she recovered. More pressingly, her modest income was needed to maintain the sisters financially. She didn't hesitate to spend her money to help them. "I had no choice," she says.

During the five years they faced poverty, Yvonne paid for all of the groceries and medications for herself and her sisters. Her $399 monthly pension from the library was the most money they had coming in, her $5000 in savings the only emergency fund should further disaster strike. Meanwhile, the deterioration in her health clearly hit Yvonne hard. She learned as well in 1995 that, like two of her sisters, she has epilepsy, though her case is the mildest.

Quebec's second referendum vote took place on October 30 of that year, under Premier Jacques Parizeau. This time, the fiery oratory of Lucien Bouchard, a popular federal politician and passionate sovereignist who would be elected Quebec's premier the following January, spurred the Yes forces forward. The vote ended with the No side winning by a little more than one percentage point. Again the sisters voted, and again Yvonne believed the country should remain undivided (the sisters never tell each other how they vote, in any election or referendum). But the charged political atmosphere was secondary to the more urgent situation the sisters faced at home as they struggled to get by financially. And they had already launched their own political battle with the Ontario government.

10: CÉCILE: BACK
FROM BETRAYAL

BUOYED BY NEW CONFIDENCE and certain that she was embarking on a new life, Cécile Dionne had fashioned her wedding as part of the quintuplet fairy tale. After all, she had made it through her rigorous hospital training in Montreal to become a nurse—the first independent choice she had been allowed to make after leaving Nicolet and turning twenty-one. Now she was marrying a man who had sought her out and courted her. He was the first man she had ever dated, and a man with whom she soon fell in love. She would wear a gown fit for a storybook princess, one made from twelve metres of silk and ten metres of Swiss lace and embroidered with seed pearls that required forty hours of hand-stitching. Slim, petite, and barely five feet tall, she looked as delicate as the bridal doll on a wedding cake. Her hair, swept up from her forehead and softly curled, was caught by a lace headband that held a shoulder-length veil. After the ceremony, with her lifted veil a frothy confection framing her face, her eyes shone so brightly and her smile was so radiant that anyone would have been able to see it was the happiest day of her life.

But she had paid for it, in spirit and in fact. This time, Cécile had promised herself, I'll get it right for Mom and Dad and me. She had allowed the press to be there, of course, and even invited all the out-of-town relatives her parents wished to be present, bearing the entire cost from her trust fund. She remembers, "In my silly head I thought that all would be fixed, that it would arrange communication between them and ourselves [the quintuplets]."

She had brought the whole family together, after years of being told it was the quintuplets' fault that its members had been wrenched apart. The white gown, the ceremony in Sacred Heart Church in Corbeil, the reception at a restaurant in North Bay—it all added up to $10,000, a small fortune that would be equal to over $60,000 today. But Cécile felt it was worth it—if only it signalled a fresh start, a happy life with her husband, peace in the family.

On November 23, 1957, just six weeks after her sister Annette's quiet wedding in Montreal, Cécile married Philippe Langlois, a technician with Radio-Canada, the French voice of the Canadian Broadcasting Corporation. Cécile was twenty-three, Langlois twenty-six.

He was working in Montreal when a story about four of the sisters having moved to that city appeared in a local newspaper. The article said that Cécile and Yvonne lived in the nurses' quarters at the Hôpital Notre Dame de l'Espérance, where they were in training. Langlois called and left his number for Cécile. When she called back, he asked for a date. The dapper young man opened up a whole new world for Cécile just by taking her to movies and concerts in the handsome island city. Very soon, Langlois won her heart. He laughed at her wry humour, was relaxed with her sisters, and quit his own job to help her sister Marie set up her flower shop business. Cécile felt lucky to have found such a man — and to have found love.

But she was so eager and innocently romantic that she missed the signs of danger. She was in love during the fifties, and though the sexual revolution and the women's movement were stirring in more worldly circles, these ideas were virtually unknown to her. She had been raised in a glass bubble, taught by strict nuns and barred from contact with boys by her parents. Like her four sisters, Cécile had known the warmth of a young man's hand in hers only once, when the teenage girls had been taken by their father on a publicity trip to a winter carnival in St. Paul, Minnesota, and were each assigned an escort for the festivities.

The first time she suspected that Langlois was a heavy drinker was the night before their wedding. They were staying in separate rooms in the Big House. "He drank a lot," she remembers, "and I could hear him getting up to be sick in the bathroom many times in the night." After their wedding, they found their motel staked out by photographers and fled to another. They didn't make love that night, but Cécile thought her husband was being considerate of her and waiting for a more relaxed time.

The next day, the couple flew to New York. There they were treated to dinner by the Manhattan-based photographer Arthur Sasse, who was well known to the quintuplets from the years when Oliva Dionne contracted him to come to Corbeil to record their lives. During the meal, Langlois kept knocking back more and more drinks. That was the first night he made love to Cécile, and as she said succinctly forty years later, "The sexual side of the marriage was not warm." Langlois was a disinterested lover, intent only on satisfying his needs. For her part, Cécile had been raised to be modest and passive, and was too shy to ask for the hugs and intimacy she wanted from her husband. "I had no experience and was never very demanding, so I was not demanding in that area either."

Initially, the couple rented a house just outside Montreal, but Cécile was persuaded by Langlois in 1959 to buy a house in suburban Dorval, near the airport. This was an idea that suited her because she had stopped working in the hopes of starting a family. Yet as had been the case with their splashy wedding, he paid for nothing himself. Though he earned a good salary at his job at Radio-Canada, he left all major, and most minor, purchases to Cécile.

Cécile soon realized that she had a problem—a husband who rarely came home till late at night, who was often drunk when he did come home, and who shared little if any of his earnings. "Sometimes he gave me a few dollars, sometimes nothing. Almost every Thursday, when he was paid his salary, the money would be gone by the time he came home. I was very discouraged in my marriage. He was never there, he was always lying to me. And I was having children with him during that time."

Meanwhile, Cécile's own money, like her sisters', was being carefully parcelled out at $500 a month by Guaranty Trust, according to the rigid schedule set up by her father. The firm's officials were rarely moved by her requests to dip into the fund because of special needs. "I was feeling so guilty every time I was asking for money. They made me feel that it was not my own money." As a result, she couldn't keep up the house payments and the family was forced to move.

A bigger problem became evident soon after the wedding. One night, six months into her first year of marriage, Cécile went to bed early. She was pregnant with their first child, Claude. Langlois had left for the Dorval airport to pick up her brother Victor and a friend, who had been visiting New York. They had left their car at Cécile's house before flying to the U.S.

She awoke in the middle of the night and found that her husband was not beside her. When she went downstairs to find him, she looked in the guest room. There she saw Langlois in one of the twin beds, lying in the arms of another man. Shocked, she grabbed at her husband to wrench the two men apart, and found herself staring into the other man's face. It was Victor.

Cécile felt profoundly betrayed. Victor had accompanied Langlois and a third man on a trip to New York one month before her wedding. The three had appeared on the popular television quiz show *To Tell the Truth* at the invitation of the producers, who thought they looked alike; the show's panel had tried to guess which man was about to marry one of the Dionne quintuplets. Because of this trip, Cécile wondered if Victor had already learned that Langlois was gay and not told her before the wedding. But in typical Dionne fashion, coming as she did from a family where feelings were repressed and secrets kept hidden, Cécile never spoke to her brother or Langlois about it, then or later, though she did confide the incident to her sisters soon afterwards. She left Victor downstairs and insisted that her husband return to their room with her. As she explains it now, "When I saw them it was too late to do anything. In my head I decided to get separated. I wanted to leave him [Langlois] then, but I went to the church for advice. The priest asked me if we

193

were still having sexual relations. I said we were. He told me to stay married. I was carrying Claude at the time."

As strange as it may seem today, neither the priest's advice nor Cécile's placid acceptance of it was unusual for the times. The Catholic church in Quebec held sway in almost all matters, including those of the bedroom. For Cécile, who had been schooled by nuns and who held that particular priest in high regard, it was natural to believe he knew best.

She had to find some way to cope with what she'd discovered. As part of her nurse's training, Cécile had attended a seminar on homosexuality and, despite her limited experience, felt she had some understanding and acceptance of what it meant. If Langlois did not reject her personally, she thought, if he would only be honest with her, perhaps they could work it out. She still loved him and they had a child coming. Maybe if they moved to Quebec City, where Langlois's family lived, things would be better. He'd live up to his financial responsibilities there, and together they could build a family of their own.

Hoping for a fresh start, they moved to that city, the provincial capital, towards the end of 1959 and rented a duplex. After Claude, Patrice was born in 1960. When the couple learned that Cécile was pregnant with twins, they rented, and Cécile later bought, a spacious house in Sillery, the city's fine residential area. Their sons Bertrand and Bruno were born in 1961, but Bruno died at fifteen months from kidney cancer. A daughter, Elizabeth, was born in 1962.

Unfortunately, all the while they were having more children, things got worse. In Quebec City, Langlois' drinking and nights out increased. Though he had played with Claude as a youngster and sometimes took him out with him at night, he showed little interest in the other children, who barely got to know their father.

"He left me alone during the nights most of the time," said Cécile of this period, when both Langlois' drinking and his sexual exploits were getting more out of hand. "One night, at midnight, he arrived [home] with two young sailors in uniform. They drank and drank and left a mess. I was afraid for the children, for my boys, that somebody would go into their bedrooms. The sailors stayed all night and left early in the morning."

Although Cécile recounted this painful past in a place and time far removed, the memories clearly shadowed her. She arrived to talk about her past carrying some notes she'd written down. Her shoulders were already slumped. She has an excellent memory for dates and detailed graphic moments, but like her sisters, has spent most of her life burying her inner thoughts. The early years of being tested by scientists and enduring their father's frequent put-downs have left the women uneasy about being asked too many questions. Cécile handles them with short, simple answers.

But ever so slowly, she opened up the layers of her adult life as though revealing the contents of a trunk that belonged to a loved one now departed. She recounted intimate, personal memories that she had long ago put away but that could still make her mourn anew, hurts that she has taken years to get past. As she recounted them, her eyes were hooded pools of sadness.

"I thought there was something the matter with me because Philippe didn't love me. That's why he prefers men and was searching for others instead of me. He said that when he was drunk, he was attracted to men.

"One night I came home from somewhere a day earlier than expected. I went upstairs to bed. Then I heard noises downstairs and footsteps on the stairs.... I phoned a neighbour to assist me. She didn't want to and said she'd keep watch and would call the police if anything appeared to be wrong. I woke up the housekeeper, who had stayed with the children, but she was too afraid to come see what was going on.

"I put on my bathrobe [and] I went to the kitchen; it was all dark. When I opened the light, I saw at least ten men on mattresses [on the floor]. I didn't look closely to see what they were doing. I said, 'I don't know you. But I would like the one that is the most decent among you to get up and leave.' One did get up, and the others all followed him and left. Philippe was coming towards me and I said, 'You, too. You leave.' I left him shortly after that. He came the day after and took his things."

It was 1963 and the couple had four surviving children.

Although Cécile and Langlois split up for a while, and Cécile went back to work as a nurse, they did not separate permanently until April 1964. That year had brought Cécile a different ordeal, and she asked Langlois to come back so she wouldn't have to go through it alone.

The four surviving quintuplets had decided to talk to author James Brough, and for the first time excerpts of their own account of their childhood were about to be published in *McCall's* magazine. Through these articles and Brough's later book, *We Were Five*, the young women were attempting, as were so many others in the early sixties, to make a statement about their own identity and a sense of independence. It was something they'd never been able to fully imagine during their first twenty years.

We Were Five was to smash the myths of childhood and youthful bliss that were fostered by government rhetoric and

196

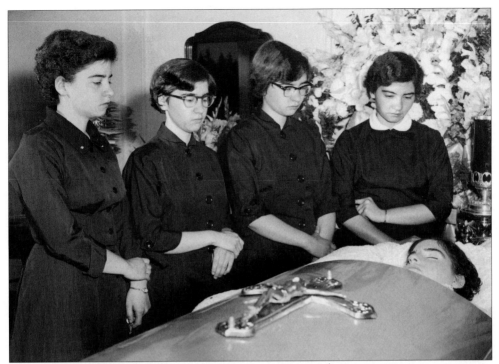

*Four surviving quintuplets stand sombre guard over their late sister Émilie at her funeral.
From left to right, Cécile, Marie, Yvonne, Annette.*

At the family's country gravesite in Corbeil. From left to right, Marie, Yvonne, Cécile, Annette.
*Photographs not credited are from the private collection of Cécile Dionne.

The quintuplets help Marie on opening day of her flower shop, Salon Émilie in Montreal, on Mother's Day, 1956. From left to right, Annette, Yvonne, Cécile, and Marie.

Annette on her wedding day at Notre-Dame de la Salette church in Montreal, greeted by her sisters Marie and Cécile (Yvonne was in hospital and couldn't attend).

Annette and Germain Allard in March 1959, with their first born son, Jean-François.
—Marcel Cognac, *The Star Weekly*

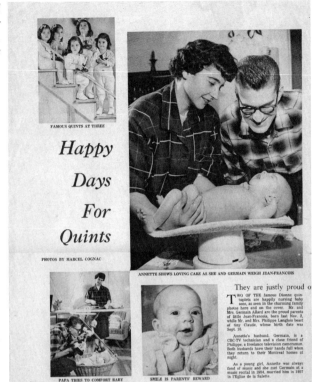

FAMOUS QUINTS AT THREE

Happy Days For Quints

PHOTOS BY MARCEL COGNAC

ANNETTE SHOWS LOVING CARE AS SHE AND GERMAIN WEIGH JEAN-FRANCOIS

PAPA TRIES TO COMFORT BABY

SMILE IS PARENTS' REWARD

They are justly proud o

TWO OF THE famous Dionne quintuplets are happily nursing baby sons, as seen in the charming family photos here and on the cover. Mr. and Mrs. Germain Allard are the proud parents of little Jean-Francois, born last Nov. 2, while Mr. and Mrs. Philippe Langlois boast of tiny Claude, whose birth date was Sept. 16.

Annette's husband, Germain, is a CBC-TV technician and a close friend of Philippe, a freelance television cameraman. Both husbands have their hands full when they return to their Montreal homes at night.

As a young girl, Annette was always fond of music and she met Germain at a music recital in 1954, married him in 1957 in l'Eglise de la Salette.

The Star Weekly, Toronto, March 14, 1959

Bottom left: Annette in 1998, visiting Notre-Dame de la Salette for the first time since she was married there.

Bottom right: Former music teacher Sister Marcelle Corneille observes Annette, who studied with her at the former Collège Marguerite-Bourgeois in Westmount.
—Clément Allard

Interior of chapel at convent of the Little Franciscans of Mary at Baie-Saint-Paul, Quebec.

—Rino Lolli

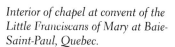

Yvonne, in her Audrey Hepburn-style hairdo and cat's-eye sunglasses, at the airport in 1968 before embarking on a world tour with a friend she would join in India.

Yvonne, in October 1998, en route to her former convent in Baie Saint-Paul, Quebec.

—Bertrand Dionne

Portrait of Cécile at age five. Painted by the artist Willy Pogany, who was commissioned by Karo Syrup and painted each of the sisters.

Cécile's graduation picture after receiving her nursing degree in 1957 from Hôpital Notre Dame de l'Espérance.

Cécile and Philippe with their twin sons, Bruno on the left and Bertrand on the right.

Cécile Dionne and her son Bertrand travelling in June 1994 to Toronto to examine historical and financial records at the Archives of Ontario.

Bertrand brushes clean the Langlois prayer stone in the Quebec City cemetery where his father, Philippe, and brother Bruno are buried in the same plot.
—Clément Allard

March 6, 1998. From left to right, Dionne lawyer
Clayton Ruby, Ontario Attorney-General Charles
Harnick, and Harvey Strosberg, lawyer acting for
the government. —Boris Spremo, *Toronto Star*

Toronto Star *cartoon of Mike Harris*
by Patrick Corrigan, February 28, 1998.

Carlo Tarini, adviser and
spokesperson for the quintuplets.

Annette, Cécile, and Yvonne in June 1998.   —Bruce Field

news media hype. It was to reveal what went on behind the picture-perfect years of simulated Christmases and choreographed family gatherings that were played out before cameras and bright lights. And it would be the first time the famous women would even hint that they had been sexually abused by their father. But the surviving three sisters say they left out graphic and specific details out of respect for their parents, who were still living.

In Cécile's case, that abuse formed a deep inner layer of distrust that would surface in her adult life. She says of her father, "He gave me a French kiss when I was a teenager. I was in the car. It happened so quickly, and he was saying, 'Look at the beautiful moon.' He asked me to be his mistress. He said, 'If you say yes, I'll buy you nice clothing.' … Before that he tried to touch me when he was in the car. He taught us to drive and felt our breasts. After supper, Mother would cry out the window, 'Who wants to go with Dad for a drive?' I knew he'd be trying [to fondle] Émilie and Marie. I was afraid for them. I said, 'I'll go.'"

Langlois knew Cécile's discomfort over how the family would react to the book and the press barrage that would follow. Indeed, the book spawned so much gossip and publicity that Cécile left her job to avoid people's stares. Langlois was happy to be needed and believed that perhaps they could still make a go of their marriage. Cécile hoped that having him back would make her feel more secure. But it was not to be. The lies continued. Once, when Langlois told her he was going to spend a weekend in retreat at a monastery in the Eastern Townships, Cécile tried to phone him and found that he had never arrived and wasn't expected. He had lied to her. After that, the couple broke apart permanently. Langlois

197

never asked to see his children again. He died of liver cirrhosis at age forty-four, in 1975.

In 1964, Cécile, now a single mother and still with no financial support from Langlois, went back to work as a nurse. The physically and emotionally demanding hospital work, when combined with arranging babysitters and raising her children in a home she could no longer afford on her earnings, left her exhausted. Some days she could barely get out of bed. Her sister Yvonne would come to help whenever possible. But even with the tight bond between the four sisters, she found it hard to tell the other two—who were married and had their own children—of her problems.

The only visit from her parents was in 1961, when Bertrand and Bruno were born; they came for the baptism. After she separated from Langlois, Cécile went to Corbeil to tell her parents the news. She was stunned when her father said he already knew she'd been in trouble. It turned out that through Cécile's earlier pleas to the trust company for emergency funds, Oliva Dionne, who was an adviser to the accounts, knew that she needed money and why. But he had never offered any help. Nor did he lend support when he learned she was on her own. If anyone else in the family also knew she was in personal trouble, no one came forward.

The pressure she now felt reminded her of the nine years she had spent in the Big House. As a youngster she had been the most good-natured of the quintet, but by adolescence she had felt burdened by a constant fear that her more fragile sisters, Émilie and Marie, would come to some harm. By the time Cécile was the mother of young children, she'd already lost Émilie. And she'd suffered the loss of her own baby, Bruno. Cécile had learned that she couldn't always protect those who needed it.

She turned to Quebec's social services department for help. Unlike a children's aid society, which removes children at risk from their homes, this was a fee-for-service agency more commonly used by parents who needed a break from their kids because of illness, financial difficulty, or an emergency situation.

Cécile had a social worker help her choose foster homes in which to place her children temporarily. She paid a boarding rate for them, which she recalls as being $10 a week. With her own history of being raised by outsiders, the plan made sense to her. Besides, she knew that she would be involved in choosing their home, and that she could visit them regularly. She also knew that if she did nothing but struggle on, emotionally and physically ill, she could lose her children completely. But if she took the steps needed to regain her health and strength, and held a job long enough to put together some money, she would be able to bring her family back together quickly. At least, that's how she reasoned, though later she was to find that most of her children didn't see it that way.

Bertrand was Cécile's most compliant child, a boy painfully shy and completely trusting of his mother. He was the first to be placed, when he was just five, in a family home not too far away. It was one of several homes he would live in over the next few years. In time, all four of her surviving children were living in different foster homes.

Every Sunday, Cécile would hire the same taxi driver to take her on her rounds to visit the kids, sometimes bringing

199

one child to visit another. On birthdays she would arrive laden down with balloons, a cake, and whatever gifts she had been able to afford or had been sent by Yvonne. It was harder to keep up the rounds when Bertrand was living on Ile d'Orléans, an island across the bridge from Quebec City. It took a costly ninety-minute ride just to reach him there. But the six-year-old was so happy living in that postcard setting of farmland and strawberry fields with Madame Gosselin, who doted on him, that Cécile put up with the frustratingly long commute for a year before she felt she had to move him closer.

She was soon forced to move to an apartment a few blocks away from the lovely family home, with its mature trees and fenced lawn. The distance was not great, but the two homes were a lifestyle apart. At night, a flashing sign from the gasoline station across the road beamed light into the apartment's front windows, a constant reminder of how different her surroundings had become. Gravel and cement formed a rough playground. Cécile tried to bring all of the children back there, then sent some away again when finances or her energy dwindled. In 1970, a month after Marie died, she moved to Saint-Bruno, on Montreal's south shore, to be close to Annette, and to try to strengthen her own family unit. "I didn't succeed," she says now with regret. "I always felt Claude and Elizabeth were reluctant with me because I placed them in foster homes."

When they were crowded together in their small Saint-Bruno apartment, the air was heavy with the tension of five people who had been isolated emotionally. After so many years of being controlled by others, Cécile was determined not to police the children's behaviour. She thought they would see that she respected them, and would cooperate as a family in response. Instead, they grew more distant.

Claude showed his anger by acting tough. Langlois had been very close to him, but had dropped him abruptly after the separation. When the children were living under one roof, Claude sometimes pushed the others around, and dealt with his aggression by learning judo and fencing. He grew remote from Cécile and lived independently as soon as he could. Today he works as a coordinator of production for a major steel company, which he wishes not to name. Divorced from his first wife, he shares custody of two children with her and has a child with his current spouse.

Patrice was the opposite to Claude, a softer boy who wanted to hang out with his older brother, who ignored him. He had difficulty making friends and studying and got into trouble in school. Cécile, single and working, experienced an agonizing cycle of phone calls from the school, frustration at home, and worry at work. In his teens, Patrice experimented with drugs. He began to have headaches and to act strangely. Eventually, he ran away and lived among some street kids. In 1979, he phoned his mother to inform her that he'd been diagnosed with schizophrenia. When he next went to see her, he was detached, pointedly called her Cécile instead of Mom, and didn't want her to kiss him. Today, he lives in a rooming house close to a hospital so he can get help quickly if he needs it. When he feels suicidal, he admits himself. Publicity about the Dionne quintuplets disturbs him.

Bertrand's story stands alone because of his involvement in his mother's and aunts' battle for money and for justice. When he moved back in with his mother at age ten, Cécile told him what had happened to her in her childhood. The boy vowed to one day give her a sense of security. How he kept that promise is a tale of monumental struggle that deserves a chapter of its own.

Elizabeth was the precious daughter who looked just like the quintuplets. Cécile placed her for a couple of years with a family who had a daughter of a similar age and who lived close by her apartment in Quebec City. When Cécile returned to her job as a nurse on a shift from 3 p.m. to midnight, she hired a babysitter and brought Elizabeth back home to live with her. But there were many months when she was too weak to work and had to take breaks to regain her strength. When Elizabeth was nine, Cécile found she couldn't manage and sent the girl back to the same foster home. In the young girl's mind, this was an unfair punishment for something she hadn't done, and she responded for a while by being uncooperative with the foster family.

When she was a child, she hadn't understood her mother's explanations of why she had been sent to a foster home. "I thought she left me, that's what I felt in my little heart," Elizabeth now says. She never knew her father, who left permanently when she was just over a year old. She saw Langlois only once more, just before he died, when she and Bertrand visited him in the hospital.

When Elizabeth finally rejoined her mother and brothers in Saint-Bruno, she was happy at first. But by age fifteen, she was having what she calls an adolescent crisis. She left home at sixteen to live with a girlfriend's family and quit high school before she finished. Her first boyfriend introduced her to drugs, which she experimented with for several years. "After three years, my boyfriend was becoming violent," she says. "I was getting scared. I was as close to the bottom as I could take. I had had one pregnancy and an abortion. I knew that was the best thing to do. My mother knew. She was sad but could do nothing about it. One day I woke up and said it was time for me to do something before it was too late."

The next years were a hard struggle for a young girl on her own with little education and no money. She moved out, rented a room, went on welfare, and stopped her drug habit. "I learned to be very self-reliant [when] we were very young. Cécile was often in her room [suffering migraine headaches], not able to take care of us." She took a series of low-wage jobs and finally got her own apartment in Montreal. This period was lonely but full of the effort to gradually improve her situation. During that time she kept in touch with Cécile frequently by phone and often had dinner with her and her aunts. Eventually, Elizabeth went back to school.

She tells her story matter-of-factly, without embarrassment. It is hard to be a Dionne, she says, but it is also a matter of pride that she has the same fight in her as her mother. At thirty-five, she has a bachelor of arts degree with certificates in social sciences. She runs a small in-house day care so she can be home for her husband, a business manager, and their two sons.

The relationship between Cécile and Elizabeth, however, is not always easy. Too much hurt gets in the way. The tragedy of Cécile's separation from her parents was played out again with her own children, though for different reasons. But Elizabeth can now recognize that she inherited her strength to survive from Cécile. "She was the model for me, that she was able to keep going."

∞∞

In her adult life, Cécile was still struggling to achieve the one thing she'd been denied for years: her own identity apart from her sisters. Marriage hadn't brought that sense of self; instead it had plunged her back into the rejections of her childhood. The people who were supposed to love her were not there, and the people who were there—the hired nurses in the hospital, Dr. Dafoe, her husband—came and went from her life at will.

Like many others in the self-seeking sixties, Cécile went to therapy sessions after she separated from Langlois and returned to them for sustenance over the years, paying only what little she could afford. Through these sessions, she started to open up emotions that she had smothered for years. She said, "I began to be angry when I went to therapy. In the early sessions, only the patient was doing the talking. I said so many things that the therapist finally interrupted me and asked, 'What was *not* done to you?'" It was a dramatic reversal of her habit of hiding what she felt, and the years were soon crowded with this personal quest for self-esteem.

The explorations of her inner feelings and reactions marked the first time she started to think of herself as an individual. Other women have used therapy to take themselves back from the role of wife or mother and retrieve the core of who they are as people. Cécile, however, says she came to her adult life with no previous identity at all. Who am I? Why doesn't my husband love me? What is normal love? Normal sex? Did my parents ever love me? How do I begin to love myself if these other people, who should have, didn't? These are the kinds of questions that Cécile confronted through counselling and therapy exercises—such as writing her feelings in journals, drawing, and other assignments designed to unlock the secrets she had never dared to face.

Quebecers took naturally to the self-help movement, which had first been popularized in California in the 1970s. It fit comfortably within the atmosphere of the province's so-called Quiet Revolution, a monumental upheaval that separated church from state, engulfed politics, and eventually affected the whole society.

Like Catholics everywhere, by the mid-1960s French Canadians were rejecting the dominant role of religion in their lives. They were responding to Vatican II, during which Pope John XXIII declared an opening of the church to modern life. New ideas on faith were embraced, the most dramatic being the decision to allow Mass to be said in languages other than Latin. In Quebec, where religious orders often controlled education, social services, and health care, the influence of the clergy became markedly reduced. Scores of nuns and priests left the church, virtually abandoning countless hospitals, schools, and hospices until the government stepped in.

The sweeping dismissal of religious supremacy in Quebec coincided with the Quiet Revolution and made way for the power-seeking provincial government. The public was awakening to its own rights and responsibilities. A generations-held tradition of dutifully following advice from the parish priest was soon eroded by a wave of therapy groups and leaders who offered self-discovery and self-reliance. Therapists' fees were more acceptable than burdensome feelings of guilt, which had often been the church's price for redemption.

Cécile was particularly drawn to a system, popular in the 1980s, called Personality and Human Relations (Personalité, Relations Humaine, or PRH). PRH was conceived in France in the mid-1960s by a priest, André Rochais, and followed the inspiration of the humanist psychologist Carl Rogers. One of Rogers' contributions was his model of a counselling relationship in which the client sets the pace for therapy and the counsellor is a supportive guide.

For more than five years, Cécile attended PRH workshops, which approach the discovery of the self by means of written assignments and group sharing. Says one group leader, "When you take the time to write, you are able to remain closer to yourself—you are better able to identify your inner feelings. When shared with the group, you are able to live these feelings."

As always, however, the bizarre part of Cécile's past came back to haunt her. Though the three sisters had declined to speak to author Pierre Berton for his 1977 book, they were approached again when the work was being made into a documentary film by the National Film Board and CBC. A representative of Berton's television production company offered the women $10,000 for the three to share, in return for a few hours' filming of them reminiscing about the past and telling how they felt about it as adults. But Cécile and her sisters were trying to escape the shadows of those earlier years and, despite Cécile's financial struggles, they refused the offer. In 1978, The Dionne Quintuplets was shown across Canada. Cécile cried when she viewed the original film footage of herself and her sisters, so innocent and lovable-looking, yet raised like caged royalty across the road from a family with whom they would never be close. Despite all the years of therapy she'd had, this documentary brought to the surface many conflicting memories and emotions.

Then Oliva Dionne died suddenly on November 14, 1979. When she went to Corbeil for her father's funeral, it was the first time she'd returned there since the mid-1960s. To Cécile's horror, she discovered that Elzire blamed Oliva's death on her and her sisters. In fact, all of the family was cold to the surviving quintuplets. She saw her brother Victor for the first time in years, but he made no move to talk to her. "The three of us entered the funeral home and were looking at the casket, but nobody came to us except Ernest's wife, Jeanette. We stayed until 9 p.m. Thérèse was constantly watching us. The next morning before the funeral, Mom said if our father was dead, it was our fault. If he had so many worries, it was our fault. After that, I sent cards to her and Pauline once in a while. They replied. I sent Mom roses for her birthday one year." The family's scars went too deep ever to be healed.

There were times when the oppressive Dionne legacy was pushed back, of course, but it was never fully absent. One of Cécile's happier periods was with a man she dated for almost four years in the early 1980s. They met through a dating service; he was separated and had five children. She had had so little caring from men in her life that almost twenty years later she remembers even the smallest of gestures, like the help this man gave her when she was setting up a room in her home for her esthetics business. In addition to her PRH sessions, she had taken a sex therapy course to see if there was something wrong with her that had led to her marriage breakup. But she learned through therapy and this relationship that, sexually, "I was okay." After Langlois, it was something she needed to know.

Unfortunately, the relationship faded out with no explanation. The man just stopped phoning her. In an era when divorce is common, many people who date in their mature years tell similar stories of abrupt ends to romance; most people simply move on in their search for another mate. For Cécile, however, rejection had become like a curse she couldn't shake. It took a long time for her to get over this one.

She also had problems dating because the men she met expected her to have substantial money tucked away. Some of the men were downright cheap, as if they expected a Dionne quintuplet to pay for everything. She never found anyone to make her feel special, and she has not dated in years. "I'm no longer interested. Love is not for everyone," she says, then adds, "Why is romance so difficult for me? Is it because we were not loved as children?"

Working steadily at her own busy esthetics business once her children were on their own, Cécile found she could manage financially with just the small extra boost from the interest on her dwindling trust fund. During those six years from 1980, her confidence rose thanks to the new pride she felt in not asking Guaranty Trust for any money. "It was so difficult to ask for the money. It was as if I was asking for charity. I never felt it was mine." The rosy period would last only until her health failed. She bought a house with the last $16,000 she received at age forty-five, but had to sell it again after a bout of vague, weakening illnesses forced her to stop working in 1986.

Elzire died that year on November 22. There were no final, soft words between mother and daughter. Cécile went to see her in the North Bay hospital when she learned that her mother had fallen and was slipping into unconsciousness. But she was too ill to attend the funeral.

Her feelings about her mother are still mixed. When she was asked if she thought her mother lashed out at the quintuplets because of frustration over her children being taken from her, Cécile said, "It depends on what's inside the person, not on the times, how they react to a child." And when she was asked to put herself in her mother's shoes, Cécile became upset. "It reminds me that my parents always said that all their troubles were our fault." She admits, however, that Elzire wasn't always so hard on her. "My mother said I had the same eyes as her mother. I used that to prevent Émilie and Marie from bad treatment. I could soften Mom, change her mind. I mostly protected them."

Cécile's health continued to deteriorate that year. She was lethargic and her spleen had enlarged to three times its normal size. It had to be surgically removed in February 1987. By the following year, she was deep into therapy sessions again, unable to work, struggling to stay afloat financially with an occasional hundred-dollar handout from her son Bertrand, who was himself only getting by.

On July 7, 1988, a steamy hot day, the three sisters drove to muggy Toronto because Guaranty Trust was preparing to close shop. The women, who had come to get whatever money was remaining in their accounts, were taken aback to find that they had to prove their financial need before the officials would hand over a cheque. The firm's austere officers interrogated the women about their finances, and argued that since they surely had enough money, they should give the remainder to their other siblings. Disgusted, Cécile's brought out a photocopy of her bank account, which she had thought to bring along. There was a total of $100 left in her account. Yvonne also recalls that incident, and she, too, was stunned by the line of questioning. "One man kept asking if we really need the money and he asked the age of every one [of the siblings] at home," says Yvonne. "He was cold, not cordial. The meeting took at least two to three hours. He never softened." But the women held firm and got their money.

Feeling desperate by 1992, Cécile finally turned to Annette, who was living alone in her three-bedroom house in Saint-Bruno, and asked if she would consider having Cécile move in with her. With the last bit of her cash from the trust, some $6000, Cécile offered to have a bedroom and bathroom enlarged to make living together less inconvenient. She helped the contractor with the labour in order to keep down the costs. Annette welcomed her sister, just as both accepted Yvonne a year later after she had surgery to have both of her hips replaced.

Cécile plunged into a major depression the next year. This was not a new experience: she had suffered from depression in her youth. "[But] those were little depressions that never healed. This time I went very low," she said. "I cried all day for many days." She still takes daily medication for depression. Typically, the emotional lows plus the medications swelled her legs and added more than thirty pounds to her short figure. Another burden to shed.

The depression was partly due to the stress of the past, which she and her sisters were reliving during the filming of *Million Dollar Babies*, a fictionalized TV miniseries based on their lives. Through the efforts of their lawyer and Cécile's son Bertrand, the three women were being paid by the film company for the right to use their name and story. Money was crucial now that all were unemployed, so they had willingly agreed. But it meant checking the script for inaccuracies and sometimes facing disputes over things they tried to have corrected. Cécile was the one who spoke out. She was also the one who, accompanied by Bertrand, was to represent the quintuplets in Hollywood to publicize the show's American broadcast.

The trip was a disaster. Cécile and Bertrand had no cash as yet and could go only if their expenses were paid, which they believed CBS was arranging. The airfare was covered and they'd been promised free transportation for a week. But when the limousine dropped them off at the Los Angeles hotel, there was no one to greet them, no car provided for them to get about, no money provided up front to pay for cabs. They'd been assigned one room to share, a mother and her adult son. They skipped the press conference and left after one night's stay.

It bothered Cécile to read a subsequent newspaper article in which the director of the miniseries said that the quintuplets would never be able to take the stress of a press conference, and that Cécile's nerves had prevented her from showing up. But despite all her troubles, Cécile has a dry, sharp sense of humour that bubbles to the surface at surprising times. After recounting this let-down and speaking

211

with remembered annoyance, she suddenly laughs. She was pleasantly tickled by the memory that the article had prompted some kind person in the United States to send her a get-well card.

Through the remainder of the 1990s, poor health continued to plague Cécile. Her left hip was operated on in July 1995, when she was sixty-one, because of osteoporosis. Her right knee remained painful, and she needed a cane to walk any distance. Then she was diagnosed with epilepsy, as Annette and Yvonne had been.

Cécile's first episode came one Sunday morning in 1995, after an all-day therapy course the day before. She was doing a homework exercise, drawing three separate pictures of what she felt "in my head, my heart, and my belly." She became agitated, thirsty, needed a nap. When she awoke, she began talking nonsense and lost all sense of time. She called Bertrand, who came and stayed with her. She recalls being "in and out of it." She could smell a bad odour, like rotting fish, but didn't know what it was.

Frightened, she visited a doctor, who referred her for an electroencephalograph, which measures electrical activity in the brain. Later, she was told there were two spaces in her brain where similar episodes could occur, "like electrical lightning." On December 8, 1995, a neurologist told her that she suffered from epilepsy and would have to be on medication—Dilantin, in her case—for the rest of her life. The noxious smell she experienced is called an aura, or simple partial seizure, and warns of a bigger seizure to follow. It also meant that the electrical storm occurred in the part of her brain corresponding to smell. Cécile says, "When I thought it over, I remembered that when Émilie died, the doctor told Dad we should all be examined." That did not happen.

Despite all of these health setbacks, however, the tide was beginning to turn favourably in another area of Cécile's life. In the mid-1990s, some of Bertrand's efforts to try to relieve his mother's and aunts' desperate financial situation began to pay off. First, their Montreal lawyer, Daniel Payette, interested a BBC producer in doing a documentary on the quintuplets. He worked out a deal that gave them around $5000 each, in exchange for their cooperation on the script.

The contract for *Million Dollar Babies* came to around $100,000, and Cécile, Yvonne, and Annette each got just under $20,000. With her share, Cécile bought a 1994 green Geo Metro, which cost her around $10,000, and paid some bills. But the money did not last long, since she had received little other income for eight years. By this time, Payette was also pursuing a fifteen percent portion of any use of their image, such as by the Dionne Quint Museum in North Bay, but this was still just a drop in the bucket. Something more was needed to get them out of poverty permanently.

Fortunately, Cécile's spirits had lifted, perked up by both the medical treatment and the feeling of encouragement she was getting from the mounting archival documents Bertrand was finding in his search for what had happened to the quintuplets' funds when they were young. The fighting mood and sense of injustice that had taken hold of Oliva when he was seeking to assert his parental rights was now surging through his daughter and grandson.

But all was not light ahead. The publication in 1995 of

Family Secrets cemented the split that had long existed between the family's two sides. There was a backlash of angry denials from the siblings, usually voiced by the articulate Thérèse Callahan, their oldest living sister. She stated that all of the allegations of sexual and physical abuse by their parents were false, without any foundation. The dispute, which played out on television and in magazine articles throughout Quebec, severed any remaining ties the women had with their relatives. Cécile was nevertheless firm in her belief that they had done the right thing. "It was the truth," she asserts.

Today Cécile insists that it was not only the hoped-for royalties that prompted them to reveal graphic details from their past. Certainly, the book did not bring in enough money to warrant exposing such painful feelings gratuitously—by 1996, when sales had peaked, each of the sisters had made around $5000. Their motive, instead, was a need to reveal the realities of their teenage lives. The story they felt compelled to tell was that they had been doubly damaged, in both their childhood and their teenage years.

Dr. Bessel A. van der Kolk, a world expert on traumatic stress and director of the trauma centre at Human Resources Institute Hospital in Brookline, Massachusetts, said in an interview in which he heard a description of the quintuplets' unusual childhood, "It sounds like nobody saw them as separate people, that no one focussed on their individual interests. No one seems to have taken responsibility and said, 'This is my child.'" When the factor of a divided family was added in, the story suggested to van der Kolk that, "it sounds like lots of people who were supposed to be their natural support system, resented them."

214

The Harvard psychiatrist says that while the celebrated five ended up as the object of admiration and envy, it seems as if "nobody knew them for who they were." Although he never met the women himself, he says he finds that, in essence, the girls were like orphans who lost their parents from the moment they were born. The result, in such cases, is often a feeling of abandonment, van der Kolk says. "It's striking how they seem to have been unable to find loving partners. You often see this in neglected children; they don't know what to look for later in life."

Though Cécile never met van der Kolk, her own thoughts on her life experiences mirror his. In an October 1998 interview, given months after she had received her settlement money and was contemplating a changed future, she was still burdened by her past and how it had affected her life. "I never felt different from the others [her quintuplet sisters], not during those first years. There was no one there to say, 'Cécile, you are one self, one person on your own.' It's more than neglect we suffered. It's rejection. We were orphans with no parents; we were abandoned children," she said. Poignantly, she added that everything that had gone wrong in their lives began with the fact that "the base of a normal childhood was lacking. A normal child, the mother presses to her breast; it creates a relationship. We did not know that from a mother. The nurses were told not to kiss us. How could we face ourselves with love when we were without love?"

Since 1995, Cécile has been deeply involved in Bertrand's mission to bring justice to the quintuplets. After they had made some money from the miniseries, she and her son could afford a trip to Toronto and an overnight stay in a downtown motel to visit the Ontario archives. She was amazed by the number of boxes of historical documents, letters, and data related to her and her sisters. An entire room was filled with these boxes, which rested both on shelves and on the floor.

The years of 1996 and 1997 tested Cécile's resolve. But despite ongoing ailments, fatigue, her distressing weight problem, and the frustrations of the Ontario government's stalling, she emerged more focused on her goal. As Carlo Tarini, the sisters' media adviser, puts it, "She grew into the role of spokesperson for the sisters. At some point when we seemed to be playing ping-pong with the government, going back and forth, she was revolted by the way they were being treated."

By February 1998, Cécile's life appeared to have come full circle. There she was on TV newscasts across the country again. But this time, it was not as a beloved child star performing in fancy outfits. This time, she was wearing her old green winter coat and hat, "an old woman with difficulty getting out of a taxi," she said when she saw herself that day in front of the province's Gothic-looking legislative building. "I was ashamed. But I told myself I was going for a good cause, and let go of what our appearances were.… It was very hard to be there. It reminded me of the time we were all photographed so often. But when we were little, they were always doing it and we were used to it."

11: THE OTHER SIDE

T HE YOUNG BOY WAS circling his bicycle on the small patch of paved land next to the highway. He rode aimlessly, sure in the way that rural youngsters are that nothing much else was likely to happen on the backwoods roadway. But he was soon surprised.

A huge Greyhound bus lumbered up and parked across the eight-year-old's riding range. Out scrambled a group of chattering Québécois teenagers with notebooks. They walked towards the nearby nursing home, staring at a stretch of land that was so familiar to the boy, pointing at the imposing yellow-brick institution set back into expansive grounds. The boy knew Nipissing Manor better by its former name: the Big House.

Spotted by the students, he was told they were a high-school journalism class doing a project on the Dionne quintuplets. Did the boy know anyone related to the sisters whom they could interview on camera? Yvon Dionne was suffused with pride. He was their nephew, he boasted, the younger of two sons of Claude, who was the last child born to Elzire and Oliva. He answered questions and happily agreed to be filmed. When the bus left, he ran his bike home and burst out with the news to his father.

Claude Dionne listened but was not impressed. Then he brought the boy plummeting down from the clouds: "You're

217

going to look pretty smart on that film with your fly left unzipped." From celebrity to shame.

That is how Yvon Dionne recalled first learning that the quintuplets had been a huge story in Canadian history. Yet some twenty years after that memorable incident, he still hasn't met his illustrious aunts, so divided does the family remain today, into two distinct sides: the quintuplets and their other siblings.

The young man was deeply troubled in March 1998 by what he felt was missing in all the publicity for the Dionne sisters. Their fight for a financial settlement had stirred up not only their personal history, but the detritus that went with it. Like all Dionnes, Yvon had felt it eroding his pride. He spent his childhood in a house next door to the one his grandparents Oliva and Elzire moved into after the Big House was sold. His unmarried aunt Pauline lived with her parents and was like a second mother to him. There was never a day that he didn't stop by for milk and cookies. Two uncles and their families lived but a sprint away; the other siblings, save the quintuplets, were nearby or visited his grandparents frequently. He believed that his grandparents were great people, and he felt proud to be related to celebrities.

But his sense of living in a big, happy family was shattered when he was fourteen. His grade nine history teacher said the class was going to study the Dionne quintuplets and would view the NFB/CBC film about them. Young Yvon was taken aback when told he could be excused. When he asked his father why, he was told the documentary was harsh towards his grandparents. He watched the film and was horrified. Just four years after his beloved grandfather had died, there he was on the screen, there was his voice, and yet Oliva's story wasn't about someone Yvon recognized. Suddenly, things he'd heard but barely understood made sense, particularly his father's paranoia about the media and about people who wanted to make friends with him.

The teenager began to pepper the family with questions, especially his aunt Pauline, whom he says was obsessed with the story and got very emotional and red in the face when she gave him answers. He talked to his grandmother about the public perception of the family, but she simply said that people didn't understand. Elzire told him she herself did not understand her five daughters, and did not know how they could have participated in *We Were Five*.

After Elzire died in 1986, there was almost no contact between the siblings and the surviving quintuplets. With the publication of *Family Secrets* in 1994, Pauline, who had maintained occasional correspondence and phone contact with Cécile, abruptly cut her off. By the time Annette, Yvonne, and Cécile won their compensation, the split between the two sides of the family was complete.

Both groups were deeply embittered about the past. But while the quintuplets felt a sadness and sense of loss over the family closeness they had never had, the siblings appeared more angry and resentful of their sisters. Certainly both groups were victims of a government takeover that destroyed family pride, reputation, and cohesiveness. Yet the siblings never shook the feeling that they had got the worst of it.

Yvon Dionne highlighted this family pathology in a letter he sent to Premier Mike Harris on March 10, 1998, after the provincial leader had apologized to the sisters for their past treatment by the Ontario government. Yvon, who acted on his own but informed his relatives of what he was going to do, chastised Harris for ignoring the quintuplets' siblings:

If you really wanted to apologize to the Dionnes you would have travelled not only to Montreal but to North Bay where the majority of the Dionne family lives. I thought because you are from North Bay you would have seen things differently. But you obviously don't. You are no different than the majority of the public who still believes that the only Dionnes that were really abused are the quintuplets.

Nobody ever thinks of the parents, my grandparents, who had their babies stolen from them. Nobody ever thinks of the way the government publicly declared my grandparents as "unfit" to take care of their own babies. Nobody ever thinks of the years between 1934 and 1942 when my grandparents fought so desperately to regain custody from a greedy government. Nobody ever thinks of the disgusting and cruel way in which the media and the government portrayed this poor French Canadian farming family.

Nobody ever thinks of the siblings of the quintuplets who saw their family torn apart by their government, and actually got away with it for sixty-four years. Nobody ever thinks of how difficult it must have been for my grandparents to explain to their children why their sisters were being displayed in cages like animals to the public. Nobody ever thinks of the river of tears that [was] shed.

So why did the parents, brothers and sisters of the quintuplets not get an apology? Maybe it is

220

because you are like the majority of the public who believed every word that was written in the two books that the quints wrote about their family. The quints claimed that they were physically, mentally, emotionally and sexually abused, so you and the public pass judgment on the family without question. Nobody ever thinks that maybe these claims are false. It must have been difficult to be reunited with a family that was not familiar to the quints. But you can also imagine how difficult it would have been to change from world famous celebrities to common farming children overnight.

I knew my grandparents very well and to this day I have not met more gentle, kind and loving people. My grandparents, uncles, aunts and my father were not only dumbfounded by these false claims but hurt beyond belief from these books. And to know that the public would pass judgment on them without question is terrible.

My grandfather died in 1979 and my grandmother in 1986. It is too late to give them the apology that they rightfully deserved. But there are still five surviving siblings of the quints who need to know that their government takes responsibility for having destroyed and ridiculed their family and parents.

Mr. Harris, please prove to me that you are not using the Dionnes to make you look more compassionate as a politician. Please prove to me that you simply forgot to apologize to the surviving family rather than chose not to. Do the

right thing and give the Dionne family, not just
the quints, the acknowledgment that they rightfully deserve.

Sincerely,

Yvon Dionne

In an interview several months after writing this letter, Yvon,
a slim twenty-nine-year-old with the characteristic intense
Dionne gaze, revealed that he had since experienced his own
break with the siblings. His fifty-one-year-old mother, also
named Pauline, had died on April 18, 1998, of bone cancer.
Separated from Yvon's father just a few years before she died,
she had been relegated by the siblings to the group they
referred to disparagingly as the "ex-wives." The two other
women in this group had long been divorced from their
Dionne husbands, and Yvon was hurt to find his mother
being treated as an untrustworthy outsider after her decades-
long marriage to Claude.

His own estrangement from the family began when he and
his older brother, Marc, had a dispute with their father over
their mother's will and what she left to them. Their aunts,
Thérèse and Pauline, stopped speaking to them. Their uncle
Oliva Jr. phoned and yelled at both young men. In the
Dionne family, it seems, people are either in or they're out.

Given all that the siblings have gone through for more than
sixty years, respect, not surprisingly, has become their family
watchword. It was a fight for respect, as much as for child
custody, that consumed their father before them. Like him, they
equate any lack of respect with the sin of disloyalty. As a result,
the siblings trust no one—sometimes not even each other.

Many requests were made to the siblings, through Oliva and Elzire's oldest living child, Thérèse Callahan, for interviews for this book. Thérèse, herself, was clearly ambivalent; she initially agreed to a meeting in North Bay but later cancelled it with a minor excuse. When her go-betweens suggested to her that she participate in a later interview, she rejected their advice.

One friend of hers, Michael O'Caine, said that he first got to know the family when he worked at Oliva Dionne's souvenir booth at Quintland. "Obviously the family is very dysfunctional. They were two complete families. The other side never got over that they were ignored in the past and that more recently they were being put down in the press," he said. "[Thérèse] sometimes gets a bad shuffle in all of this." O'Caine said that he urged her to take part in this book, but "she was mistrustful. She doesn't want to give someone a chance to hear their side."

In telephone discussions about potential interviews, Thérèse was at times warm and gracious. At other times, she would be suddenly hostile to the idea, offering the explanation that her brothers didn't trust that their side would be told fairly. In saying this, she essentially repeated the very phrases her father had used with reporters in the 1940s, when he was asked to give the family's viewpoint. "We don't feel anyone can be fair to both sides and tell the truth," she said. Thérèse also made it clear that the siblings did not want to be associated with a book that would give full hearing to the quintuplets. Instead, the siblings have arranged for a book telling only their side to be written by a Franco-Ontarian acquaintance who has been researching Dionne history.

Clearly, the siblings' bitterness is so deep-seated that almost anything written without their approval is taken as a slight. Thérèse said that early press reports about her mother, for example, were demeaning because reporters described her as hugely overweight. (Even this small reference is significant in the family rift. The three surviving quintuplets say that their mother always blamed their birth and the events afterwards for her weight problems. This ignores the fact that Elzire gave birth to a total of fourteen children, and that photos taken of her show that she was large, though not obese, and remained overweight long after her children were grown.) This suspiciousness has in the past led Thérèse to agree only to interviews where her view alone could be expressed.

In November 1995, she spoke out in a Quebec magazine, *Dernière Heure,* in an interview that she said she gave "to save the honour of her parents" after the publication of *Family Secrets.* Asked to recall her first memory about the quintuplets' birth, Thérèse spoke of the move to send the older children away from the household. She said, "We were helpless because it was the first time that we left the house without our parents. We begged to go back to them."

Thérèse was then five years old. Dr. Dafoe would not allow her and her siblings to return home until the babies' hospital had been built almost four months later. Whooping cough was rampant in the area at that time, and there was even talk that the parents themselves would have to vacate the farmhouse. A scene in the fictionalized TV miniseries *Million Dollar Babies* poignantly portrays the children as they must have been in reality: confused and crying, baby Pauline clinging to her mother before being pulled away, then all of them driven from their home in their father's truck like refugees from a conflict they would never comprehend.

Thérèse, who was frail, was sent to live with her mother's

aunt, Donalda Legros, while all the other children were sent to their father's brother Léon's home. She explained, "This is a period that has marked me, since I can still speak of it today." Her mother was too ill to visit her for the first two months; her father came only from time to time.

To this day, Thérèse still believes that the government could have chosen to help them by building a bigger home that could have accommodated the whole family. She blames the government for the fact that the Dionne family remains divided. "We returned to find our parents completely depressed. They were no longer in control of their own house.... [Neither] my father nor my mother ... had much hopes, the ambience remained rather bitter.... After the birth of the quints, our parents became very sad and very preoccupied, which put an end to our [previous] happiness when, in our young minds, all had seemed to revolve around us. The problems really began with their birth, but not with them. Day by day we prematurely became adults because we had also been subjugated to what our parents had to endure, the removal of the quints and the denial of the right to visit them."

Contrary to what the surviving quintuplets have said about the family's reunion in the Big House, Thérèse insisted, "Their return was a true celebration." She spoke of joyful moments, all of them together. "At our home, for example, we sang almost all the time while working or simply for the pleasure of singing.... Almost every night, there were instances when we'd play cards, other games or where we'd sing and dance."

Thérèse also presented an image of Elzire that was very different from the quintuplets'. "My mother was the most down-to-earth person. Even when she had additional work, she took the time to receive visitors. And when we, the children, wanted to speak to her, she never was hesitant to listen, she always gave us advice. My mother didn't have a lot of education, but she had a wisdom that was instinctive. Beat us? Throw us to the ground? I never saw her do such things!"

Of course, this bucolic picture of life in the Big House leaves out the fact that from the age of eight, Thérèse was sent away to boarding schools and was often absent during the time the quintuplets were living there.

On the delicate subject of whether she had been jealous of the quintuplets, Thérèse answered abruptly. "I could have been envious of all the luxuries they had. We had but two dresses a year. But it stopped at that." In a telling glimpse of the fate of the siblings, she said that the other Dionne children "had to say in confession that the quints were put on this earth for a great reason, while we were here to serve them. That didn't upset us, except that we needed time to realize that we also had value. It took me some forty-five years to realize that I had some intelligence."

At age forty-five, Callahan returned to school and obtained a bachelor's degree in French and a master's degree in education, all while raising a family of four sons. She said, "I needed to prove myself. Because until then, each time I met people, it was always to recall the difference between the quints and the rest of the siblings. They were inquisitive of them and never interested in us." She added that she always felt less important and less well raised than her five famous sisters. "People always said we were less refined."

When asked what shocked her most about *Family Secrets*, Thérèse said, "Perhaps all the accusations of sexual abuse by my father. But all the disparaging remarks about my parents and brothers and sisters hurt me terribly. Reading that my mother was physically violent with them upset me terribly because my mother was a saint. If my mother wasn't an angel, no one was! Despite all she had to endure, she could still smile through the tears."

On the subject of her father, she said, "I want to first speak of the accusations of the abuse of power. He could never have been guilty because he administered the quint's funds according to the directions of the government." When asked whether he had ever sexually abused or harassed her, Rose-Marie, or Pauline, she gave an emphatic "Never." Nor does she believe that he touched or harassed the quintuplets. When asked why, as adults, they would say such a thing, she answered, "Perhaps they feel the need to write a sensational book. A number of fictional elements ... to assure it would sell."

She and her husband stopped contact with the quintuplets when *We Were Five* was published. But she believes that the problems really began when the children first moved into the house and found they no longer had all of the attention. "Until then, the whole world saw them as princesses but at our home they were considered as other children. They were accustomed to being adored, but my parents did not bow down to them. They loved the quints, but at the same time they loved their other children."

Question: "Would you like to reconcile with them?"

Answer: "No, not after the two books. They've hurt us too much."

In the beginning, the public saw only hastily snapped photographs of the five Dionne children who'd been born before the quintuplets. They were Ernest, almost eight; Rose-Marie, six; Thérèse, five; Daniel, three; and Pauline, eleven months. They were usually caught by the camera unawares: two boys and three girls looking confused by all the fuss. Though they were healthy and attractive, they were no match for the captivating image of their five identical sisters, who were taught to perform for an audience. The older Dionne children were farm kids who wore practical clothes and were overwhelmed by the curiosity directed at them.

In the early months, when the babies still lived in the farm-house, tumultuous changes affected the lives of the Dionne couple and their five older children. First, half of their living space was closed off to them; then a virtual quarantine was placed on the household, so they could have no guests of their own; and finally the older children were sent away. At the same time, Oliva Dionne saw a flow of money unlike anything he had ever known. The Red Cross alone was spending $300 a month (the equivalent of $3000 today) on the salaries of nurses in the house. The Dionnes were even able to employ a maid and a helper with private donations that arrived by mail.

When the quintuplets were moved to the hospital across the road and began to be besieged with commercial contracts, Oliva made attempts to capitalize on their fame and bring in income that would improve the lot of his other children. He first signed an exclusive contract with the *New York Daily News* for pictures of the rest of the family, then agreed to use the older children in commercial endorsements like the ones their sisters were doing. The makers of Crown Brand corn syrup, the Canada Starch Company, did use the siblings in an advertising layout. But the idea didn't take hold with many other companies.

It is impossible to look at Oliva Dionne's actions at this time, says Robert Bérubé, a Franco-Ontarian educator who has studied the Dionne family, without understanding that the parents and their other children were also exploited. Bérubé is the author chosen by the siblings to write a book describing their version of events. He says, "There was abuse of power against the family. First it was the doctor, then it was the government, then it was the priests. The parents were supported by Franco-Ontarian associations, but there was a price to pay. There were conditions. They had to give up power to the nuns and priests to run the school, and they even ran the Big House. Go back to the 1940s and see how Quebec was governed by the church. The priest had so much power. They would walk in the house—you had to greet them and be very polite. They controlled the communities."

Bérubé goes on to say, "The quints were heavily influenced by their husbands, nuns, and priests. The siblings completely dispute the sexual abuse. The quintuplets believe it happened, but what is their interpretation of assault? According to a nun, if you touched their hand, you violated them. I firmly believe that Mr. and Mrs. Dionne were honest people with a lot of integrity. They suffered unjustly at the hands of the government and other interest groups."

But Bérubé's assessment sometimes mixes together historical fact and the siblings' opinions. Of course, some of what he notes—for example, the pressures brought to bear on the Dionnes—is indisputable. So too, the nuns who taught the quintuplets clearly must have had an influence on them. Nevertheless, the three surviving sisters made their allegations of sexual abuse as adults, and were fully aware of the meaning of what had been done to them. Moreover, they have stuck to

229

the same basic story for more than three decades. As well, Cécile insists that she was not influenced by her husband during the short period of her marriage, and she maintains that the nuns and priests did not turn the quintuplets against their parents. "Dad was always suspicious of the nuns. I talked to Dad before getting married. He spoke about 'intruders' in our lives, and he talked of Father Gustave Sauvé as one. I told him then, 'It's untrue, he never told us bad things about you.'" For their part, the siblings fail to take into account that because of the extraordinary events, their parents were irrevocably changed, and had handled the quintuplets differently than they had their other children, whom they'd raised from birth.

Bérubé's research into historical archives, however, has given him insight into the times. He says, "Those francophone associations had a negative effect. They didn't treat Oliva with respect. They were fighting for a principle, and he was fighting for his children. His passion burned him out.... Getting the quints back took a lot of money. If you look at the Dionnes' last house, it was a small house. Mrs. Dionne left only a few thousand dollars [on her death]."

Bérubé maintains that his intent, and that of the siblings, is only to refute the misrepresentations of the past. In particular, they want to challenge the notion that Oliva Dionne became a harsh, controlling figure in the quintuplets' lives. In reality, the siblings believe, he was a victim of the situation, caught between the government and the power groups challenging it.

The quintuplets believe that the trouble between the two sides began when they moved together into the Big House, and at least one neighbour concurs. Émile Contant, who was close in age to some of the siblings and whose father had been a hunting partner of Oliva's, remembers, "The brothers and sisters had it good in the Big House. The quints didn't. The brothers got money, bicycles, trucks, and cars; they had all the toys. They had a love/hate relationship with the quints. They [the siblings] were upper class for the area, but they're the ones who are bitter." In a community that then had only twenty houses in an eight-kilometre area, neighbours like Contant could see much of what was going on.

But the siblings are either unaware of or refuse to acknowledge how tense and difficult the reunion with their sisters was. They seem to believe that what went on in the Big House—the insensitive treatment of the girls by their parents, the coldness of their brothers and sisters towards them—was normal family behaviour. They insist that the ultimate split in the family came much later, with publication of *We Were Five*. Audrey Dionne, who was married to Daniel when that book was published, says, "I was shocked [that the book stripped bare the family's history]. I said, 'My God, why did they do that?'"

Each of the siblings was thrust into an unprecedented situation for which they never could have prepared. Their unhappy reactions to so much upheaval were natural. What made the breach between the two sides of the family so unique and lasting, however, was that the siblings' hurts were validated by their parents, while the quintuplets were left to adjust on their own. When the quintuplets were older and looked back, they came to the conclusion that their parents and siblings already had a tense, troubled household because of the original family division, and it had been convenient to label the five sisters a disruptive force when they all moved in together.

Seven years old at the time of the quintuplets' birth, Ernest was the oldest of the Dionnes' earlier children. When he was interviewed in 1984 by the *Toronto Star* on the occasion of the quintuplets' fiftieth birthday, Ernest wept when recalling the past. His face flushed, he shook with emotion, and his eyes filled with tears. "You never get over something like this," he explained. "The whole family was never the same. People said terrible things to me when I went away to school in Ottawa. We had a normal family life, then everything changed. They took my father's pride, he never had a chance.... I believe my father did the right thing, the best he could. If he hadn't, things would have been much worse for the quints."

Throughout his life, Ernest remained in the Corbeil area, settling with his wife first in the guards' building in front of the Big House, and then building a red-brick bungalow just up the road and across from the original farm. He and his wife, Jeanette, had six daughters. He worked as a stationary engineer in North Bay and took over management of the farm when Oliva died, running it until he himself died in 1995, at the age of sixty-eight.

The second child, Rose-Marie Dionne, married Maurice Girouard, a car salesman, in a wedding that was large by Corbeil standards. For a time, the couple lived near Montreal and occasionally visited Annette and Germain in Saint-Bruno. Rose-Marie, dispatched by her parents, was the first family member to arrive at the convent where Émilie died. Her husband later became involved in the adult quintuplets' trust account when Oliva asked Girouard to replace him on the advisory committee. The couple, who had two daughters and two sons, moved to St. Catharines and eventually divorced.

Ill with cancer for years, Rose-Marie died at sixty-six in November 1995.

Thérèse Dionne, a retired high-school music teacher and mother of four, married Tom Callahan, a superintendent at the Johns-Mansville wood fibreboard plant in North Bay; he died in 1987. For many years, she has acted as the spokesperson for the rest of the siblings. When she was interviewed in 1984 by the *Toronto Star*, Thérèse expressed the sentiments of many of the family members when she said that the publicity about the original Dionne homestead, which was being turned into a permanent museum at the time, was bringing the old hurts back. "They're crucifying the family again. They talk about a shack. That was our home and it was no more a shack than any other around here that existed in 1934. During the Depression there were no castles in North Bay—though I can't speak for Toronto.

"It's like before. Nobody would believe what we suffered. Half the people had no clue there was anyone else in the family. We were second-class citizens. They [promoters and journalists] had to always elevate five. So they lowered the rest so five would look better. It was a regular hell."

In a recent telephone conversation, Thérèse said that she had worked so hard "to please my parents" that she had had a nervous breakdown at seventeen. "I was doing my studying for grade thirteen and my grade ten piano, with music history and harmony, all at the same time. Every time I came home and had good marks, they were so happy. Mother appreciated education even though she left school at age eleven." According to Thérèse, Elzire wanted all of her children to have an education, yet the quintuplets were forced to study homemaking skills until they were twenty-one and finally free to make their own choices. Cécile says, "Dad wanted us to be with the nuns at Nicolet for at least two more years, and we didn't know then that it meant until we reached the age of majority."

The fourth child, Daniel, was widely known as the black sheep of the family. The quintuplets recall that their father was hard on him and handed him the chores that Ernest didn't want to do. As a young man, Danny had a reputation for getting into trouble. At sixteen, he was sent to a private school in Hull, Quebec, where he was remembered for borrowing the teacher's car and getting drunk. A binge drinker, he had started to drink at an even earlier age; he became violent and abusive when inebriated but often couldn't remember what he'd done wrong the next day.

He married Audrey Caissie, a French-Canadian girl from New Brunswick, when she was seventeen; they had four sons and a daughter before divorcing seventeen years later. The young couple lived for a time in Toronto, where Danny worked in shipping for Eaton's department stores. They moved to North Bay and bought a house with his share of Émilie's trust account after she died, around $10,000. Like Thérèse's husband, Danny got a job with Johns-Mansville, as a set-up man for machines. In 1960, he and his wife bought the Dionne homestead from Oliva for $5000, moved in upstairs with their children, and opened the downstairs to the public as a museum. They were soon overwhelmed with traffic and visitors, and the number of people coming through and asking questions was more than Danny could take. It brought back all of the old memories that he disliked talking about, his wife said. They sold the farmhouse after only two years.

Audrey had first met Danny while both were visiting Toronto. She didn't make the connection between him and the famous Dionne quintuplets until he took her to visit his family at the Big House. When he said he had to call ahead from Callander so that someone would unlock the gates to the house, it dawned on her who the Dionnes were. She remembered that her mother had worn an apron with a picture of the five little girls' faces on it.

Today, Audrey rarely has contact with her ex-husband's brothers and sisters (as one of "the ex-wives," she is no longer considered family by the siblings). Yet she says of the Dionnes, "They were a decent family before the quintuplets were born. If left alone, they would have been a beautiful French-Canadian family. It's all because of what the government did. Danny was an alcoholic because … of what the government put the family through."

When Audrey met the family in the Big House for the first time, she saw the division between the two groups immediately. The quintuplets were always together, and they kept their distance from the rest. "Yet there was lots of joy in that house," she says, referring to parties with music, Christmas gatherings, and the like. She describes Elzire as a very strong presence within the household, and a typical French-Canadian mother. She never heard Oliva raise his voice.

After she and Danny divorced, Audrey moved to Sturgeon Falls with their five children and supported them by working as a waitress, then managing restaurants. Though she and her kids were only an hour away from most of the Dionnes, they rarely saw their relatives again. Danny, who was married to his second wife, Marie, for eleven years, died of cancer on January 5, 1995, just four days before his brother Ernest.

Pauline Dionne, born eleven months before her five sisters, was often considered "the sixth quint." She was an adorable child herself, and was the only one in the family with golden curls. For her early schooling she attended classes with the quintuplets, who were being taught by a private tutor in the nursery, but later she was separated from them like the other siblings and sent away to a fine boarding school.

Pauline was an art teacher and a nun for several years, then spent almost two decades caring for her parents until both passed away. She never married. Because she spent so many years away from teaching, she was unable to get work after her parents died and was left to live meagerly. Pauline, the daughter who most resembles her mother but for the fair hair, carries the past with a heavy heart. One nephew describes her as "a wounded bird," adding that her anguish only got worse when the adult quintuplets exposed the secrets of the family's years together.

Though she had kept in contact with Cécile into the 1990s, Pauline broke that off abruptly after the publication of *Family Secrets*. According to Cécile, "In 1992 she wrote us a letter asking us on our next birthday to write a notification in the newspaper that we forgive Mother and Dad. I wrote back saying it was monstrous to ask us that. Things have been bad since then. When I went into the Ontario Archives in 1995 in Toronto, I phoned Pauline to reassure her not to be afraid of the miniseries [*Million Dollar Babies*] because ... I had told the producer to respect Mom and Dad. She was nice on the phone, but after she wrote us to say it wasn't true that Mother and Dad were respected in the miniseries." The quintuplets have not heard from her in years.

Oliva Jr.'s birth, the first to follow the quintuplets', was publicized internationally as part of the continuing fascination with all things related to the Dionne girls. Elzire was quoted as saying, "This one will never go away." Cécile remembers her mother bringing the new baby to the nursery. She says, "He was so very protected and deeply loved. He was Dad's favourite."

Known as Oliver, he was in the Royal Canadian Air Force and emerged as "a tough guy and strict with his kids," according to one insider. Divorced from his first wife, Glenda, with whom he had one daughter and two sons, he later married Lil Corbeil.

Victor Dionne, born almost two years after Oliva Jr., was an audiovisual technician, then worked in the North Bay psychiatric hospital as a janitor. He still lives near North Bay, but has been too ill to work in recent years. He never married.

As far back as 1955, Victor expressed to a reporter the bitterness felt by the siblings about their famous sisters. That Christmas, when the quintuplets didn't come home for the holidays, Oliva Dionne had called a press conference to publicize his belief that "outsiders"—he meant Annette's boyfriend, Germain Allard—had turned the sisters away from their family. Victor, who was then nineteen, was quoted as saying, "They act as if they are queens or something." In the same article, Victor said, "My sisters keep changing their stories and contradicting themselves. They said they never met any boys at home and never had any parties or fun there. That's a lie. I was at college and used to bring my friends to the house for parties. The quints used to sit and laugh and make fun of them and then run up to their rooms." Yet Victor apparently maintained contact with Cécile; he travelled to New York with her fiancé, Philippe Langlois, shortly before their wedding, and stayed once in their Montreal home after the couple married. But he had no further contact with his sister after that fateful night.

Claude Dionne, the baby of the family and the only child who was born in the Big House, lives in a house that, like Ernest's, is just short steps from his parents' last home. He saw them daily before they died. He married a woman named Pauline and had two sons, Yvon and Marc. He was a nurse's assistant in a North Bay psychiatric hospital, then a switchboard receptionist there, and is now retired.

Yvon says that when he was growing up, his father was "caring and generous, but he had a strong, bitter side." The sisters remember Claude as a baby they played with. Years later, at Oliva's funeral, Cécile says, "Claude didn't even say hello to us. He seemed to have rejected us. I feel he had a lot of aggression; he put on our shoulders all that our parents endured."

It's impossible to know just how long the legacy of mistrust and misunderstanding between family members will go on. Many members of the third generation, nephews and nieces of the quintuplets, are in stable family relationships and are highly successful in their jobs. Yet few of them would speak openly about how growing up as a Dionne affected them.

Richard Dionne, one of Daniel's sons and a nephew of the quintuplets, says of his generation that though many did well, "emotionally they don't know how to talk about [the past]." In

some cases, their parents—a sister or brother of the quintuplets—warned them that they were not to be interviewed for
this book. Over the years, the children have learned the hard
way that going against the family's demand for silence is
considered treachery by the siblings.

Those who do go on record speak of the Dionne family as
having known chaos right after the quintuplets' birth that
changed all of their lives. Richard Dionne describes his father,
for instance, as an alcoholic who became physically abusive
when he drank. "He'd show up drunk, hear that the kids had
misbehaved, and give the strap," he says. Richard seemed to
get the worst of it. He was frequently taken aside and whacked
with a leather belt or a piece of wood. His sister was once
beaten and locked out of the house until three in the morning
after forgetting to reheat some french fries when she was ten.

Of his grandfather Oliva Dionne's reaction to the quintuplets' birth, Richard says, "Before that, his kids worked along
with him. He was strict but always there for them. After the
quints were born, he was so focused on getting the other kids
back. The Dionnes are fighters. It's only natural, as a fighter
and a father, to go after your kids. They neglected the other
children, though it was not their fault."

Richard recalls that when he was five or six years old and
living across from the Big House, tourists would often stop and
ask him questions. He got into trouble with his father when he
was caught trying to conduct a child's tour of Dionne land-
marks. Today he believes his father never dealt with how he was
affected by events in his childhood. He describes photos his
father kept in his old scrapbook, many taken when the quintuplets and siblings all lived together. Richard says, "You can

see they were two separate families just from the way they were dressed and how the five sisters were grouped apart." The scrapbook ends after Émilie's death.

Daniel's alcoholism started early. Richard says, "He was very attractive, my mother must have thought she was marrying a prince. He had the Dionne name and everybody thought that the family was wealthy." But there was no evidence of wealth in Daniel's life. When his mother died, he was left around $10,000, as were all of the other siblings except the quintuplets, who were left nothing. Richard says that he believes the actions of the Ontario government resulted in the entire Dionne family—Oliva, Elzire, and all of their children—becoming "dysfunctional." And he believes that his generation of Dionnes has also suffered. "We got the hand-me-down baggage, too," he says.

A niece of the quintuplets, who asked that her name not be used in this book, said in an interview that her father's experiences had so damaged him that when he had children of his own, he was abusive physically and sexually. She also said that her father rarely mentioned his famous sisters. "It felt like a forbidden subject. Even my grandfather and grandmother rarely spoke of them," she recalls.

The woman broke down and cried when she described being repeatedly sexually abused by her father. "I was always scared of him, even as an adult. We were brought up never to say anything, to keep our mouths shut, because we were the Dionnes and we had to look good. There were always those little secrets. There was no place we could go for help.

"It's sad. I know a lot of families that drift apart. This family was torn apart."

12: A PROMISE MADE

A S HE WATCHED THE throng of journalists pressing forward with its battery of invasive media technology that February 26, 1998, one man was crying. He scanned their every move, ready to pounce if anyone came too close to the three sombre women at the front of the room, but the man was sick at heart. Tears came to his eyes because he had failed.

Bertrand Dionne had promised his mother, Cécile, that she would never have to expose herself to public scrutiny again. Now here she was at a press conference being broadcast on national television, laying bare the hidden facts that had caused her and her sisters such great shame. Her disclosures, which ran so contrary to the background of wealth and glamour these reporters had unearthed through research in their newsroom libraries beforehand, riveted the normally skeptical audience.

"Poverty-stricken" was how the journalists would describe his mother's and aunts' circumstances, and Bertrand knew specifically that meant that all three women were living in a house with wintry drafts inside, and that between them they could barely pay for necessary prescription drugs.

"Kidnapped from our parents" was a dramatic phrase used by Cécile, and Bertrand knew its human toll: a once-proud family humiliated, its members bitterly divided for more than half a century.

"All this abuse," another of Cécile's phrases, would be used by the media to summarize the years of exploitation. Bertrand knew that exploitation had been initiated by the Ontario government, which had displayed the five babies as if they were part of a circus act, used them to create a flourishing tourism industry, and left them ill-prepared for ordinary life.

All this passed through thirty-six-year-old Bertrand's mind during that pivotal press conference in Toronto, when it was too late to retreat. In the end, going public turned out to be the apex of a campaign he had launched years before. Yet in his heart, Bertrand felt he had let Cécile down. "There was my mother in front of a million people with a sign—'Justice, Not Charity'—like homeless people begging," he said. "I had promised her seven years before that she would not have to go out in public, and I like to keep my promises."

Months after the press conference when Cécile, Annette, and Yvonne consented to be interviewed for this book, Bertrand also agreed to tell his story. It was time, he said, not only to reveal what had happened to the quintuplets in their childhood, but also to show the effect that unnatural fishbowl upbringing had had on their adult lives and on their children's lives.

When did it start, this compulsion to fight back on his mother's behalf? Certainly all children have a natural sense of fairness when they are young. If they learn that their parents have been wronged, it marks their worldview in a defining way. Few, though, devote themselves entirely to fighting the injustices of a previous generation. The task looms too large, and the odds against winning are too insurmountable.

No one faced heavier odds than Bertrand. When he began researching his mother's past, he had no money, little education, and was not fluent in English, the language of the majority of materials concerning his mother's and aunts' history. It took several years before anyone even gave him an encouraging opinion on whether he would win any compensation for the quintuplets. Even then, he was advised to go after only the small amounts of money that were owed to the women for the unauthorized use of their pictures and names. No one believed Bertrand would ever get a hearing, let alone restitution, from the Ontario government—at least not until he met his first supporter in 1994.

Bertrand's fight for justice truly began back in 1970, when, as a boy of nine, he read in the newspaper that his aunt Marie had died and saw press photos of her with his mother and her two other sisters. Bertrand was then living in a foster home and had a habit of collecting empty pop bottles at the park after baseball games and returning them for a one-cent refund to buy candy. His mother was famous? How could that be? The boy knew Cécile to be poor and struggling, not rich and celebrated.

When he was ten and living with his mother again, he began to accompany her on walks after dinner. He understood that she was ill and wrapped in periods of sadness. She often stayed in her room and needed some activity to lift her energy and spirits. During one of these walks, Bertrand first asked about the mysterious circumstances of her glamorous past. So began the story that would later consume a decade of his life. Night after night, Cécile brought forth another piece of the puzzle, and by the time he was fifteen and a teacher asked, "How come you're a Dionne and you're dressed so badly?" he was burning inside at the injustice of what had been done to him and to his mother.

Bertrand's childhood probably should not have nurtured great loyalty. He was often separated from his mother and siblings, shunted from foster home to foster home, teased and picked on as a stranger at new schools. Yet he grew into a fiercely loyal and extremely compliant child. In fact, he was the child Cécile sent away first because she knew he was the most likely to accept the situation. Perhaps because he had lost his twin brother, Bruno, who died at fifteen months, he identified closely with his mother and her identical sisters. He accepted Cécile's explanation that she had to work to support them after his father left home, and that it was too much for her to keep a job and care for four children on her own. As he got older, his understanding only deepened. "I was never really mad at my mother. I always understood she had an abnormal life," he says.

His first placement was in a foster home in Quebec City, not far from the apartment to which Cécile had moved. He found the woman who ran the home strict—she had taken in too many children. Bertrand was not happy, but he trusted that his mother would find him a better home. She did, though at some personal cost. The wood-and-stone bungalow of Madame Gosselin on pastoral Ile d'Orléans, an hour and a half from Quebec City, offered Bertrand doting care and unfettered play. Madame Gosselin spoiled him with fresh strawberry pies, and encouraged his independence by allowing him to drive a tractor in the field.

But the trip to visit him was too long and costly for Cécile, and Bertrand was not happy at school. (Once, a teacher spotted him sucking his thumb during the bus ride home. The next day, the teacher brought a pacifier to school and made Bertrand use it in front of his classmates.) After a year, Cécile moved Bertrand to the home of Monsieur and Madame Boucher in Pont Rouge, near Quebec City. Looking back, Bertrand makes the surprising statement that he is grateful to Cécile for placing him there and giving him the opportunity to live in a normal family household, a situation he never knew in his mother's home.

At nine, however, he was moved again, this time to a group home where he spent a long, unhappy year in a strict environment. But it was close to Saint-Bruno, where Cécile had moved and was trying to set up house for all four children. The family was reunited when Bertrand was ten.

In those five years he spent separated from his family, Bertrand had lived an ironic reversal of his mother's young life. Although he was the son of a woman who was once treated like a princess, he had been the pauper boy shuttled from place to place. He came home to a loving, albeit troubled mother, at ten, practically the same age Cécile had been when she was thrust into a life with a mother she hardly knew.

On rejoining his brothers, sister, and mother, Bertrand had to learn responsibility quickly. He was the one Cécile relied on to go to the store for groceries. He learned how to fill in the amount on Cécile's signed blank cheques, and how to go to the bank—a child reaching up to the teller's wicket—to have her passbook brought up to date. One time, he saw that there was only one cent left in the account. He recalls feeling older than his ten years.

Eventually, Bertrand finished high school and went to work. He had already carried so much responsibility for so many years that he felt ready to ease Cécile's burden and make money on his own. At sixteen, he had a girlfriend and a job bagging groceries. At nineteen, he was living in Montreal, selling shoes by day and working as a bouncer at a discothèque at night. These were the free-wheeling 1980s, and the flashy Stanley Street disco, the Limelight, was a wildly popular club that also had a separate basement room where gay men met and danced together. At last, Bertrand came to an acceptance of himself. "It was the first time I saw people like me. It helped me to accept who I am, to know I'm not alone," he says.

Today he is open and comfortable about being gay. But he struggled with that identity for an uncommon reason: his father's homosexuality had deeply hurt his mother. Bertrand feared that being gay meant he was like Philippe, and he was ashamed of his father, not because of his sexual orientation, but because he treated his mother so badly. "At first I had to deal in my own mind with being homosexual. I knew my father was, and I felt I was not like my father in the way he was to my mother.... I felt alone about it. How will I ever tell Cécile? ... At age nineteen or twenty, I turned to tell her in the car at the very same time as she turned to me and asked if I was gay. I said no, but I don't know why I said no.... At sixteen, I was living with my girlfriend part time and I was having fun with her, but I was hiding myself to myself. I kept everything inside. I didn't want to hurt my mother." When they finally talked about it, Cécile accepted Bertrand's lifestyle without judgement.

About a year later, Bertrand began working in a downtown Montreal hotel as a doorman, a car jockey, a bellboy, and a part-time concierge. But he felt his life had no strong sense of purpose; then something clicked, and Bertrand began thinking again about his mother. "I realized that—in that part of my life that I had been living for me—I realized that Cécile had no money at all. I woke up." He decided he would start a quest for justice and security for Cécile. He was twenty-six years old.

Bertrand inherited the look characteristic of his grandfather Oliva: an intense gaze and a wiry physique that make him appear ready to spring into action. When he's at ease, laughter splits his features into a wide grin, but his casual uniform of jeans and T-shirts barely hides the determined personality within.

Before he could begin his campaign, he first had to clear his own debts. Meanwhile, he gave Cécile a few hundred dollars whenever he could, to help her get by. His efforts began randomly in 1991 as he cast about for more money for her. He tried to sell Cécile's wedding gown—the Montreal designer's fantasy of lace and seed pearls—offering it to the Dionne Quint Museum in North Bay, but he was told that its non-profit board had no money to buy either the dress or the bed she had used in her marriage. He next called General Motors and asked if they had a charity fund, explaining that the quintuplets, whom they had once used in advertisements to sell cars, were now poverty-stricken. He was told that the company did have a department that funded non-profit charities, but that their largesse did not extend to individuals.

"I had a feeling that the quints had been robbed," Bertrand said. He remembered that the NFB/CBC documentary he had seen had shown "all those people who went to see the quints, the big mansion, the nice dresses. I saw there was a lot of money over there." He needed more information to find out where that money had gone. Working discreetly from the hotel when he was on the night shift, and with the help of a co-worker, he would slip behind the front desk and send out faxes of requests for research and help. On Cécile's behalf, he wrote to the Children's Aid Society in Nipissing district on December 19, 1991. The agency director said they had no files on the Dionnes. He referred Bertrand to the Parry Sound district CAS, whose director wrote back that there was nothing to indicate "any involvement in the matters of the Dionne family" and referred Bertrand full circle to the Nipissing branch. Progress was going to be slow.

He wrote to the Archives of Ontario on January 29, 1992. It took a year for officials to respond with a list of the documents available in their Dionne files. He drove to Toronto, slept in his car overnight to avoid hotel costs, and began sifting through the roomful of archival material. He got copies of as many papers as possible.

Like a hound on the scent, Bertrand started digging up telling details in the most unusual places. In a library sale, he picked up a book on federal statistics of 1939 and noted huge differences in gasoline taxes (they'd been hiked to six to eight cents a gallon in Ontario during the years that the Dionnes drew an estimated 350,000 American travellers annually; this compared with Quebec's two- to three-cent tax for those same years). The Ontario government had clearly capitalized on the babies' popularity, and Bertrand was out to prove it owed them in return.

At this time, he was working at the hotel and devoting one day a week to helping his mother and aunts in Saint-Bruno. He did the grocery shopping and accompanied them to doctors' appointments. Any spare time he had was spent looking for a lawyer who would take the case on a contingency basis. He couldn't afford lawyers' hourly rates, so he offered instead to buy them dinner or a drink in exchange for an opinion or advice on who to see next. That interview style soon racked up charges on his credit cards, which were cut off for non-payment. His long-distance phone bills also soared, though Bertrand says that when he told the Bell Canada payment office he was doing research to help his mother, who was a Dionne quintuplet, credit was extended to him.

He was laid off work because of a back injury in 1993 and was evicted from his apartment because he couldn't pay the rent. By this time, the mounting pile of information he'd gathered from original documents, old press clippings, provincial annual reports, and more was all-consuming. He copied every relevant article and report, stacking up boxes of information that would later fill shelves, file cabinets, and most of the floor space of a room. At the same time, Yvonne was due to have her double hip operation and would need a lot of help, especially since Quebec hospitals were so short-staffed. Bertrand went to the hospital at 8 a.m. every day and stayed with Yvonne until she had dinner and fell asleep. He put off going back to work.

Circumstances were sweeping everything along in their path like a tsunami rushing in from the sea. Bertrand decided to go along with it and gamble on the biggest risk of his life:

he would devote all of his time, energy, and thoughts to the project and not return to his job. If he failed, he not only would have brought insurmountable debt on himself, but his mother and aunts would be devastated.

In May 1993, Bertrand had some good luck. He was referred to a Montreal lawyer, Daniel Payette, who specialized in intellectual property, a growing field in law based on the question of who owns ideas and images. Payette said Yvonne, Annette, and Cécile Dionne had a good chance of getting some income because any business, individual, club, or non-profit organization that sold products bearing the quintuplets' name or image, or even charged admission based on their name or image, owed a percentage of the money they earned to the sisters. Bertrand finally heard someone else say what he had believed for much of his life.

The mild-mannered Payette, meanwhile, knew he was on to something big when he got a phone call from his mother, Lise Payette, a prominent Quebec journalist, former politician, TV interviewer, and writer of spectacularly popular Quebec television dramas. This high-powered woman was not easily impressed by the personalities who sought legal counsel from her son. But this time was different. She told Payette that the Dionne quintuplets had been her idols when she was a girl growing up in a poor neighbourhood in Montreal. Payette, who had spent a decade practising law in Quebec and had clients who were popular literary figures and TV celebrities, is still amazed by the enduring fascination with the Dionnes. "These are the only ones my mother was impressed with," he says with significance.

Payette's career in law came after a ten-year stint as a sociology teacher at a local college. Now forty-six, he still conveys an academic aura, with his somewhat rumpled appearance and his soft-spoken, methodical manner. As soon as he met Payette, Bertrand believed that he'd found the right lawyer to pursue his case. For their first appointment, Bertrand arrived in worn jeans, carrying a bagful of ragtag articles that he spread across the lawyer's desk—paper cut-out dolls, pencils, pens, mugs, T-shirts—all bearing drawings or photographs of the five identical youngsters' faces. As he looked over the strange collection of goods, Payette told Bertrand that he had a winnable case.

Payette's father, André Payette, and his mother had both been CBC journalists in Paris for the French station Radio-Canada when he was born. Young Payette grew up and was educated in France during the quintuplets' most private years, and so had known little about the Dionne history. All he had heard recently about the three surviving sisters was that they had lived in virtual seclusion for more than twenty years. He was intrigued when Bertrand said that these same women would now be willing to do publicity interviews if necessary. Payette realized early on that, eventually, the women would have to take their story to the press.

But first, how to start bringing in some money for them to ease their desperate straits? At the time, none of the women was able to work. Annette had discovered she had epilepsy, and had recently mortgaged her house to help her son pay off a bank loan. Cécile had moved in with her because she was broke, was suffering from a painfully deteriorating hip, and was slipping into a depression. Yvonne was also becoming immobilized by two damaged hips and was expected to join her sisters after her surgery in the fall.

Payette decided that his first move was to get control of the women's image rights, copyrights, and name usage. All of the appearances and endorsements they'd made as children had been arranged by their guardians through legal contracts that stipulated a rate of payment for the rights. Those contracts were still in operation, but only a few businesses and organizations using their names or images had sent reports or money to the women's guardians or trust account since 1955, when they turned twenty-one, and none had sent anything since 1957.

Payette's instruction from the three survivors was to regain their rights without initiating any lawsuits, which they didn't want and couldn't afford. So he decided that the only way to force businesses to honour these contracts might be through the threat of the publicity that would come with a court action. Thus Payette began the first act in a logical, step-by-step process that had the most modest of beginnings.

On behalf of Yvonne, Annette, and Cécile Dionne, the lawyer sent a letter to the Dionne Quint Museum asking for a percentage of income from ticket sales and from sales of items bearing their likenesses or names. As with every letter he would eventually send out, the lawyer stressed that the sisters wished to settle their rights without making a claim for the past. "We could sue you for the past, but we will not if you respect their rights in the future," he wrote.

Though the women were living in a quiet town outside Montreal, their life story seemed destined to pick up steam again in faraway North Bay. Just as it had been with their sensational birth, the *North Bay Nugget* was first off the mark.

And it all started with an unlikely report from a 1993 civic meeting during which the town council discussed the women's request for modest payment for the use of their names and images by the museum.

The reporter covering that meeting wrote about the request in the next day's paper. Stories from the *Nugget* are regularly sent electronically to the Canadian Press, an agency that supplies articles to ninety-six member newspapers across the country, but rarely do items about civic business make it beyond the Ontario news desk. That night, however, the CP editor in charge recognized a bigger national story in the local report.

Back in 1934, CP was called a "newswire operation," a term that's been made obsolete by the emergence of the silicon chip. Then, the story of the Dionnes' birth had been communicated by telegraph and transmitted worldwide by copper wire. Sixty years later, news of their present situation travelled by satellite. In the flash of time it takes for communication between linked computers, the surviving sisters' request for compensation from the museum that bore their name had reached every major city in Canada and scores of smaller ones as well. From then on, as the sisters' quest grew, the small-town newspaper that had been there from the very beginning stayed on top of the story, like a beacon highlighting for the national press the enduring significance of the quintuplets to Canada.

Before long, an agreement was reached with the museum — ten percent of its revenue now goes to the sisters. The same deal was negotiated with manufacturers of Dionne memorabilia in the North Bay area. The amounts coming in were small, but Payette's strategy was to build a fund that would pay for the cost of going after bigger fish.

Payette had taken the case on a contingency basis, an arrangement that is allowed under Quebec's legal system, which is different in its origins from that of the rest of Canada. He and his law partner liked to take on a few of these riskier cases as a service to clients who otherwise couldn't afford to hire them. Referring to the Dionne case, he says, "We absolutely don't know if any money will come of it.... We'll be methodical and see where the money is available most quickly. And build on that to get more documents and go after bigger areas."

Payette started with Canada, but eventually finalized contractual arrangements in the United States, Great Britain, France, and Australia as well. The bulk of the deals centred on the use of old film footage taken of the quintuplets as babies and children. Two major American film companies—Fox-Movitone, which later became Twentieth Century Fox, and Pathé News Inc., which was eventually bought by the eccentric American billionaire Howard Hughes—had acquired from the guardians exclusive film rights to the five girls. Payette analysed all of the contracts made on the girls' behalf from 1935 through the 1940s, focusing especially on those made for films and newsreels.

Film rights are financially lucrative. Usually, the film company that holds the copyright on footage charges $100 to $150 a minute for its use. Even cases where five- to six-minute clips had been used in documentaries would prove important to Payette's mounting war chest. But getting compensation wasn't easy. So much time had passed that some businesses assumed they were the sole owners of their past files, photos, and films, and Payette was largely unsuccessful with the American film companies. Payette's partner, Chantal Carbonneau, says, "We were told that the archives [which originally belonged to Pathé News] were assigned to CNN. However, CNN denied this information. We were then unable to negotiate any agreement. We had negotiations with Twentieth Century Fox in 1994 but were unable to conclude any agreement. We also sent a formal notice to NEA [Newspaper Enterprises of America] but without any response. Since our clients didn't want to take legal procedures, we suspended our file."

In Canada, meanwhile, Payette went after the National Film Board, which had made *The Dionne Quintuplets* with the CBC in 1978 using footage from the 1930s and early 1940s. According to Payette, the NFB and the CBC had bought their archives from many sources, including a Los Angeles-based film library that owns the three Hollywood movies made with the quintuplets. Other footage was found in a government file and used without seeking anyone's permission, Payette discovered.

The NFB subsequently made video cassettes of its documentary and sold them in response to media requests for archival footage. Payette told the film board that the Dionnes were willing to forgo any share of past sales, but he insisted that they authorize each future sale, and that they receive royalties of ten percent on those. He says he spent close to fifteen hours over a six-month period in negotiations with government lawyers for the NFB, but in the end he won their cooperation on a deal.

The CBC, however, which is a public broadcaster and, like the NFB, under the jurisdiction of the federal department of Canadian heritage, refused Payette's demands. He argued his case with CBC lawyers, but never reached an agreement. The CBC insisted that its archives were its own property for its own use, and that its material originally came from the National Archives of Canada. Payette countered that since there was no CBC television network in existence in 1934 (CBC radio started in 1936, CBC-TV in 1952), the company had no footage that was originally its own.

The CBC asserted that the newsreels were public information to which the Canadian public had rights. "Like all public figures, the Dionnes were filmed because they were part of the news. That puts the film into the public domain," says director of business affairs Liz Jenner. According to Payette, the Crown corporation remains the only business that refused his request for a percentage of royalties for the women from the archival newsreels.

When their months of dispute ended in a stand-off, Payette advised Bertrand, and later Carlo Tarini, the sisters' media advisor, not to grant any interviews to the CBC. They followed that advice until early 1998, when the Canadian media grabbed hold of the Dionne story and the two men decided to accept all the hard news coverage they could get, including by the CBC.

Even before all this happened, Bertrand had read in a newspaper that Cinar, a Montreal filmmaking company, was planning to make *Million Dollar Babies*, a TV miniseries about the quintuplets (based on a 1986 fictionalized account of their childhood, *The Time of Their Lives*, by John Nihmey and Stuart Foxman). When Payette heard about it, he knew that he had a chance to win the first decent cash award for the women, and that he could earn enough to pay for making future deals. Fortunately, Cinar's lawyer was a specialist in copyright law, and the two quickly came to an agreement. According to Payette, "She saw that it was better to do the film with the Dionnes and not against them."

The deal Payette arranged brought in around $100,000. A salary of $8000 was separately arranged for Bertrand, for his role as caretaker and driver for the three women, who were checking the script. The money paid off his credit cards, but he still needed occasional handouts from Yvonne when he couldn't afford his rent or food. Nevertheless, he was beginning to see some light ahead after three years of reaching out in the dark.

In total, the small contracts with the museum, memorabilia manufacturers, the NFB, and the like eventually brought in some $35,000 a year. Payette gets fifteen percent of that and the rest is divided into equal shares for the quintuplets. The $8-million, four-hour miniseries, licensed by Cinar to the CBC in Canada and to CBS in the United States, aired in 1994. Each of the women received close to $20,000 for her cooperation with that project.

Like a skilled conductor, Payette orchestrated a position from which the Dionnes could proceed to bigger and better things. He travelled to Cannes, France, to meet with producers from Britain's BBC, and eventually convinced them to do a documentary on the three sisters. Though this would mean only a small amount of cash, it would start to bring the sisters' current situation into public view.

While international publicity was helpful in alerting Canadian media to the enduring worldwide interest in the sisters, Payette still felt that Canada was where the story had to be told. He tapped into interest from the Quebec publishing house Libre Expression, and Jean-Yves Soucy was signed to write a book that would both bring in revenue and, hopefully, arouse public indignation over what had happened to the quintuplets in the past. "At that time ... there was publicity for the book in French Canada," remembers Payette. "Carlo [Tarini] was retained by the publisher. I said the most important part now was not the lawyer but public relations."

Carlo Tarini's audacious flair came to him early in his career. At twenty-five, unknown, and virtually clueless about computer technology, he had scored big by getting Bill Gates, the co-founder and chairman of Microsoft, to endorse a new computer product made by Ogivar Technologies, a client of Tarini's. In fact, Ogivar was only the second client Tarini had managed to sign on to a recently launched solo business. "I was always an entrepreneur at heart," he remarks. "I have the psychological profile: a lack of respect for authority and a conviction that I'm always right. It's a similar profile to juvenile delinquents." The statement is vintage Tarini: bold, irreverent, ambitious, with just enough self-deprecation and humour to catch the listener off guard. This style would later prove crucial to Cécile, Annette, and Yvonne Dionne.

In 1985, Ogivar was the first Canadian computer company after Compaq in the U.S. to come up with a new kind of 386-based PC, or personal computer. Tarini's gut instinct told him that this was a major breakthrough for a homegrown company. The problem was that Microsoft was still in the process of developing the software it required, and in the meantime the trade press was ignoring the new computer.

In 1986, Tarini arranged a seminar for Ogivar, invited top corporate buyers like Bell Canada, and tried to get Bill Gates to attend. He rented the tony Ritz-Carleton hotel in Montreal and the Westin Harbour Castle in Toronto, blowing the full year's marketing budget. The Toronto-based general manager of Microsoft Canada said he would come to the seminar, but doubted that Gates would show up. He himself had yet to meet the company's legendary leader, though he'd been with Microsoft for several years.

Undeterred, Tarini sent messages, letters, and a packet of information to the vice-president of international marketing in Seattle, as well as to Gates himself. Tarini recounts his strategy, savouring every detail although more than a decade has passed: "The seminar was slated for January and it's now December and I'm still working on trying to get Bill Gates. It's near Christmastime. I go out and buy a pair of black business shoes, cheap. I ask for two shoeboxes and put one each in a box wrapped in bright Christmas paper—I figured that would make sure it got to them—with a covering letter titled 'How to Get Your Foot in the Door.' I send one to Gates and one to the international marketing guy in Seattle and FedEx them. The VP called and said, 'We got your package.' He said that Bill would be in Spain at that time and couldn't come but that he supported the project.

"I jumped on it and offered to come right away with a video crew and film Gates giving a message as to where the company is at with developing the software." Forty-eight hours later, the twenty-five-year-old Tarini was in Seattle, setting up his video equipment in a conference room and preparing to tape a salute to Ogivar.

"[Gates] didn't show till two hours late. He said, 'You're the guy who sent the shoes. Very clever. We need good marketing guys; you should think about it.' Then he reads my notes for two minutes and repeated ninety-nine percent of it on the video. I wrote the French translation phonetically, and he read it. At the seminars, it was announced that although Bill Gates couldn't attend, he would have loved to be there. At that moment, Gates suddenly appeared on a giant screen speaking in both French and English." Tarini says, "We signed a lot of sales that day." The use of "we" is a clue. It was Tarini's client that made the sales, but when Tarini's on the job, he's *in* it.

Jumping from this brief, heady encounter and the instant success it brought to years of knocking on closed doors on behalf of three desperate women would not seem a natural move for a hustling marketing strategist. But Tarini got caught up by their story.

Born in Quebec to Italian parents, Tarini remembers that the story of the Dionne quintuplets was the first book he ever read in English, in a junior high school Great Canadian Stories course. "When I met them for the first time, it was like meeting major stars. I was impressed, respectful of who they are.... I was meeting a part of Canadian history," he recalls.

By the time Tarini met Cécile, Yvonne, and Annette, it was 1994 and he'd developed Impact Communication Marketing, a successful specialty marketing agency for high-tech companies. Impact operates out of a spacious five-room office-condo that Tarini owns in a renovated building with brick interior walls and pine wood doors in fashionable Old Montreal. He has four full-time staff as well as freelance technical writers, translators, and coordinators.

His unusual diversion from the computer world into the world of the Dionnes came through a friend, an author who got him into marketing for some writers and for Libre Expression. The company needed help launching *Family Secrets*. Because of the book's subject matter, requests for interviews were coming in from the English-speaking media, and the publisher called on Tarini because he is fluent in both English and French.

Tarini soon learned that the Dionne women had told the controversial story of their teenage years to Jean-Yves Soucy because "they needed money for groceries, and they shared the royalties with Soucy." The book sold about forty thousand copies in Quebec, he says. Sales in English Canada were negligible, which Tarini says was due to poor distribution. But the publicity blitz he created sparked a huge media response in Quebec, and the story was picked up on newswire services. Excerpts ran in *La Presse*, the Montreal-based French-language daily newspaper. Canada's national newspaper, *The Globe and Mail*, ran a front-page story about the book's launch and mentioned the allegations of sexual abuse.

To prepare the women to give press interviews, Tarini spent a good deal of time with them. His facility with the media impressed them, and was noticed as well by Bertrand. As the two men became friendly, Bertrand began to tell Tarini about the research he'd been doing. "Bertrand started telling me that the real story of the Dionne family is about Ontario government intervention and the mismanagement of their trust fund. Plus the government used their trust money even to pay for toilet paper at Quintland.

"At first I doubted it; it was too strange to be true. Bertrand came with a huge green suitcase [full of archival material].... I brought it all home to look at the financial documents. I see the toilet paper listed. The building [costs]. The quintuplets paid for their own jail."

Tarini repeats the story as he learned it, and the fire of indignation that fuelled his efforts to help the women is rekindled. His emotions break through in expressive hand gestures and the rapid-fire delivery of facts. Yet that passion did not obscure his vision of how he personally could fit into the picture. He realized it was a chance to do something he believed in and make his mark at the same time—an opportunity Tarini was not about to miss.

He soon gained the trust of the quintuplets, and was delegated the family's media spokesperson. All media requests, quotes from the women, arrangements for a lawyer, etc., went through him. Initially, of course, Bertrand had no money to offer him, but Tarini wasn't fazed. For the first months, he worked on the file as a volunteer, with the understanding that if the sisters ever won compensation from the government, he'd get paid.

It was not long before Tarini realized that the project, which had quickly become a full-time job, would be no shoo-in, but a frustrating series of closed doors. Yet Bertrand had seen at the Soucy book launch that Tarini had what was needed: the combination of easy schmooze and hard sell that worked with Quebec television and print reporters. For his part, Tarini knew that in the Dionnes, he had the goods that would grab the media. "It's a phenomenal story. These are three ordinary-seeming women. What makes them extraordinary? They were born as extraordinary, treated that way. And then dropped."

After Tarini sent press releases promoting Soucy's book to the U.S. national networks, NBC's *Dateline* contacted him. An assistant producer came to Montreal to look into filming the three sisters, but she found them too uncomfortable speaking in English on camera. She decided not to go ahead. Next, a CBS reporter came and interviewed the women for a morning breakfast show, live by satellite. The sisters appeared ill at ease. Tarini realized he had his work cut out for him if he was going to continue promoting the women to the media.

At the same time, Daniel Payette was recommending to Bertrand that he would have to hire an Ontario lawyer if he wanted to go after the provincial government. Payette felt he could go no further than to send an opening letter to then-premier Bob Rae, which he did in late 1994. The Quebec lawyer was not involved in the women's later negotiations with the Ontario government, and so did not share in their eventual settlement. But Bertrand credits Payette with having taken a big gamble at the start. The risk he took opened the door in a case that others had declared impossible to win.

13: JUSTICE, NOT CHARITY

IN THE EARLY 1990S, Bertrand was bolstered by public reaction to a notorious Quebec child-abuse scandal that was known as the case of the Duplessis children. These were children who had been wrongly placed, and frequently physically and sexually abused, in psychiatric facilities when Maurice Duplessis was premier of Quebec (from 1936 to 1939 and again from 1944 to 1959). His was an autocratic, repressive era referred to as the *grande noirceur*, or the Great Darkness.

For Bertrand, public compassion for these children, who as adults had begun telling their stories in the press, was a positive sign for his own cause. Some three thousand surviving former inmates of the institutions had been seeking compensation and apologies from the government, the church, and the medical profession. Their stories were chilling. In the 1940s and 1950s, the numbers of children in orphanages had swelled. At the time, federal government subsidies for psychiatric patients were, at $2.50 a day, far more generous than provincial education grants of seventy-five cents for orphans. The federal allotment was available only for medical institutions, so religious groups that were in debt or simply seeking more funds had their orphanages redesignated as asylums for the mentally retarded—with the province's blessing.

Thousands of Quebec children, the majority of whom were born to unmarried mothers and considered social outcasts in the arch-conservative, church-dominated society, were spirited away to these asylums and committed. Orphans and children from destitute families also ended up there, all falsely diagnosed as insane or retarded. They were released in the 1960s after Duplessis' Union Nationale government was finally defeated.

The widespread publicity sparked by a 1991 book, *Les Enfants de Duplessis*, brought to light an ugly complicity between politicians, physicians, and religious leaders. The scandal struck a chord with Bertrand. He saw similarities to what had happened to the quintuplets, who had been damaged by the wilful acts of politicians and medical professionals, and poorly served by clergy who did nothing to interfere.

Watching the controversy mount in Quebec, Bertrand felt certain that he was also on track to win a settlement—without resorting to a lawsuit—from the government of Ontario, which was then being led by Premier Bob Rae and his socialist New Democratic party. The first letter to Rae was written by Payette on November 11, 1994, and signed by Cécile, Annette, and Yvonne. In it, the sisters said, "We were a scientific curiosity, an object of exploitation for tourists, and we still carry the effects of that life.... We have suffered all our life.... We are asking for compensation for past and present suffering." On December 13, Rae responded that his attorney-general, Marion Boyd, had their file and would communicate with the women soon. Payette then wrote to Boyd. After more than a month had passed, the quintuplets wrote again to Rae and said that they hadn't yet heard from anyone about the case.

When Louise Hurteau, the lawyer for the attorney-general, finally contacted Payette, he advised Bertrand that it was time to seek the help of Ontario counsel. He also expressed the opinion that it was unlikely the women would get more than $120,000 from the government—a figure he based on individual settlements that had been made with Canadians of Japanese descent who were interned by the federal government during the Second World War. It was an opinion Bertrand simply would not accept.

With no funds to pay another lawyer, Bertrand tried to proceed alone. He wrote Hurteau on March 15, 1995, then blanketed her with papers supporting his case, including a list of contracts that had been made by Ontario officials on behalf of the Dionne quintuplets, as well as a passing of accounts by Judge Plouffe that indicated the guardians were spending close to half of the profits. He sent quotes from Dr. William Blatz's book *The Five Sisters*, in which the scientist refers to 500,000 visitors coming to see the girls. He included the *North Bay Nugget* of December 4, 1936, in which Welfare Minister David Croll, then in charge of the children, said they were "the best industry any town can have," drawing tourists from across the continent. Croll also said that "millions" had been spent by visitors to the town in the last season.

Bertrand added excerpts from the *Collected Studies on the Dionne Quintuplets*, written by a team of scientists headed by Dr. Blatz, in which it is said that "the Dionne quintuplets are becoming aware of the crowds gathered to watch them." Dr. Dafoe says in the preface that, before the study, the girls had "reached the stage at which they were equal to normal children in hardihood." He also included a copy of Pierre Berton's book

The Dionne Years and a recent letter of support from the author that began, "The Ontario government owes an enormous unpaid debt to the Dionne quintuplets, who were exploited shamelessly in the 1930s for the benefit of the tourist trade."

Warming to his own fury over the story, Bertrand added his personal opinion that the treatment of the quintuplets by the government had been "an indignity against the human race." This last bit, in French, was in capital letters—which is, as any frequent recipient of critical mail knows, a signal that the writer's frustration has reached the boiling point.

In sum, Bertrand said it was time that the government of Ontario recognized what was owed to the women. He asked for $10 million on their behalf and topped the packet of papers with a picture of the five little girls clowning for photographers with their hands up in the air as if they are being robbed. (That amount, Bertrand now says, was a starting point for negotiations. Later, on advice, he dropped the specific figure and left it open to negotiation.) A copy of the entire missive was also sent to Premier Rae.

Whether it was the red flag of angry capital letters, the mound of facts, or the fat sum requested that aroused attention, Boyd replied to the weighty letter on April 11, 1995, saying that Hurteau would look into the matter and make a recommendation to the attorney-general. Hurteau then phoned Bertrand and asked for more specific details of how the compensation money would be used. She said she would meet with him herself on behalf of Boyd, whose schedule was too busy to allow for an appointment.

Bertrand travelled to Toronto on May 24, 1995, for the meeting. He later recalled the situation with humour: a young man with no money in his pockets, wandering the downtown streets asking passers-by how to find Ontario's legislative buildings. Two different people sent him in the wrong direction.

But Bertrand eventually found his way, and walked into the lawyer's office with detailed requests in hand. He also hand-delivered a second copy of the entire package of background material to Rae's office, to assure himself that the premier received it. He told Hurteau that he wanted a $700,000 house for all three sisters to live in, to be built in a choice location. He had found a parcel of land in the Saint-Bruno mountain area and priced the construction through a Laval, Quebec, firm. In addition, he asked for $1 million for each of Cécile, Yvonne, and Annette, plus $5000 a month for each of them for the rest of their lives.

He had figured it this way: The house had to be big enough for all three to live with privacy from each other. The lump sum payment of $1 million each would secure the women financially so that they'd never again fear a lack of money. And the $60,000 a year per sister would cover their bills and travel expenses. Bertrand left the meeting under the impression that Hurteau would recommend that the Rae government agree to the house, the cash, and the monthly stipend. She later phoned him and said that his request was reasonable. By June, however, the Rae government was no longer in charge.

An election campaign had been under way in Ontario in May 1995. Never neglecting to cover all bases, Bertrand had written to Mike Harris, the leader of the Progressive Conservative party, and asked for his support. On May 25, 1995, Harris,

269

whose political riding is in North Bay, wrote back, "As a resident of North Bay, I am familiar with and have sympathy for the situation experienced by the sisters throughout their childhood. I understand negotiations are currently under way with the Ontario Government. If I am in a position to be able to address this issue following the upcoming provincial election, please be assured that your concern and request on behalf of the Dionne sisters will be given our full attention."

Two weeks later, Harris *was* in a position to help, having won the election and become premier of the province—just as the Liberal Mitchell Hepburn had done fifty years earlier on a promise to curb spending. Nevertheless, due to Harris's promise to help the sisters, Tarini thought they'd struck gold at last. "I said, 'Don't worry, this will be done in three months.' Harris is the guy whose marketing campaign was 'I keep my promises.'"

But the new government was even worse than the old one when it came to getting back to people. It wasn't until September 8, 1995, that Bertrand received a letter from Louise Hurteau, now acting for the new government. She asked for an accounting of what the three sisters received as income, their monthly expenses, their health reports, and the costs of the house they would construct if they received compensation.

The delays were dragging out, so Bertrand let Hurteau know that if he didn't get a firm answer from the government in six months, he'd take the matter, which he had kept confidential so far, to the media. The following February, when his patience had run out, Bertrand learned that Hurteau was on maternity leave. He wrote the department warning that he required a response by February 23, 1996, or he'd go public. He heard back from Kim Twohig, a lawyer for the new attorney-general, Charles Harnick, who had worked on the case with Hurteau; she told him that the settlement he'd requested was too high. Bertrand thought it was just another stall. He wrote Premier Harris on April 10, 1996, saying that nothing was yet settled.

Meanwhile, he and Tarini turned their attention towards retaining a lawyer who had easy access to the right government officials. Tarini, who devours national and local newspapers with his breakfast, knew of Clayton Ruby's reputation as a human-rights lawyer who takes on difficult, controversial cases and is able to garner widespread publicity. He contacted him. Ruby, however, recommended another Toronto lawyer, Bill McMurtry, whom he felt was a better choice for insider negotiations with the newly elected government. McMurtry was the brother of the former attorney-general, Roy McMurtry, who had been a prominent Tory politician and was currently the chief justice of Ontario. Bill McMurtry, who considers himself a Red Tory, which is to say a liberal-minded Conservative, was not a man who backed off from trying to change government thinking on issues.

At first glance, McMurtry said it looked like an easy assignment. He sent out a long letter requesting some movement on the settlement and an answer by May 28, 1996. He never heard back, and when he tried to reach government lawyers and aides, his calls went unanswered.

Premier Harris finally replied to Bertrand on July 22, 1996. He apologized for the delay and assured him that "the Government of Ontario is fully prepared to enter into discussions with the Dionne sisters regarding the possibility of compensation." Harris added that the Crown law office would give the matter its complete attention.

Nothing more was heard for a year.

As time dragged on, with no movement on the government's part, McMurtry was faced with a decision. According to Tarini, the lawyer made it clear that he couldn't continue with the case if the ultimate goal was to sue the government. McMurtry, a well-known litigation lawyer, had represented the government in the past and expected to do so again in the future. In effect, he wished to avoid suing his own potential client. He offered instead to mediate the matter, but government officials continued to stonewall him. In the end, McMurty wrote Tarini that he and Bertrand had no choice but to take the plight of the surviving Dionne quintuplets to the media.

Bertrand had nothing left to lose. He had lost his car in the fall of 1997 because he couldn't meet the payments on a loan. And he was evicted yet again in December 1997 because he couldn't afford his rent. He moved to a run-down flat over a store in a working-class Montreal neighbourhood.

In searching the file that Bertrand had created, including yellowed and faded newspaper clippings, Tarini had discovered that the *North Bay Nugget* had been the most consistent in its treatment of Dionne news as an important story. During his research in 1996, he called John Tollefsrud, a reporter who had written about the women from time to time, and told him that the sisters were pursuing a settlement and an inquiry. The reporter and Tarini kept in touch. Tollefsrud's stories, which were sent out nationally by Canadian Press, moved other newspaper and broadcast reporters to start taking more interest in the Dionnes' plight.

By 1997, fed up with the governement's stonewalling, Tarini called Tollefsrud again and urged him to try to get answers from the government himself. Tarini credits the reporter with exposing the province's delaying tactics when he quoted Brendan Crawley, the communications officer for Attorney-General Harnick, as saying that the Dionne case was "under active consideration." Tarini and Bertrand watched for something to happen. Nothing changed.

Tarini was certain that the fight would be played out in the court of public opinion and that the government would have to act. But the Canadian press was unexpectedly slow to go all out on the women's story. Says Tarini, "I tried early on. I sent out so many packages to national news reporters and national news desks, trying to interest them in the facts of the sisters' exploitation. I sent copies of reports highlighting what had happened."

It seemed to Tarini that the miniseries *Million Dollar Babies* had already burned the story and negated its impact. "People thought they knew it all from watching that show. They didn't connect that it was an entertainment package, not factual news, and it wasn't up to date." Frustrated, Tarini turned to the market that had responded before. He once again approached the big U.S. networks: NBC, ABC, and CBS. If he was able to connect with them as he had done just two years earlier, their coverage would kick-start the Canadian media.

Producers at ABC's *PrimeTime Live* were the first to say yes. Tarini studied their ratings versus those of CBS's *60 Minutes* and decided to proceed with the ABC newsmagazine show. His instincts were right on. Spurred by advance promotion of the episode, which was to run on November 26, 1997, Canadian newspapers and magazines began to print detailed feature stories about the Dionnes.

On the night of the *PrimeTime Live* broadcast, McMurtry—who by then was off the case—received a fax from the government stating that the province wanted to set up a fund to cover research into children's issues in the name of the Dionnes. McMurtry sent the information to Tarini, who fired back a letter to Attorney-General Harnick saying that idea was nice, but it still didn't address the issue of the public inquiry.

When the three women appeared on the popular U.S. show, Cécile Dionne told interviewer Sylvia Chase that the fairy-tale story of their childhood had never been true, that after being used by the government to make money, they were left poor in their later adult years. The sisters were beginning to open up on camera, in English.

The day after the broadcast, November 27, Brendan Crawley told reporters that the government was not going to compensate the surviving Dionne quintuplets because their adult circumstances had nothing to do with their exploitation as children. Harnick added that he had great sympathy for the women, and that the government was looking for some kind of gesture to recognize their "historical role."

Tarini realized that the government was trying to put a negative spin on the story, trying to make it seem that the women wanted money without adequate reason. So he turned the spin around, putting the focus on the sisters' request for a public inquiry. He stressed that the money they were after was their own, and that it had been stolen from their trust account while they were still bringing in a fortune for the province.

Media interest heated up. Tarini saw a chance to grab some of the spotlight being directed at the much-publicized November 19, 1997, birth of septuplets—the result of fertility drugs—to Bobbi and Kenny McCaughey in Iowa. He assumed correctly that the story would be a cover article in that week's edition of *Time*, so he called the magazine and spoke to a researcher, who told him the gifts had already started to come in to the McCaughey family. "It was already sounding like the Dionne story all over again," Tarini said. He sent a package of background information on the Dionne quintuplets, which prompted editors to ask for a message of advice from the sisters.

Their message, in the form of a letter to the parents, appeared in the December 1 issue of the magazine. Signed by Annette, Cécile, and Yvonne Dionne, it reads, in part, "Our lives have been ruined by the exploitation we suffered at the hands of the government of Ontario.... We sincerely hope a lesson will be learned from examining how our lives were forever altered by our childhood experience."

Newsweek was next. Tarini called the competing weekly U.S. news magazine and set up a phone interview with the women that resulted in a full-page story in a similar issue on the septuplets. The publicity was starting to pay off. Thanks to the renewed international interest, the Canadian media finally caught on. News reports, feature stories, and editorials sprang up in the English and French press, in big cities and small towns, in newspapers and magazines.

After months of not responding to the many inquiries that Tarini made, Attorney-General Harnick finally phoned him. Tarini recalls, "It was 5:05 p.m. on a weeknight, raining hard, when most people would have left their office. I told Harnick, 'It's about time you called, after the twenty-five messages I left you.'"

But Harnick's words were not encouraging. Tarini remembers being told by the attorney-general that the request for a settlement for the surviving Dionne quintuplets was "without merit," that the women would be better served by a lawyer than by Tarini, and that "an inquiry wouldn't be in their best interest." Tarini shot back that the three women couldn't afford a lawyer because of their impoverished state.

A day later, Tarini read a Canadian Press report that said Harnick had talked to him for an hour. "An hour? I timed it at seven or eight minutes!" Tarini fired off some 150 pages of archival documents to Harnick to show a sample of what an inquiry would reveal.

The following day, December 5, 1997, he received a letter from acting Deputy Attorney-General Andromache Karakatsanis saying that the Ontario government would pay for the cost of a lawyer to represent Yvonne, Annette, and Cécile Dionne in their further negotiations with the government. Tarini had just the person in mind. He called Clayton Ruby, and this time convinced the lawyer that he was needed. Moreover, Ruby agreed to take the case at the government rate of $192 an hour—less than half what he normally charges.

Tarini wrote back to Harnick that Ruby was the Dionnes' legal representative, then immediately read in the newspapers that the province would pay the women's legal fees. The leak was a clear signal to the marketing man: "Finally, we were getting somewhere."

In an interview in the trendy Montreal restaurant Prima Donna—Italian in name, art deco in décor, Japanese on the menu—Tarini tucks into his sushi with the same gusto he brings to his story. This is the part he relishes most—the period between late 1997 and 1998, when he and the international media engaged in a publicity dance choreographed beyond his wildest dreams. Not even Tarini was always sure which side was leading and which was following.

In December, as the Canadian media turned up its coverage of the story, Harnick said in the legislature that the Dionnes had no legal entitlement to a settlement but that the government was looking at "the moral issue." So when Tarini received an interview request from the nationally distributed *Globe and Mail*, he invited reporter Estanislao Oziewicz to his office and opened up the mass of files he and Bertrand had collected to show that there was far more than a moral issue involved. On December 22, 1997, a front-page story in the *Globe* detailed the Ontario government's involvement with the quintuplets and revealed that the Archives of Ontario were missing the minutes of guardianship meetings from 1934 to 1937.

The story also highlighted an incident that was first described by Pierre Berton in his book twenty years earlier but never resolved: David Croll, the welfare minister who had been appointed to oversee the quintuplets' wardship, had refused after resigning from that role to hand back to government officials his records of the contracts and negotiations he had handled on the children's behalf. Croll later burned these records.

Two national TV networks pursued Tarini for their investigative magazine shows, the CBC for *The National Magazine* and CTV for *W5*. He gave the nod to *W5* when the program offered to pay for a forensic audit, albeit a non-exhaustive one, of the Dionne quintuplets' trust fund account based on documents that filled one room of the province's official archives.

In February 1998, *W5* hired forensic accountant Frank Vettese to dig through fifty boxes of files on the girls' guardianship. Interviewed by reporter Rosemarie Thompson, who was tenaciously following the Dionne story, Vettese estimated that the province owed the women $2 to $3 million just for charges to their trust account. He also said that when he factored in the rejected $1-million New York World's Fair contract, the monies owed to the quintuplets added up to a grand total of $22 million in today's dollars.

A blizzard of news coverage occurred in early 1998, sparked alternately by both sides. Harnick's office told the press of a meeting between Ruby and the attorney-general, but Ruby said no such meeting took place. (The lawyer says he had only three minutes with the deputy attorney-general.) Premier Harris, when scrummed by reporters, said an offer was on the table. Ruby went public with the news that there was no offer. Harnick scheduled a meeting with Ruby, but then rescheduled it. Tarini countered by telling reporters exactly where and when the two men were to meet, and revealing that the purpose of the meeting was to come to a deal. "I say 8 a.m., Ruby's place. At 7:45 Harnick walks in. The news crews are all there with their mikes. They wait him out. An hour later he comes out. No deal. I tell Bertrand and he tells Cécile. It's a major let-down."

Tarini goes on: "We were becoming a pain in the ass to Harris. Bertrand goes on TV with a *North Bay Nugget* newspaper clipping from years ago that says Harris's father held an option to purchase the Big House at a greatly diminished price from its original cost. The *New York Times* is on to the story. This story is not going away. Harris was being scrummed all over the map."

Harris blasted the media for bringing his elderly and ailing father's name into the picture. The premier stressed that Deane Harris's involvement in the late 1950s had been on behalf of a local tourist operators' association he had headed, and had fallen through in the end. Harris's father, a Lake Nipissing resort owner, had in late 1958 urged local politicians to pay $32,000 for the mansion plus its three satellite buildings and 9.7 acres of land and then develop it as a district museum, including "a Dionne Memorial Wing" to draw tourists. But nothing came of the idea, Harris's option eventually expired, and the home was sold to a nursing home operator. An indignant Premier Harris told reporters, "Here is a gentleman who I guess because he is the father of the premier—eighty-four years old and not very well, recovering from chemotherapy—unfair and untrue and actually slanderous allegations are being made.... He had an option, the option expired. He lost the $50, the $100, whatever you lose on behalf of an option, on behalf of the tourist industry in the area."

But at last an offer of compensation came. The government brought in a high-profile lawyer from outside its own legal department, the treasurer of the Ontario Law Society, Harvey Strosberg. He met with Ruby and presented him with an offer of $2000 a month for each of Cécile, Yvonne, and

Annette. In exchange, the women had to sign a waiver that freed the government from legal responsibility. And there was a gag order: If the offer was revealed to the media, it would become void. Tarini calls it "the silent offer." Ruby faxed it to him, he faxed a copy to Bertrand, the three sisters turned it down flat.

Tarini recalls, "In a conference call I spoke to Cécile. I said, 'Three months ago Harnick said there'd be no money. Now it's $2000 a month each.' Cécile said, 'It's nowhere near what's owed and I want an inquiry.' [Annette and Yvonne concurred.] Ruby and I explained the danger of refusing. Two weeks before, Harris had said there'd be no inquiry because, he said, by the time there would be a report the women would be dead. Now they turn around and offer them $2000 a month for life. How short a life were they expecting?"

It was time for a bolder strategy. Tarini suggested they go public with a press conference. Ruby decided to stage it at the Queen's Park media centre—right under the Tories' noses. Tarini arranged for a Liberal MPP to book the room under the topic of children's issues, to keep the real purpose of the press conference under wraps.

At this point, Tarini had to weigh his instinct for a tell-all dramatic move against his personal knowledge of the women's reluctance to expose their situation publicly. True, they had told the story of their unhappy childhood in a book just a few years earlier. But they had not revealed that their adult lives had fallen apart, and that they were living in unconscionable circumstances.

Tarini was counting on public compassion. "I knew we'd

have to do a press conference eventually. I always believed at some point they'd have to reveal themselves to the public—to face their pain and what their situation really was. After *Million Dollar Babies*, people still thought they were living in Arizona or a Florida condo." Much to Tarini's surprise, the women agreed to the press conference. He had kept them abreast of all the negotiations, and frustration and anger had taken hold, giving them the confidence to face the public again.

Tarini gives this account of what happened: "When you do a press conference, the phones are ringing off the hook. Everybody wants to interview them, everybody's pitching, complaining, 'You gave an interview to CTV, not us.' A guy from French Newsworld says, 'We could give you good visibility, we'll broadcast the press conference live.' That guy gets Toronto Newsworld onside. You can't beat an hour of broadcast, live.... It doesn't bother the women. They know it's time to do it. Their only worry is they have nothing to wear. I said, 'Wear your own clothes.' That's all they've got, shabby coats."

The women and Bertrand travelled to Toronto by train but were delayed on the tracks and arrived late. Tarini, who had taken a plane, arrived before them. "The press conference is at 1 p.m. I'm at Ruby's office, a reporter from CBC calls, asks, 'Where are they?' She wants to talk to them. She guesses they're on the train and sends a TV crew to the train station. Cécile sees them and is pissed off because she was tired and unprepared. Most people would freeze in their steps, but the sisters carry on like pros. Bertrand calls. I say, 'Where the hell are you? The press conference is in half an hour.'

"Bertrand drives up in a cab. The women aren't nervous.

We have to go down to Ruby's basement because Cécile's using a cane and can't get up the stairs. It's a narrow staircase to a library full of musty old books. We sit down with Ruby and go over what's going to happen. I'm a perfectionist and I have the greatest respect for Ruby. But I have a feeling inside this is D-Day. I want to coach them more. I'm the professional and I'm getting hyper. They're the victims about to face a wall of reporters, cameras, and lights, and they're calm. I was there at 8:15 in the morning at Ruby's office, fielding calls. Ruby's cool as a cucumber. I feel we're headed for the edge on slippery terrain. He's so relaxed I ask myself, Does he know what this is all about?"

Ruby ordered sandwiches for the group. The sisters calmly munched chicken salad, but Tarini was too nervous to eat. He brought forward a sign that he'd made. "I brought it on the plane. I had discussed it with the sisters. I said, 'People are so confused. What do the Dionnes really want?' A previous newspaper story said they wanted $10 million. That wasn't so, but that story and number kept cropping up. I needed to make it visually clear. I knew there would be a photo. The sisters and I and Bertrand discussed what it is they really want, and the phrase came from the conversation. It was a sentence from Cécile that we narrowed down: 'Justice, Not Charity.'"

The words may have been Cécile's, but the concept was pure Tarini. Three months earlier, at a Montreal awards ceremony honouring Quebec artists, most of them from the province's larger cities, somebody had arrived with a sign that said, "What About the Regions?" The sign was seen everywhere in newspapers the next day. The image stayed with Tarini.

After they'd eaten, the group went to meet the media at the province's legislative building. "At the press conference I was nervous," remembers Bertrand. "I was there to watch if any journalist would not respect them. Cécile wore an old, green, all-weather coat and leggings. She was tired and needed her cane," he recalls.

Tarini picks up the story: "They walk up the steps to the first floor media centre. It's packed. They sit there against the right-hand side of the wall. Every network, local news stations, three national networks—everybody has cameras, everybody's panning in, they're really in their faces. It starts becoming unbelievable. It's a celebrity circus all over again. They're just sitting there, not upset. I am. Bertrand is too. We are mystified at how they have already become news just by their presence.

"At 1 p.m. we start the press conference. They go up and sit at the table. I pass out the press kits, a copy of the offer, at five minutes to go. I see a journalist look at it, dialling her cellphone while reading it. She says to her editor, 'You're not going to believe this.' She describes the $2000-a-month pension with total disgust. I'm surprised. The media are definitely not impartial. The story strikes a nerve. Cécile has the sign next to her. I've got [second] thoughts about it. Are we going over the top by using it?

"Ruby starts off. He goes over the offer, introduces the three sisters. Cécile reads a prepared statement and fields questions. One from Radio-Canada, in French, is not sympathetic; she handles it well. Once she's finished, she whips out the sign from a green garbage bag. The sisters stand and get up and hold it together. The next day they're on front pages across the country."

14: VICTORY
AT LAST

CLAYTON RUBY, CLAY to his friends, was the perfect man for the job of Goliath-slayer in a confrontation with the Ontario government. Ruby was already an outspoken opponent of Premier Mike Harris and the tight-fisted policies that had placed deficit-reduction before the needs of the poor, the sick, and the homeless—policies that were anathema to a lawyer who had long been at the forefront of human-rights causes.

In his early career, Ruby had acted for U.S. draft dodgers and Vietnam War protesters. He also had organized one of North America's first community legal clinics, dispensing advice and aid to the hippies of the 1960s. Now, at fifty-six, Ruby has retained much of the slim, intense appearance of his intellectually restless youth. He carries himself with an elegance that would easily, but mistakenly, suggest more familiarity with upholding the privileges of the élite than with righting the injustices done to the underdog. But that is exactly what he does, in an eloquent and media-savvy way. Ruby says he agreed to act for Annette, Cécile, and Yvonne Dionne "not because I thought it was a winnable case, but because it was more a moral obligation, that some lawyer ought to do it, that given their historical position, any Canadian ought to feel an obligation to them."

For those who can pay Ruby's full fee, it is in the stratos-pheric $500-an-hour range. But there are cases he takes on for far less because they belong on the broad stage of a civil-rights champion. Known for his advocacy of Canada's Charter of Rights and Freedoms, he has wielded it, Bible-like, in widely disparate cases. He has acted for a convicted Palestinian terrorist in Canada, for example, and for the controversial Church of Scientology. He represented Nova Scotia Micmac Donald Marshall at a 1989 federal inquiry into his wrongful murder conviction. A fearless provocateur, Ruby has slammed Ontario's judges as political hacks and Toronto's police force as racist.

His public persona is that of a tiger who goes after his enemies with jungle swiftness and relentless intent, staking out his territory, roaring and pouncing. No sooner did the Harris government find itself up against Ruby than it called in a prominent lawyer to replace the civil service legal depart-ment that had been handling the Dionne file.

Harvey Strosberg, treasurer of the Law Society of Upper Canada, was a weighty choice to face Ruby. Though Ruby is a governing officer, or bencher, of the society, and though he and Strosberg sit on the same decision-making committees, it is Strosberg who now presides over the body that for two centuries has overseen Ontario's legal profession. Strosberg, in effect, is chairman of the board of the largest law society in the country.

The two men know each other well, of course, both of them elected members of that inner sanctum of Ontario's lawyers.

They also share the privilege of dining in specially designated quarters in historic Osgoode Hall, built in 1829 as the society's headquarters and later expanded to house law courts and, for a time, a law school. As benchers, Strosberg and Ruby eat and glad-hand in a room set off from the huge and noisy barristers' dining lounge, which the ordinary mass of lawyers may attend. They are both power brokers in their profession, star members of Toronto's clubby legal establishment.

At fifty-four, Strosberg resembles, in appearance and style, a Hollywood casting director's choice for the role of the Godfather: black-suited in fine fabric, cigar-wielding, powerful. He lives luxuriously, works furiously, networks continually. He came to the law from a scrappy, middle-class background and a preference for the football field. As a civil litigator, he has cultivated a reputation for ruthless, rapier cross-examination and exhaustive investigation of his cases. An artful strategist, he can be hard-nosed in trial but butter-smooth when negotiating an out-of-court settlement.

Not shy of controversy, the entrepreneurial lawyer came up with a novel idea in 1998 to finance lawsuits for those who can't afford them through private investors. If the case fails, the investors lose their gamble. If the case is won, the investors get their money back, plus annual interest of twenty percent. Critics thought this was a way around contingency fees, which are not permissible in Ontario, but Strosberg defended the system as a way to finance cases that would otherwise never get heard. He has also become the master of the class-action lawsuit, an American concept that has been imported into Ontario courts only recently.

Strosberg's clients usually differ from Ruby's. While the latter is best known as a human-rights champion who regularly appeals to the court of public opinion, Strosberg is a leading litigator of torts cases, where monetary damages are sought, and has made his name in civil courtrooms and backroom deals. He had acted for hockey legend Bobby Orr in his fight against the mishandling of his finances by his agent, Alan Eagleson. (Strosberg won a settlement on that case and a few years later the former international hockey czar was convicted of fraud both in Canada and the United States and went to jail.) Strosberg was also counsel for some one thousand Bre-X investors whose money went down the tubes in the gold-mining scam. And he was lead counsel in a $3.5-billion lawsuit launched on behalf of people infected with hepatitis C through tainted blood.

But perhaps his most significant case saw him representing the federal government against former Canadian prime minister Brian Mulroney in the infamous Airbus scandal. Mulroney had sued the government for libel after the justice department wrote Swiss authorities in 1995 that the former leader had defrauded the government of millions of dollars through Air Canada's purchase of Airbus jets. Strosberg's swift resolution of the case saw the government apologize formally, say it had no evidence of wrongdoing, and pay Mulroney $2 million in legal fees.

Attorney-General Charles Harnick turned to Strosberg late in the course of the Dionne case. By that time, there was no question that in the battle for the hearts of the public, the government was losing ground. In fact, the case that had been declared "without merit" by Harnick's own legal department had turned into a public-relations nightmare.

Though it was Harnick who brought in Strosberg, it soon became clear that the lawyer's instructions were coming directly from the premier's office. Ruby was a worrisome adversary for the Tories, and they wanted the case resolved quickly. Both lawyers also wanted a speedy resolution. At the government's rate of pay—$192 an hour—they were losing money each day the negotiations dragged on.

Strosberg's task was to come up with a deal quickly and quietly (especially quietly, as his client now wanted the whole case wrapped up without further media attention). He soon produced an offer of settlement, but it was not only rejected, it also sparked a turning point that favoured the Dionne sisters, since its contents outraged the public even further.

The final straw came on the day following the sisters' press conference, when Harris, in response, said he would put the money in the women's accounts whether they accepted the offer or not. "I have asked the attorney-general, as we have offered, effective March 1, to facilitate and transfer $2000 to each of the Dionnes," he said. The three women, at age sixty-three, were being treated like children again, receiving doled-out allowances over which they had no say. As Ruby puts it, "They didn't want a welfare-like pension. From the beginning, we had documents that showed they were wronged. They wanted money that was theirs, not a pension."

Strosberg saw the disaster speeding towards him like a runaway train when he leaned of the sisters' impending visit to Toronto. He insisted on talking to the premier personally. He understood this was no longer a legal battle they were waging but a political assault that could damage the government severely if it wasn't stopped.

Public pressure and the media also had a role to play. After my front-page article revealing details of the quintuplets' desperate situation appeared in the *Toronto Star* on March 2, I wrote a column urging the public to speak out on their behalf. An avalanche of 6,000 faxes and letters of support swept into the newsroom, and I delivered them to the premier's office that week — all reported in news columns and stories I wrote daily. The pressure was intense, as was evident by the swiftness of a response. As a savvy strategist, Strosberg knew when to cut his losses. He had learned from the Mulroney case a valuable lesson that now came into play: when a mistake is made, recognize it and deal with it immediately. He had turned that case around in less than a week and saved the federal Liberals from further embarrassment.

When the hurtling train hit, in the form of the sisters' press conference, Strosberg began casting about privately for opinions on what would be a reasonable lump sum to offer the women. The figure of $2 million came up often enough to seem fair, and he let that be known to the premier.

That week, Ruby called the women to see if they would consider Strosberg's suggested sum. They said no. "They had to make a hard decision to refuse that," Bertrand remembers. "But they had to pay Carlo and expenses and divide the money and try to buy a house. They're owed more than that." The women felt justified in refusing the $2 million offer, an amount that would have seemed huge to others in their financial straits.

Ruby and Strosberg got down to business in unusually

informal settings. Two of their meetings were held over dinner in public restaurants. Although the press was after them both, trying to find out what was going on, none among the pursuing pack found them.

The final head-to-head deal-making session took place somewhere no one thought to check: at North 44°, one of the city's finest restaurants, an art deco temple to casual elegance smugly named for Toronto's latitude on the globe. Situated in the upper reaches of the city's core, North 44° is a gathering place for affluent baby boomers and well-heeled food groupies who like their ahi tuna pepper-crusted and charred, not cooked, their martinis shaken, not stirred.

It was there that Ruby and his common-law spouse, Harriet Sachs, met Strosberg and his wife, Cathy, on March 3, over fine food and, compliments of Ruby, who is something of a wine connoisseur, four bottles of superior burgundy. During nearly four hours of discussion, both women repeatedly shushed their partners as the numbers battle—$1 million? $2 million? $3 million?—reached higher decibels.

Though the table of diners had tried to go unnoticed, the presence of the two colourful lawyers was enough to cause a buzz of interest. At one point, Cathy Strosberg kicked her husband under the table. He had started the negotiation with a lowball offer that all four knew wouldn't be acceptable. Cathy Strosberg saw herself and Sachs as buffers in the fray. One man was asking for the moon, the other was offering too little money. Having the women there would prevent the disputants from becoming locked into polarized positions. Or so they thought.

There was a pause at $3 million. Ruby phoned his clients in Montreal but they turned it down, a refusal that had even

Bertrand wondering if they were making a terrible mistake. At $4 million, they struck a deal. It was finalized the next day at 2 a.m., as Strosberg, accompanied by his wife, sat in Ruby's home, each man arguing out the terms of the agreement and checking with his clients. It seemed odd to Ruby that it was Debbie Hutton, one of Harris's inner circle of so-called whiz-kid advisers, and not the elected attorney-general, who was on the phone giving instructions to Strosberg. Ruby spoke to her as well. He had thought Harnick would at least want to appear to be in charge. Nevertheless, the deal was approved.

It was over, or so it seemed.

Choosing Strosberg to battle Ruby had turned out to be a stroke of genius, but perhaps not for the reasons the government had intended. In early rounds, this had appeared to be a contest of giants—the commanding Strosberg versus the combative Ruby. But in truth, the two men were cut from the same legal cloth. They barrelled through all of the objections and demands, and quickly came to an agreement that made both sides look good—the surviving Dionne sisters and the daughters of the late Marie for their dignity and perseverance, Harris and his crew for coming up with a decent amount to make up for their early poor handling of the case.

In a noon-hour press conference on March 6, 1998, Harnick announced the settlement. But a surprise followed that caught both Strosberg and Ruby unawares. Indeed even Harnick himself seemed unprepared for the element that next emerged. He read from a page he had been handed shortly before taking his seat in front of a wall of reporters, with Ruby and Strosberg on either side of him. Suddenly, the lawyers heard Harnick say that the Harris government would grant "a factual review of the role of the Ontario government in the affairs of the Dionne quintuplets between the years 1935 to 1944." Both lawyers were momentarily stunned. Ruby had tried four or five times to include a provision in the final deal for some kind of investigation, but Strosberg had bargained hard and the sisters, who had been told there would be no inquiry, had finally agreed to release the government from any further responsibility.

Harnick, looking grim and pale, proceeded to verbally fall on his sword on behalf of the Harris government. Harnick read, "This is clearly a case where our government—and probably I in particular—allowed process and legal technicalities to get in the way of people and compassion. The premier made it very clear that this was not our finest hour."

Harris, for his part, was so contrite that he flew to Montreal, bearing a President's Choice coffee cake, to personally apologize to the Dionne sisters. He was accompanied by a miniskirted Debbie Hutton, she of the advisory team that had so miscalculated public interest in the Dionne quintuplets.

From Ruby's perspective, an inquiry meant that the whole matter of the Dionne quintuplets' exploitation, both personal and financial, was open again despite their signed release. "I intend to keep on pressing for more money," he vowed. "We'll go back to the government for every penny. It's not a question of giving money or a gift, if it's money that was stolen from the quintuplets' trust fund."

Hired now by the sisters to be their counsel for the inquiry, Ruby was dismayed to learn that the government appointed to head the review a retired octogenarian, a former Supreme Court of Ontario justice who, it turned out, had been acquainted with some of the players from the quintuplets' childhood history. Justice Gregory Evans made some fateful comments to the press, however, that soon caused such a hubbub that his only way out was to resign.

When he'd barely started his probe, Evans, a former integrity commissioner, said he had found no evidence that huge sums of money were missing from the sisters' trust account. As unusual as it was for a judge to comment on a matter before him, Evans showed further indiscretion when he said that years ago, when he had viewed the sisters on display at Quintland, he had not thought they were being exploited by the government.

After the comments were reported, Evans travelled to North Bay, where Yvonne, Annette, and Cécile were appearing at a charity fund-raiser for the non-profit Dionne Quint Museum and a centre for troubled children. He met with reporters, with the women, and with Bertrand to assure them that he believed he had an open mind on the inquiry. He learned, however, that Ruby and his clients expected the inquiry to address a range of issues that went far beyond checking the contracts made on behalf of the five girls. They were also asking him to look at the moral obligation of the government. Evans decided, as he told the press, "that wasn't my deal." He resigned on May 23, 1998.

Once again, Ruby seized the opportunity. He handed Harnick a list of ten people, nine of them prominent women judges and/or human-rights advocates, whom he would accept for the inquiry. He refused all of the attorney-general's other suggestions. One of his choices, Judge Gloria Epstein of the Ontario Court general division, was appointed on June 25 to head the inquiry, which lasted nine months.

✌

Tarini's greatest hunch and the riskiest move of his career paid off. Though he'd tallied close to $100,000 in expenses, he ended up with a sweet reward for his efforts. The women had worked out a deal that would give him around twelve percent of their total. For a number of reasons, his share in the end turned out be the odd figure of 11.41 percent. For one thing, the women decided to pay the difference between Ruby's fee from the government and his normal rate (an amount no one will reveal). That came off the top, and Tarini then got his share. After expenses, he netted under $400,000—he won't be more specific—for more than three years of work.

His efforts didn't end with the money he got from the Dionnes, though for a man with a spouse and young daughter, the rich payout was a happy, hard-earned prize. The government's surprise offer of a judicial inquiry launched what Tarini calls phase two of his involvement with the surviving quintuplets.

Today his office is filled with copies of archival documents, press clippings, academic studies, and old books. A visitor who wants to do research there is ushered into his so-called war room, where papers are stacked in chronological order and by subject all around a hexagonal desk for easy perusal. It would be impossible to read it all, even over several days.

Tarini's conviction that more money is owed to the women, and that it was originally stolen from them, is right on the surface of what he says. So, too, is his abiding anger at the injustice of it all. "I've seen enough financial statements to know that the government is the culprit here. They got the money from their [the sisters'] piggy bank and spent it like drunken sailors. The government didn't use any basic business practices. They just had expenses going out without any revenue coming in to Quintland. They couldn't generate money from admission because the public was against visible exploitation. So they exploited them covertly."

He advised the women to go ahead with a CBC *Life and Times* documentary, which aired in October 1998. He liked its timing—halfway between the hype over the $4-million deal, and the next big news story, the judge's report in April 1999.

Ask Tarini if he has a strategy that will influence the Harris government to give a full accounting of what the women are really owed and what was taken from them, and the master communicator comes up with an enigmatic answer. "There's a French expression: *'Un petit train va loin.'* It means: 'A small train travels far.'"

Just watch me, he's saying.

Bertrand was also paid for his efforts with fifteen percent of the net amount received by Cécile, Annette, and Yvonne. In total, the young man, who had been broke for almost all of his life and had lost virtually everything during the years he worked flat-out on the project, ended up with less than $500,000. He bought a black Chevrolet Camaro—the sporty Z28 model—and some new clothes, fixed up his apartment, paid his bills and the debts of a former boyfriend who had helped him, and got a new haircut.

He then spent the bulk of his new fortune buying Cécile a house in Montreal. "I knew she would never feel secure enough to buy one for herself," he said. He spent months supervising its renovation. The house is registered in both of their names, but Bertrand signed a legal paper that says his share is a loan from Cécile and will pass on her death to her estate. This was done to avoid family jealousy or inequity.

Bertrand dismisses the fact that he has already spent all of his money with a characteristic grin and what can only be described as a Gallic shrug of insouciance. "I believed in what I was doing for Cécile. I know I'm able to work. I'm only thirty-seven; later my life will be more normal. I'm not worried about myself."

On a visit to Quebec City in August 1998, when the money had been won and the judge's inquiry started, Bertrand toured the homes he had known as a child. He started in upscale Sillery, the leafy residential district that had been his first home. The two-storey brick house, with its wrought-iron fence and ivy-covered chimney, had had ten big trees around it, which Bertrand counted to see if they were still intact. "I always remember this house. I didn't understand why we had to move."

He also went to the cemetery where his father, Philippe Langlois, and his twin brother, Bruno, are buried, father above child, in the same plot. In the more than twenty years that had passed since Langlois died, neither Cécile nor her son had ever had the money to travel to that city and buy a monument dedicated to the two family members buried there. The grave site was marked with only a simple flat prayer stone that read "Langlois."

That August, after Bertrand had found a gravestone-maker and carefully selected a grey tombstone of Vermont granite, he returned to the cemetery. There, he knelt down to whisk away with his bare hands the dry, loose earth that had crusted onto the stone marker. He carefully pulled out the long grasses that obscured the name that was a part of his heritage and that of his dead brother. He turned his head and eyes away from view.

As he bent lower, intent on his task, cleaning even after nothing remained but the prayer stone and the name, he appeared absorbed in a prayer of his own making, a promise fulfilled and a bond finally acknowledged.

For the sisters, the settlement and the inquiry marked the start of a new phase of their lives, one that they had sought so diligently and that would bring them full circle to their extraordinary beginnings.

Annette was careful with the sudden infusion of $1 million that was her share. In fact, the adult lives of these famous women had been lived so simply for so long that they celebrated their victory with a modest shepherd's pie. Eric and his fiancée brought a bottle of champagne to the celebration, but they decided not to open it until after the inquiry delivered its report.

Annette gave each of her children $5000 and put the same amount in an education fund for her grandson. Six months later she bought a smart, two-bedroom condominium apartment just blocks away from her former home, which she was fixing up to sell. The faded white aluminum siding had already been given new life with a sunshine shade of yellow.

As ever, she paints a bright face on whatever she can. Her optimism has revived. "I'm not troubled by depression any more," she says. "I have the power to get rid of what depresses me. I had good therapy." On a triumphant return trip to North Bay in May 1998, during which she and her sisters raised funds for local community causes, Annette said that despite all of their trauma, she was glad to know that the quin-tuplets had made the ordinary people who visited Quintland happy during the difficult Depression years.

At Eric's engagement party a few months later, she found herself pleased to see Allard again, despite all that had passed between them. It was the first time in twenty-five years that the children and their parents had been in the same room together, the first time the couple had seen each other since Charles' graduation eleven years before. Annette says, "Gerry came over and we spoke of the past. I don't have anger at him, just regret."

Coincidentally, Allard broke up with his long-time girl-friend just weeks later, and has seen Annette several times since. Annette says that it feels good to be friendly again, but adds a cautionary note, more for herself than for anyone else: "It brings back the past too much."

Yvonne remains careful, even though money is no longer a problem. She had bought a 1992 Chevrolet for $14,000 the year before her operation, and she continued to drive it after she got her $1 million from the Ontario government. She still rises at 5 a.m., in the convent mode, and does exercises to keep her bones strong. She keeps a replica of the metal pins that hold her hips in place, as if to remind herself that she is only loosely fastened together. And she still worries about her sisters, saying everything is happening too fast for her to feel assured it will all work out.

Today, as she confronts living on her own again, she's uncertain about her future. Her own small house, which she kept but never stays in any more, would need major repairs before she could sell it or move back in. "The situation is delicate. Cécile wants to live in Montreal, Annette is leaving her house for a beautiful condo. They don't need me as much as they did before. It hurts a bit. I like the closeness of being together." Annette says of Yvonne, "I think she's attached to our living together: She stayed here for the company. She doesn't make the effort to communicate with others." But Yvonne has a different explanation: "I stayed here because I loved them."

Prompted by the interviews for this book, Yvonne began to ask aloud some questions about her past that she had long dismissed and says she normally doesn't "waste her time" thinking about. Were their parents capable of raising them when they were born? What would have happened if they had been returned to Oliva and Elzire once they were healthy? What would have happened if they'd been sold to the Chicago World's Fair? Was their mother able to love them?

These questions seem to come not from the resourceful adult woman, but from the child whose voice Yvonne usually keeps silent. No matter how it's explained, she still feels abandoned by those who were meant to protect her.

For Cécile, this fight was about dignity as much as it was about money. She was intent on having the inquiry to find out what happened to the money that was supposed to be in the trust fund. "If it was your money and it was stolen, would you want it back?" she asks.

Today, she has moved to her own house with the help of Bertrand, who is joint owner and has overseen renovations that include wiring for a future elevator and bathroom lift devices, should her health deteriorate. She is careful with her money and is getting advice from an investment counsellor. She regularly sees a Montreal chiropractor for neck aches and back pain. Dr. Jean-Philippe Marcoux is a specialist in the top two vertebrae of the spinal column, and he also practises a method of counselling that helps unlock what he calls the "secrets and memories in the body" that prevent healing.

He spoke of Cécile with her permission. "She's carrying so heavy a load of her own reality and that of the previous generation. She has a really deep past, one of the extremes. She feels she has no place in the world because she feels rejected and used by everyone. At the psychology level, she's extraordinary. At the body level, it's what happens to everyone. We lock away our secrets. We can have a better life, a healthier life, if we look at reality and drop the damn suitcase of secrets."

To that end, there is one path she has decided to take on her own. She has become the spokesperson for Kids Help Phone, a national, bilingual, toll-free helpline set up to respond to troubled and abused children and youth. To start, Cécile wrote a letter of personal support for the organization's fund-raising campaign; the letter brought in "a great response, because she's such a presence in Canada," says Jane Anderson, a donations manager. In it, Cécile wrote, "We were the children everyone looked at and nobody saw. Over the sadness inside, we had to smile and perform. I wish that we could have poured our hearts out to someone who knew that we were just children, like any others, and that we needed the same freedoms, the same understanding, the same love. Today, a tragedy like ours need not happen."

Cécile also planned to travel to high schools across Canada to speak to students and raise awareness of the hotline, but she had to put the trip off for a while after an accident landed her in the hospital in the fall of 1998. The morning after CBC-TV aired a documentary on the surviving quintuplets on its *Life and Times* series, Cécile, waking early to let out her cat, Tin-Tin, had a spell of dizziness. She toppled down three stairs to the back door and landed on her face, breaking her nose and four other bones. She required seven hours of plastic surgery, had her jaw wired shut, and spent two weeks in hospital (during which she contracted pneumonia twice).

Despite all of her setbacks, however, she has come to see personal dignity as her true birthright. "I'm proud to be myself, that I found myself. The troubles I had made me strong. Because of that, I am still here today."

Epilogue: **COURAGE AND INSPIRATION**

I T WAS LIKE A SLAP in the face. As they approached their sixty-fifth birthdays, hopeful of finding serenity at last, Cécile, Yvonne, and Annette Dionne instead found more distress.

The report of Madam Justice Gloria Epstein—a weighty three-volume tome of more than one thousand pages that cost taxpayers approximately $1.4 million—was delivered to the three sisters and their two nieces on April 14, 1999, weeks before their May 28 birthday. Though it claimed to be the final chapter in the quintuplets' saga, it raised more questions than it answered and left them with a heavy decision to make.

As part of the negotiations that had culminated in their $4-million settlement, the women had agreed to release the government from any further responsibility towards them. As well, the attorney-general had said that the judicial review would not be made public unless the women themselves chose to disclose all or part of it. Of course, they would have preferred to close the book on the past in a private manner. But instead, as Cécile, Yvonne, and Annette waded through page after page of the report, they found that its version of their own story didn't always ring true. "This does not tell us the truth. We feel they are protecting someone," said Yvonne Dionne, shortly after reading the report. All three sisters said that facts were left out and past events were explained in a way that protected people in the government of the 1930s and 1940s and in the sisters' own family. Yvonne said, "I told the judge [when she was being interviewed for the report] I was not thinking about getting more money. I only wanted to know the truth."

Though it purported to be a factual review that would give the women closure, the report in the end left them disappointed and hurt. They felt that excuses of the past had been used again to explain away the prolonged separation from their parents and siblings, the years of being poked and prodded by scientists, the excessive spending by the guardians of the children's trust fund money, their public exhibition, and the failure of the government to prepare the family for a realistic reunion. Such excuses, first espoused by the Mitch Hepburn government when it said that its main concern was the quintuplets' safety and well-being, served to divert attention from any criticism from that time, as well as to obscure the government's responsibility for an abnormal situation it alone had created. Instead of excuses, the sisters had hoped to find some moral assessment about the ethics of what happened to five defenceless children.

Madam Justice Gloria Epstein's full mandate was spelled out in an Order in Council of June 24, 1998. She was to conduct "a review of the reason(s) which led the government of Ontario to become involved in the affairs of the Dionne quintuplets, and the manner in which those affairs were handled, by considering the issues which have been identified by the Dionne quintuplets as their concerns; to take into account the social, historical and economic context of the period in which the government of Ontario handled the affairs of the Dionne quintuplets, as well as their family and community circumstances." And, the mandate stated clearly, she was to do this "without expressing any conclusion about the criminal or civil liability of any person or organization."

Her instructions allowed for the use of any documentary or other material that Justice Epstein considered relevant, and she was free to interview any person whom she considered to have material information. The order made clear, on the other hand, that the review was "not a formal inquiry with calling of witnesses or the participation of parties." This meant that people who were interviewed could say what they liked without contest or cross-examination by lawyers for interested parties.

To carry out this task required a considerable team, which was led by Epstein and lawyer Chris Paliare. They hired the services of a private investigation company and a major accounting firm. Documents were retrieved from the Ontario Archives in Toronto, the Dionne Quint Museum in North Bay, and a number of other relevant sites. Advertisements were placed in newspapers, directing members of the public to a web site, and asking for information such as original documents, contracts, or personal records pertaining to the government's involvement in the Dionne quintuplets' affairs.

Six historical reports were commissioned from a group of historians who prepared papers describing various aspects of Ontario life in the 1930s; a private symposium was held in which the essays were presented and discussed. A psychiatrist and a psychologist were retained to interview the three sisters, to determine if any psychological or emotional harm came about because of the way they were handled by the government. Support staff was hired, and further professional help was taken on for extensive legal research.

More than two dozen people were interviewed, including the surviving quintuplets and three of their siblings. Cécile, Annette, and Yvonne were interviewed separately and at length one day at the upscale Ritz Hotel in Montreal, where the judge and counsel were staying. Fact-finding trips took members of the team to North Bay, Montreal, Ottawa, and Windsor, and elsewhere. Author Pierre Berton was interviewed, as were several academics who had written essays for the *Journal of Canadian Studies'* special Dionne issue. (At least one of these academics was canvassed for his opinion on whether the quintuplets' settlement from the government had seemed adequate, though the question had nothing to do with his area of research or expertise.) Fay and Jimmy Rodolfos in Woburn, Massachusetts, were also visited over two days by a private investigator from Forensic Investigative Associates Inc.

When Attorney-General Charles Harnick announced that Judge Epstein would head a factual review of the Dionne quintuplets' years under government custody, he told reporters that Epstein has "an excellent reputation as an active sitting judge and [is] certainly a very contemporary person." Clayton Ruby said the Dionnes liked Epstein because of her history of involvement in women's and children's issues.

In July 1998, Judge Epstein travelled to Quebec's Eastern Townships to meet Annette and Cécile at an inn where they

were staying for a few days. At this first meeting, the quintuplets found someone far different from the government's
earlier choice, Justice Gregory Evans. During their few hours
together, Judge Epstein told them a little about herself and
said her family was very proud of her for taking this case. The
women found her to be charming, attractive, and stylish.

Epstein, aged fifty, had attended York University, graduated from Queen's University in commerce in 1972 and from
the University of Toronto law school in 1977; she was called
to the bar two years later. A well-respected family lawyer with
her own firm, Gloria J. Epstein and Associates, she was
appointed to the bench in the Ontario Court, general division,
in June 1993.

Judge Epstein knew the issues of special concern to the
Dionnes. Ruby had set them out in a June 17, 1998, letter to
Harnick. He asked for the investigation to address specific
questions about contracts for endorsements and appearances
by the quintuplets and the monies they brought in, and about
whether the financial trust was administered for the sisters'
benefit. Ruby also asked for an assessment of the psychological and emotional harm caused by their years under government control, and by the government's failure to make proper
arrangements for their family reunion and their future as
private citizens.

When they finally received the report, what hit the three
surviving quintuplets so hard was the sense that they were
reading a story that had been washed clean of dissent. They
felt that the report was markedly selective in the facts and
comments it chose to include, leaving out those that were
critical of the guardians' spending habits or that would have

shown how badly the public was misled by the government. For Yvonne, Annette, and Cécile, the report was more telling in what it left out than in the details it chose to cover so extensively.

Reeling from this immense let-down, the sisters wrestled with a decision: whether to reject the report publicly. They knew that by revealing the report's specific contents, they would open themselves up to yet another controversy to be played out in the media. Or should they try to go straight to Premier Mike Harris, in private, as he had suggested during his apologetic visit to them after they won their settlement?

In an April 23, 1999, interview at her long-time home in Saint-Bruno, shortly before she was to move to her new condominium for a fresh start, Annette Dionne, along with her sisters, was in a mood to expose the report. "We want the public to know the real truth so that [what happened to the quintuplets] can't happen to others, so that a future government can't get away with hiding facts and controlling people's lives." Yvonne Dionne, added, "I don't think they [the review team] want to believe what happened."

In fact, the sisters had felt when being interviewed that the review team betrayed an unwillingness to give full credibility to the stories the sisters told of their family life in the Big House. Yvonne added an unsettling point: the lawyer who questioned her for the review asked her pointedly why the sisters had felt they had to write *Family Secrets*, and said that it was not a nice thing to have made such allegations against their parents.

In a separate interview, Cécile appeared crushed by the dismay she felt over the report. She said she simply couldn't accept it. "They seem to have a prejudice against the quintuplets. I felt it that way when they asked me questions about the siblings. They seemed to have their own opinion formed [after talking to the siblings]." (Four of the siblings—Thérèse, Pauline, Victor, and Claude—had been interviewed in North Bay.)

After several days of discussion among themselves and with their advisers—Bertrand Dionne, Carlo Tarini, and Clayton Ruby—the three women and their nieces chose to avoid the media and go directly to Premier Harris with their concerns. To that end, they sent him a letter, dated April 25, 1999, asking to meet with him within a week. The timing for even a quiet confrontation couldn't have been better: Harris was in the midst of a pre-election frenzy and was reviving his popularity in the polls by flipping up promises like flapjacks.

While she was awaiting a response, a despondent Cécile said, "Really, I don't expect anything." She said that what the sisters needed emotionally was a full acknowledgement of what had been done to them. She was upset that the report would stand as a document of record when she and her sisters believed it had missed the heart of what had gone wrong. "Even with so much detail, it's very superficial about the difference in the way that we were handled in the early part of our lives, then shipped to the other side [the family in the Big House] without any inspection. They threw us away without any concern. That was awful."

Annette also commented heatedly on the same point. "Not to prepare us for life—for the future—that wasn't to our advantage. Managing our money only? What a preparation!" Says Yvonne, "They [past government officials] were using us and we were bringing lots of money to the province. No set amount went into the trust fund. They spent what they wanted." Cécile says, "I can't accept that they were spending all that money only for good reasons."

Their April letter was the first in a volley of exchanges between the women and the government that stretched over two months. The sisters had written Harris their opinion of the judge's review, stating that they were "surprised to find many errors on basic facts, mistakes, and were also disappointed to find interpretations that differ with what we had experienced." Of the report's findings, they said, "In many cases these are based on only half of the story; the other half is left out or barely touched on." They noted that the report was not checked with them for accuracy before it was published, "though the offer was made." Finally, the women suggested a meeting before the expected election .

Their letter and deadline had a clear impact. They were answered on May 4 by a phone call to Bertrand from Debbie Hutton of the Premier's Office; she said she was getting a copy of the report for the premier and promised to set up a meeting shortly. On May 11, Harris himself wrote to the women. Explaining that he was by then engaged in campaign activities for the June 3 election, Harris said he wanted to give the report and a future meeting "the time and attention they deserve," and suggested they meet sometime later in June.

The sisters wrote back to Harris the next day, stressing that it was urgent that he meet with them while he was still in a decision-making position, since he was the premier who had finally brought some progress to their long pursuit. "We are aging, frail and are not able to withstand much more," they wrote. "Nevertheless... we have come a long way in our quest for justice and do not intend to leave this half-finished." In response, the premier dispatched to Montreal Attorney-General Charles Harnick—who was not running for re-election—to meet with the women on May 18. Clayton Ruby, Carlo Tarini, and Bertrand Dionne were also present, as were the sisters' financial adviser, Montreal notary Claude Prévost, and two people from Harnick's office. At that meeting, after much consultation, the sisters came up with their list of requests. They asked that the judge's report be corrected, that some monies still owed to them be earmarked to help Canadian children who are victims of abuse, and that they be granted increased compensation beyond their earlier settlement.

To advance the discussion, Prévost next sent Harnick an assessment of some questionable expense claims and decisions made by the quintuplets' guardians. Prévost found that "at least $375,000 of expenditures from the trust fund were needless for the Quintuplets from 1934 to 1944." He contested these expenses on the grounds that the mainte-nance and operation of Quintland, professional fees for lawyers and accountants, and charitable donations were mostly "associated with elaborate surroundings that had been developed as an environment in which the Quints could live and still be accessible for public viewing." Prévost pointed out that the Guardianship Act of 1935 allowed the capital and income of the children's estate to be used only "for the benefit and advantage of the said children." Instead, he wrote, it was directed to "a tourist attraction used to entrap the Quints and for such things as toilet paper and for public washrooms." He claimed Quintland "turned into a significant windfall for the Government of Ontario both directly and indirectly," and that the sisters considered these expenses "a diversion of funds and as such morally unacceptable."

In addition to that depletion of the trust fund, Prévost included the $1-million loss when the government refused a contract to allow them to be exhibited in New York under conditions that promised to improve upon the environment of Quintland. In total, the fiscal expert wrote, the 1999 value of the lost income, based on consumer price index calculations and an average yield of compound interest of 9.3 per cent, would have been $49,904,553. In light of this, he said, $10 million would appear to be a reasonable request, and he called for the women to receive "a significant and fair financial compensation of an additional and final $6,000,000."

Two days later, Harnick wrote to the women to assure them that "the Government of Ontario will continue to assist you to bring closure to this difficult part of your lives." The premier, he said, "continues to be committed to ensuring that your concerns are addressed." He informed them, however, that Madame Justice Epstein had refused to meet with them or their representatives, having been "advised by her counsel that it would be inappropriate for her to receive further submissions or a critique of the Report." Oddly, another letter from Harnick followed the next day, restating Judge Epstein's position on meeting with the women about her report. "After due consideration," Harnick wrote, "she has concluded that such a meeting would not be appropriate given the extensive work and thoroughness which went into its final preparation. Indeed, Madam Justice Epstein has expressed confidence in the Report and its conclusions."

Harnick went on to insist that the premier could not meet with them before the election, but had every intention of doing so afterward. Even in the event of a change in government, Harnick assured the sisters, "any of the three Party leaders would be pleased to keep this commitment. Indeed, you have Premier Harris' word that he will do everything in his power to assure that this is so." Nevertheless, there was a warning in the letter. So far, the judge's report was being kept confidential by both sides. But, Harnick wrote, should the women ultimately "make public the Epstein Report, in whole or in part, or if you were to comment upon the Report's contents or conclusions, we will assume that its completely confidential nature, which was safeguarded by the Ontario government as part of its commitment to you, will have been waived by you."

In truth, Harnick's admonition was beyond the terms of the original order in council and was a stretch on his part. The order read that the attorney-general would not disclose the report without the consent of the three sisters and their two nieces, "unless all or any part of the report has been made public." This is a clear reference to content and says nothing of the women's right to comment on their general satisfaction or unhappiness with the report.

The flurry of correspondence continued. On May 26, Harris again wrote personally and spoke of meeting with the sisters shortly after the election. Annette, Cécile, and Yvonne, along with their nieces, responded immediately with a letter stating, "We trust in you."

While waiting for that meeting, Clayton Ruby sought to obtain from Judge Epstein a copy of the studies that helped form her review, as well as notes from the private symposium of historians and a computer disk of her full report. Review counsel Chris Paliare wrote back that there was no transcript of the symposium, that the historians' reports had been given to the Archives of Ontario, and that Judge Epstein had had the disks containing the report erased, to keep the information confidential. Meanwhile, Tarini was pressing for a meeting before the start of summer holidays, when some of the principals might be away. Harris finally agreed to see them in Toronto on June 28.

For that meeting, Prévost had accountants from the major firm of KPMG Forensic and Investigative Accounting Practice, crunch the numbers Prévost had calculated for the sisters and come up with an independent assessment of what was owed to them. The firm arrived at a slightly higher figure than Prévost's, $50,674,749. This confirmed the women's resolve to press for what they believed was a fairer settlement package.

The three sisters rose before dawn in order to be ready for the first flight of the day from Montreal to Toronto. As always, their physical and emotional energy was drained by the effort to remain calm, collected, and confident that they were within their rights when confronting the premier of Ontario. They were accompanied by Bertrand, Tarini, and Ruby.

They were to meet at the Bradgate Arms, a quiet, exclusive hotel in a tree-lined residential area away from Harris' Queen's Park office. The premier arrived with only Debbie Hutton for the one-hour meeting. True to his word, Harris was attentive to the women's claims. He said that he would need time to think it over and that Hutton would be in touch with Ruby. But he ultimately sent the sisters off with nothing more than a question: how would he explain to taxpayers any additional payment made to the Dionnes?

Cécile shot back a question of her own: why were no similar explanations needed for taxpayers years ago when the government was spending the money that was supposed to insure the quintuplets' future security? Both sides left the meeting without answers. Once more, the women were waiting for politicians to decide the next chapter in their story and to determine what new direction their long journey would take.

With so much time and effort, not to mention money, put into the judicial review of their lives, Yvonne, Annette, and Cécile had truly hoped for a final and full accounting. Unfortunately, they found themselves disappointed yet again.

Nevertheless, the three surviving quintuplets face the future with more hope than despair, more dignity than vulnerability. But the end of poverty that came with their initial settlement from the Ontario government has not fundamentally changed their lives. They are still humble women, grateful for the public's embrace of them when their dire situation became known. They are still surprised by their own ability to spark international interest, and they continue to be cheered by the countless letters they receive from people of all ages. Some write about taking a cue from the quintuplets to survive periods of pain and suffering; others, those who lived through the 1930s, thank them for having been a ray of optimism in an otherwise grim time.

Since their 1998 foray back into the limelight, the women have once more been taken up by others as symbols of hope. They've received numerous requests to appear on behalf of causes ranging from breast cancer to epilepsy awareness. So

315

far, they have chosen Kids Help Phone, Canada's helpline for troubled and abused children, as their focus; Cécile has become that organization's national spokesperson and has begun to attend workshops to boost her ability to reach out to and encourage youth when she travels across the country on the agency's behalf.

Sadly, the women will never fully obtain closure on their traumatic past—too many stakeholders remain, too many people are still affected. They will always be the central figures of a spectacular chapter in Canadian history. And their saga is so extraordinary that it represents far more than personal tragedy; what was done to them can serve as a cautionary tale about the human potential for self-advancement and greed, especially in the ugly realm of child exploitation.

But unlike most victims of circumstance, Annette, Yvonne, and Cécile Dionne retain a remarkable ability to inspire the public with their inner resolve and strength of character. Though the women themselves hardly credit their impact on others, they inherently recognize that their long fight for justice can help them salvage some good from their unusual past.

INDEX